D0591850

Baron Philippe

on…

WINE

"Wine is a woman—uncertain, coy,
and hard to please. Every time you draw her cork you risk
disappointment, but when she's on form—and because she's
a professional she mostly is—what bliss!"

WOMEN

"…I earned the title of 'womanizer.'
I would have preferred 'woman lover' but there it is,
seducers can't be choosers, and I really didn't care a damn
what they said—I loved the game. By now I had broken
all the rules and it didn't matter if the satisfaction lasted
a minute, a day, a week, a year—few lasted longer."

WAR

"The German tanks drove into the courtyard
and hoisted the swastika flag above the gate. Then they
went looking for me, turned the place upside down, and
when they couldn't find me, took potshots at my portrait
hanging over the mantlepiece in the drawing room."

and
THOSE CELEBRATED LABELS

"My new idea for the labels was good.
Change them every year, give each vintage a personality
of its own, find the right artist and leave the design to him.
I would offer wine in payment for the label. Wine for art.
Art for wine. I was so excited about artists and new designs
that I even told the bank manager all about it the next day.
I got all the credit I asked for and more."

Please turn the page for the marvelous reviews of
BARON PHILIPPE

"Baron Philippe is undoubtedly a man of phenomenal energy
with a versatility of activities and he is very good company."
The Atlantic Monthly

"The erotic strain in these memoirs is wide and deep,
and one comes away convinced that Baron Philippe takes
more pride in his sexual conquests than in the success
of his vineyards, his skill as a race-car driver or his
translations of Elizabethan poems and plays....
This Rothschild is a credit to his extraordinary lineage."
The Los Angeles Times

"The book is frothy enough to have come from
Champagne instead of Bordeaux, but the bubbles are floating
in a world one might not have seen otherwise."
Newsday

"The overall picture that we get from this candid, genial autobiography is that of a **bon vivant** who loved the good life in a score of ways...and always a connoisseur of connoisseurs where French wines were concerned....All this may sound like life in another world, and in a sense it is."
John Barkham Reviews

"Beautifully rendered by Joan Littlewood, the well-known English director....She projects the easy grace and camaraderie that have made him devastatingly attractive to women."
The Chicago Sun-Times

"There were mavericks among the Rothschilds and one of the most outrageous, as well as charming, must be Philippe."
United Press International

Thank you Tom Maschler for persuading me to finish the book, Anne McArthur Murray for making it presentable, Peter Rankin for patient counsel and Les Preger for stories of the Jews in Manchester.

JOAN LITTLEWOOD

Baron Philippe

The Very Candid
Autobiography of
Baron Philippe de Rothschild

BY
JOAN LITTLEWOOD

BALLANTINE BOOKS
NEW YORK

Copyright ©1984 by Joan Littlewood and
the Baron Philippe de Rothschild

All rights reserved under International and Pan-American Copyright
Conventions. No part of this book may be reproduced or transmitted
in any form or by any means, electronic or mechanical, including
photocopying, recording, or by any information storage and retrieval
system, without permission in writing from the publisher.
Published in the United States by Ballantine Books, a division of
Random House, Inc., New York.

First published in Great Britain in 1984 under the title *Milady Vine* by
Jonathan Cape Ltd., 30 Bedford Square, London WC1, England.

Library of Congress Catalog Card Number: 85-90867

ISBN: 0-345-33040-4

This edition published by arrangement with Crown Publishers, Inc.

Cover illustration by Paul Giovanopoulos

Manufactured in the United States of America

First Ballantine Books Trade Edition: March 1986

10 9 8 7 6 5 4 3 2 1

Contents

III   It's the Wrong Time and the Wrong Place

About Joan

IT was in 1976, while I was still grief-stricken after the death of my wife, Pauline, that an extraordinary, feminine creature appeared in my life. She was herself in a similar state, having a year earlier lost her great man: Gerry Raffles. I remembered productions of their Theatre Workshop I had admired.

At the end of May I motored alone from Paris to Vienne, a small town thirty miles south of Lyon. She had stayed there in hiding, isolated, living near the river bank where Gerry died. I wanted to help, if I could. Joan was standing in clogs and slacks outside a small, whitewashed hotel not a hundred yards from the river Rhône, suspicious, reticent, not to say hostile. I talked. We lunched together and afterwards I read her passages from my translation of Marlowe's *Tamburlaine*. First one phrase, then another roused enthusiasm or sharp criticism. It took time, but I felt that a ray of light might be slowly moving in her distressed mind. I had been shocked and startled by her appearance, but it was not long before I was overwhelmed by her knowledge of the Elizabethans, her sense of theater, her humor.

Later on in the year, when she had overcome her distrust for a strange "humanoid," as she called me, so unlike, opposed even, to all the friends she had known and loved, I managed to persuade her to visit Mouton. That was the experience which was to promote our everlasting understandings and misunderstandings.

Joan loved the place: the skies, the landscape, the vines. She went tramping round the countryside, listened to the stories of my sixty years' work on the site, and pored over my translations of English poets. Perhaps she found a little solace at Mouton. Above all, she was captivated by the quality of the people who work there and kept in touch with them—and me. She was still averse to any social activity but occasionally we would work on translations together. When I was asked to write a little about myself in English I tried to enlist her help. She was cagey. If it wouldn't take long she would jot down a few anecdotes for me, but that was all. She came to Mouton, shut herself up in a remote outhouse and worked night and day. At the end of a week a pile of spicy stories appeared. I was amazed to find that they were my own. I'd forgotten I had even told them to her.

What a piece of luck for this mischievous, unharnessed, wicked Philippe, who often thinks of himself as a boy in an old man's shape, that such a rare person should manage to capture the absurdities of his life. Once engaged on my story I knew she wouldn't give up. She didn't. The pile of pages grew taller. Now you have them: and if now and again you hear her laughter between the lines it is because she knows me better than I know myself . . . sometimes.

Joan, my love to you. It is Mouton, your home forever, if you wish, which begs you to carry on, not to stray too far from the one you call "The Guv." He reads your lines, which cover seventy years of his life, with tears in his eyes. Never stop being the Joan I met in Vienne on the Rhône.

Baron Philippe

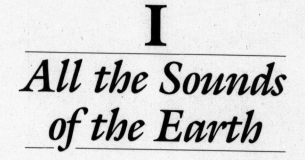

I

All the Sounds
of the Earth

1

All the sounds of the earth are like music.

OSCAR HAMMERSTEIN II

HERE I am, trying to relax in my uncomfortable but handsome armchair, beside a crackling log fire which threatens to smoke me out at any moment. It is the first time this season the fire has been lit. The harvest is in, the autumn leaves are cluttering up the pathways, the Virginia creeper in the courtyard is turning red and there is a distinct nip in the air. This is the way to keep life's storms at bay. When I first came here, sixty years ago, it was the only way to keep warm. I stretch my legs, admire my new black velvet slippers and turn to gaze into the fire.

I must tell you that this scene is quite uncharacteristic of me and carefully produced for the photographer who has just left. I am not in the habit of sitting at the fireside on my own, looking pensive. It just struck me that it might make a good opening, and even put me in a storytelling mood. Didn't our remote ancestors spend their winter evenings round the fire, rolled up in their hairy coats, telling stories of their remote ancestors? Luckily, since then, some clever chap invented the chimney piece. Pity he didn't find a way to stop it smoking. I seize the poker and stir up the logs, sparks fly, flames light the room, but what a smoke. I'd better open a window.

The library is the right place for reminiscing. The books my wife, Pauline, and I collected will bring back memories. In a corner on the lower shelves are the huge tomes, bound in dark red and gilt, which recount in minute detail the family's financial deals and catalogue their acquisitions, endlessly dull and seldom opened, if ever. They don't tell any secrets. There is nothing of the human story of the first Rothschilds, who lived in Frankfurt two hundred years ago. That's not long when you come to think about it, not in a vineyard anyway. A vine can live a hundred years. I have a flask of 1690 somewhere in my cellar, though I'm afraid opening it would be like unsealing a tomb.

The fire spreads its warmth and the smell of burning pine is rather pleasant.

It's high time to begin my story.

I suppose you think I got off to a good start, born with that outsize silver spoon in my mouth. Well I didn't. It was, "Philippe, no!" "Philippe!" "It's a naughty self-willed little thing." When I started talking, Miss May, my nurse, drummed it into me that "I" was bad manners, one mustn't talk about "I" and "me."

They sent me to the right school in a smart horse-drawn carriage, with a top-hatted groom on the box. The other boys arrived on foot. Not surprisingly, I became shy and hesitant. I even stuttered. Best to keep myself to myself.

But to begin the story decently—whatever may happen later —my father, Henri, married my mother, Mathilde Weisweiller, in 1895. He was twenty-three, she was twenty. I've no idea where, probably in Paris, and surely a brilliant affair like all Rothschild weddings. In 1896 my brother, James, arrived on time, and two years later, sister Nadine. I appeared on the scene in 1902, April 13, in a little prefab in the Faubourg St. Honoré: thirty rooms, plus ballroom. The street door was big enough to admit four tall giraffes, walking abreast. You can

still see the house, it's now Le Cercle Interallié. In my childhood, it was a hive of activity with chambermaids, parlor maids,
kitchen maids, the chief cook and his soup maker, the sauce
maker, pastry cook and assorted vegetable preparers and pantry boys, tweenies, footmen, coachmen and valets de chambre,
various. And we had very decent neighbors, the British Embassy and the Élysée Palace. We had a little trouble with the
Elysians once. It was my father's fault. He had brought back a
wagonload of monkeys from Egypt, plus Mahomet. Mahomet
was coal black and he and the monkeys did what they liked.
One morning we were informed that the Élysée had been invaded by a collection of small primates who were disturbing a
critical cabinet meeting and did we know anything about it?
Mahomet and I had a lot of fun trapping them. They liked the
chandeliers best.

I enjoyed that house. I could sneak over the embassy wall
when no one was looking and explore, but my father wanted
to move—he was afraid the increasing traffic would damage
his priceless Latour pastels, and the eighteen Chardins he had
inherited. He was being a bit silly—the house was as solid as a
rock—but he had set his heart on building a new one. The
work had actually begun when war intervened and we had to
stay in the Faubourg St. Honoré for the duration. He gave the
ground floor to the Inter-Allied Club. I used to stand at my
bedroom window watching all the top brass to-ing and fro-ing
in the courtyard. Joffre, Pétain, Foch, French, Haig, Pershing
. . . what a parade of scrambled egg.

I never liked the new house, La Muette, and I thoroughly
disliked Pa's country mansion. It was in the grounds of a ruined
abbey, Les Vaulx de Cernay, set in the pretty rolling countryside south of Paris, known as the Île de France. The château
had been restored by Violett-le-Duc—a great mass of phony
Gothic.

As you will have gathered, my father was a rich man, one of
the richest men in France, but he managed to dispose of his
wealth with no difficulty at all. He built two hospitals, naming

one after himself and my mother, and financed scientific research and any new invention which took his fancy. He built a car factory, Unic Cars; a mustard factory ("Ily n'y a que Maille qui m'aille"); a soap works, Monsavon; and decided it would be a good idea to try canning pheasant and partridge! They were all successful, except the canning, but he managed to lose money on every one of them—he would sell out at the wrong time, entrust the running of the place to an acquaintance down on his luck, or some passing embezzler who had taken his fancy. One of his dearest friends, who seemed to be running Monsavon very successfully, suddenly shot himself and the company went bankrupt.

My father was mad about cars when they were the latest thing and each one was made individually. André Citroën and Louis Renault opened their factories at the same time as my father opened Unic, but they nursed their companies along. Pa never even attended a board meeting, he didn't like boards and had never sat on any board of directors. Maybe he was clever. I was too cross with him to know, he was such a dabbler. In the end Renault bought him out and built Unic lorries.

He gave his father's collection of rare books to the Bibliothèque Nationale. The cabinet containing the catalog was enormous; the only way to get it into the building was to knock a wall down. He was a compulsive giver. He gave to everyone who approached him. His mother was a confirmed do-gooder, but my father went a little too far. He just could not say no.

Some of his ideas were considered peculiar too. He didn't think pregnant woman should be put in prison, and he treated his servants with an old-world courtesy usually reserved for ancient relatives.

His parents, Laura Thérèse von Rothschild from Frankfurt and her husband, James, were both third-generation Rothschilds. They were keeping the loot strictly within the family. Who else could afford the dowry? When I knew Grandma Thérèse, she had long been a widow: stern, buxom, always in black, with a snow-white jabot. She wore mourning for her husband to the end of her days. She never managed to speak French well; her faux pas in that thick German accent made me burst out laughing. Then her eye would light on me with deep disapproval. She never approved of me. Her favorite companions were rabbis or priests—whichever were available.

What a puritanical lady; she wouldn't allow wine in her house, even the word was forbidden in her presence. Yet strangely enough she was the first member of the family to visit Mouton. She had inherited it from her husband and she cherished everything that had belonged to him. After his death she visited all his estates, and in due course arrived at Mouton with her two young children, Henri and Jeanne. The whole village turned out to greet them, but what she found there must have shocked her to the core. She immediately set about building a house for fallen women. No one had told her that marriage was not a popular institution among the locals; in fact it was almost unknown. The poverty of the people upset her: the children without boots, the haggard women. She went around the village distributing largesse and good advice. That one visit had such an effect on my father that he never went back. She did, regularly, and her plain little daughter, Jeanne, went with her.

They would set off with a pile of trunks crammed with baby linen, dress lengths, household goods and medicines, and catch the steam train from Paris to Bordeaux. Then, wiping the soot from their faces, they'd load themselves into a handsome cab and cross to the other side of the town to wait for the little train which chugged along the riverside to Pauillac. At Pauillac the *calèche* from Mouton would be waiting for them.

The journey from Paris to Mouton took them the best part of twenty-four hours. Grandma Thérèse must have enjoyed traveling; she was always trundling along with all her baggage, from her Paris home at 42 avenue Friedland to her country house, the Château des Fontaines at Chantilly, thence to her seaside villa at Berck-sur-Mer, where she started a clinic for consumptive children.

Young Henri and Jeanne had to spend all their holidays helping her with those dying children. The experience marked my father for life. The old lady decided that he would have to be a doctor. Reluctantly he obeyed, studied conscientiously, passed his exams promptly, but hated the thought of practicing medicine and, except during the war, never did. He disliked doctors as a race, especially the successful ones. He had a horror of suffering and sickness; he wrote excellent papers on child care and children's maladies far in advance of his time, but he couldn't bear to have a child anywhere near him. I recently came across a story he wrote about a dying boy of five. The parents, who are very poor, idolize their child, who keeps calling in delirium for a clown he saw at the circus. When the doctor gives up hope the father goes to the clown and asks if he will visit his son. The clown agrees, he comes, sit with the boy and returns daily until the child recovers and sits up smiling.

The story amazed me. When we were children we never saw the man who wrote it. What was wrong with us? I think my father was happier in the land of the poor.

The first time he ever came to my bedroom I was pretty sick with the measles. He walked in, sat at the end of the bed conferring with our family doctor, Zadoc-Kahn, then left, with never a word to me.

Although we seldom saw him, his presence filled the house. One was aware of a huge Olympian figure, hidden somewhere in that huge rambling house, but we children knew that it was more than our life was worth even to be seen. I would dash along the corridor and press myself into the wall if I heard his footfall.

Most of the time he was shut up in his study, chain smoking, drinking liters of coffee and writing. He loved writing—medical papers, short stories, plays. He wrote so many plays he could have kept all the Paris theaters going till Doomsday. The only trouble was that they all seemed to be about doctors. Nobody gave the author much encouragement; my mother's friends treated him and his writing as a big joke. I think they influenced me, though I didn't know it at the time. It's very easy to laugh with the gallery and easier still to mock with the orchestra stalls.

Only now, fifty years later, I begin to rediscover my father. While looking through his books recently I came across a letter which showed me how much young Baron Henri loved the theater, in all its forms. In 1909 Diaghilev was planning to bring Russian ballet to Paris for the first time. Suddenly the subsidy promised by the tsar was withdrawn—one of his favorite ladies, a ballet dancer, had been rejected by Diaghilev. The tour was off. My father, with two others, Nicolai de Benardaky and Max Lyon, guaranteed the required sum. The company came and took Paris and the world by storm. Diaghilev allowed his angels to attend the dress rehearsals, and gave them free seats for every performance. My father was delighted. He never left the place.

Later that year a play of his, *La Rampe* (The Footlights), was accepted for the Gymnase, a good theater and a good company. He was over the moon. Theater was a refuge from life for him, as for many others.

His home life couldn't have been much fun. When I was only seven I knew that he was no longer happy with my mother. They never went out together and only met when they had to. Mamma went her own sweet way. She may have had lovers, probably did. I would have been the last to know.

If my father ever came upon her in the house, it would be because she was preparing some lavish entertainment for her fancy friends. He couldn't stand these people at any price, so when the house was buzzing with them he'd skulk in his study or disappear altogether.

Mamma had quite a crowded schedule.

Stag hunting Wednesdays and Saturdays in the forest of Rambouillet; the Duchesse d'Uzès, master of hounds, or should I say mistress?

Recovering from and reliving same.

Giving orders, visiting her twenty horses at L'Abbaye des Vaulx de Cernay.

Attending race meetings if the crowd was fashionable and she could show off her latest outfit—she wasn't particularly interested in racing.

And of course there was the season at Deauville. Papa built a house for us there and for once I had a little freedom, cantering along the beach on Twister, my pony and best friend. Mamma spent her time gambling, or taking her promenade along the esplanade with papa's banking relatives. They had a house there too, and Cousin Édouard, the elegant baron, always came for the races. If she ever found herself at home in Paris her little white and gold *carnet-de-rendez-vous* was far too full to allow much time for us.

Everyone thought her pretty and charming, and, since she was also rich and spendthrift, she was very much sought after.

We would be taken to her room in the evening while she was dressing to go out; and not allowed to speak unless we were spoken to. She'd ask if we'd behaved ourselves and done our homework. Then she'd dismiss us with a peck on both cheeks and back we'd go to the nursery. We were left entirely in the hands of Miss May, our very strict Scottish nanny. She spoke only Highland English, the best, she assured us, taught us awful tags and nursery rhymes, rebuked our bad manners and dirty fingernails and cured our collywobbles with gruel and indigestion powders. My stomach has never recovered. Despite my father's army of cooks, we were fed the most boring, unappetizing meals. There never seemed to be anything I liked until one day I discovered chocolate gâteau. After that, whenever ma had a tea party in the offing I'd steal into the pantry and scrape bits from the top layers. I was never found out.

2

Dancing on a volcano.

COMTE DE SALVANDY

WHEN I was twelve the world went wild, one of those periodic attacks of madness to which the human race is prone. They were having their war and everybody seemed to be enjoying it, in their own peculiar way, with military bands playing, soldiers marching, flags everywhere and tears. Everybody was busy. Papa's car factory was being turned over to ambulances, mamma was being fitted for a nurse's uniform, Miss May was knitting long khaki socks and crying over the Belgian children. What about this child? Me. "Oh, the Rothschild boy? He has everything." I was nobody's darling. There was Mademoiselle Yvonne Grémy, who taught me the violin when I was eight. As I gave my rendering of "The Meditation" from _Thaïs_ and she placed her slender hand on mine to correct the fingering, I nearly fainted. I was madly in love with her but she didn't fancy me at all. In fact she abandoned me, said my musical potential was nil. No, the only living creature who adored me was my pony, Twister, and she was far away.

School was dull but home was worse. Everybody was so busy

joining up and dreaming of *La Gloire* that there was nobody left to make us a hot meal. Papa was shut up night and day in his lab at L'Abbaye des Vaulx de Cernay. Even so, he managed to write a play, this one about jealousy, a man's suspicion that his ten-year-old child is not his. It was performed at the Marigny and dedicated to a young actress called Juliette.

Mamma, looking very chic in her dark blue and white uniform, was busy with her nurse's training course and papa suddenly appeared in khaki with red velvet flashes on the collar. Now at the age of forty-two he was a practicing doctor for the first time.

Shut away in his lab he had invented a new treatment for burns and designed an ambulance that could make use of the treatment in the front line. Mamma studied the technique and went to the front with the burns unit.

Papa at once wrote another play: *La Femme d'aujourd'hui* (The Woman of Today).

My father was very bright when he had to face reality. He invented air-tight tubes to preserve the soldiers' jam and meat paste. They were like the toothpaste tubes which came much later. He might have been happier if he'd been a poor man and had to work for his living. As it was he didn't get any credit for his good work. My mother was awarded the Croix de Guerre for hers, but then of course she was prettier.

On my way home from school I kept a sharp lookout for doves and fishes. Doves were the first planes the Germans sent over, mainly to scare us; they were so light they could only carry a few small bombs and the pilot had to open the door, select one and drop it carefully onto the target. Zeppelins were those beautiful silver fish of the sky which had appeared over Paris once or twice, on reconnaissance, bringing everybody out on the streets, more amazed than frightened. I, for one, refused to go to a shelter. I didn't want to miss anything.

In 1918 the Germans were only forty-four miles away and threatening to wipe Paris off the face of the earth. "Not one stone will be left standing on the other," said the Kaiser's aide-de-camp, "then perhaps they will make peace." The shells from Big Bertha, the Kaiser's mightiest peashooter, began to fall on Paris. One landed on the church of St. Gervais, when all the people were at mass; very few survived. Another landed on our school. We had all been sent down to the cellar when the shelling started, so we had to escape by the ventilation shaft. It was then that my parents decided to pack me off to Bordeaux. Big Bertha changed the course of my life, the first female to do so.

And Bordeaux? More school, the Lycée Montaigne. At first the name meant nothing to me, Michel Eyquem de Montaigne, merchant, 1533–92, mother of Spanish-Jewish origin, sometime mayor of Bordeaux and a pupil of George Buchanan, who also tutored Mary Queen of Scots' erudite son, James I of England. I began to read his essays and I was held, delighted. I found the lines which had inspired Shakespeare, Marlowe and Webster, and when I learned that he had retired to his château at the age of thirty-five to write, and declared himself unsuited to marriage and paternity, I decided that he was for me. As you have guessed, I was beginning to fancy myself as a solitary dreamer and even scribbling doggerel verses in the corner of my exercise book.

Of course I visited La Brède and sat in Montesquieu's study.

> *Souvent on a dit gravement des choses puériles,*
> *Souvent on a dit, en badinant, des vérités.*

I decided to escape from the misery of school into books, so I closed the door on the gloomy apartment on the rue du Jardin Public and browsed. Sometimes my room became a proper Disneyland. A family of gray mice would appear and play round the table. I made a maze with white flour to amuse them. It got me into terrible trouble with the eagle-eyed Miss May, who was still mounting guard over me.

I wasn't doing so well at the lycée. I knew nobody and the rigmarole was quite different from my Paris school. Monsieur René Salomé, tutor, arrived, sent from Paris to chivvy me along. What a bore. I had to think up some cunning tricks to give my two watchdogs the slip, but once out of the house I'd race down the road to the docks, the liveliest place in Bordeaux, especially when the American fleet was in. I watched the doughboys unloading their ships and tried my English on them. They were tickled pink.

My side of the family has always prided itself on its English connection and I'd been taught English since babyhood.

I asked if I could drive one of the cranes. They let me. I stayed all day. After a while they let me join in their ball game. We laughed a lot, then they had to leave for the war, and the place would seem very desolate until, inevitably, the next batch arrived to be packed off to the slaughter.

One empty weekend—and weekends at Bordeaux could be very empty—I thought I might take a look at my grandmother's property Mouton, near Pauillac, some sixty kilometers away. It was somewhere to go, at least.

The train journey wasn't very inspiring, the countryside looked empty and so flat. There were tumble-down buildings here and there and a few new châteaux with old turrets; but where were the deer parks, the gushing streams stocked with salmon, romantic ruins reflected in artificial lakes? This was very different from the world I knew. As we rumbled along, stopping at every hut, I began to notice the vines. I hadn't recognized them, those endless straight lines of wire and stave supporting the trimmed branches. What workmanship. How did they manage such perfect alignment?

We passed a small Romanesque church. It looked good: sandstone, simple lines. There were glimpses of the broad river Gironde, it gave a touch of life to the scene.

Beyond Pauillac I kept a lookout for this place Mouton. Where was it? What would it be like? There were vines, vines everywhere and a straggling street bordered with hen runs.

Where was the big house? The pediment of a huge stable dominated the scene, and beside it a group of smiling characters stood waiting for someone. Could it be me? There was a grave old man in a wide floppy hat, who turned out to be my grandmother's representative, the Baron de Miollis; Gustave Bonnefous, *maître de chai*, obviously a personage . . . a stocky chap with big moustaches; Émile Gerbaud, barrel maker; and a small group of horny-handed blokes in thin blue suits. What are they wearing on their feet? Wooden clogs, sabots. There was a bright-eyed boy, Roger Ardouin, and Merilda the cook, a tall, very beautiful woman who stood apart, holding her little daughter, Odette, by the hand.

"Welcome, young monsieur," said the old baron.

The others gave their berets a tug.

"You'll be hungry, Master Philippe," said Merilda. "I've made you some cabbage soup and a noodle cake. Odette has put a warm brick in your bed. Say bonjour, child."

But the little girl was too shy to utter a word. We turned to enter a farmyard. The smell of dung and urine would have knocked you down. Merilda turned aside. "You've brought out a bottle of the best, Monsieur Bonnefous?"

"Do you like fishing? Can you catch frogs?" It was the boy, Roger. I found it difficult to understand what any of them said. Such a strange accent, swinging and tangy, and such friendliness from people who'd never set eyes on me before.

And the food! I'd never been allowed to taste onions or garlic and I'd never heard of cabbage soup. It landed on the table in an enormous tureen, steaming hot, gales of garlic filled the room when Merilda lifted the lid. Then there was sea bass stuffed with herbs and roast beef garnished with *ceps*, freshly gathered in the nearby woods of Béhérré.

That night I drank wine for the first time in my life. At home it was forbidden; my father drank Évian water. I might be given a few drops to color the water on special occasions, but there was no taste in that. Red beef and wine which smelt like violets. I was drunk. "In the morning you visit the *chai*." The way the word was pronounced I thought it was some holy temple. These dark strangers might worship anything. I discovered later it was their wine and their women, in that order.

After breakfast I was conducted across the reeking farm-yard. Ducking the clotheslines hung with long johns, ladies' drawers and petticoats, we came to an ancient stone shed, the chai. Inside it was as cool as a cave, barrels lay in rows on their sides. Monsieur Bonnefous tapped one for me.

"Taste it," he said.

Three or four of them watched me.

"Savor it. . . . Spit it out. On the floor, where else? You won't spoil the carpet."

They all laughed. I looked—the floor was of beaten earth. What a change after the terrible chic of my home.

The boy Roger showed me how to harness a horse and spear frogs. I killed enough to make us a feast. He asked me if I was a good shot.

"Of course," I said. "What is there to shoot?"

"Only thrushes," he said, then led me over to the vineyards and started banging away. It is a practice which I have forbid-den in my old age, but I have to confess I enjoyed it then, and a fat lot of notice the local youth take of me now.

Most of all I enjoyed getting dirty, trampling through mud, coming back with filthy hands and no one waiting to scold me. It was my idea of paradise.

3

Adieu la vie, adieu l'amour
Adieu toute les femmes
C'est bien fini, c'est pour toujours
De cette guerre infâme.
C'est à Cràonne, sur le plateau
Qu'on doit laisser sa peau
Car nous sommes tous condamnés
Nous sommes les sacrifiés.

SOLDIER'S SONG

ARMISTICE, and I am back in Paris. Delirious crowds on the streets. For the first time in my life I roam the town from dawn till dusk, on my own, jumping on cars, laughing and singing with strangers. The flags and the bunting are out again. Joy everywhere, except in nearly two million homes where young men's lives were mourned, or among the survivors blinded or maimed. In every bus and train there was a compartment *"Réservé pour les mutilés de la guerre."*

My brother, James, came home from the front and of course, as a war hero, an aviator to boot, he couldn't move without a flutter of pretty birds around him. Even my darling mother joined the club. "My son James," she'd say, proudly. "He came through without a scratch." The aviator was the pukka hero, the only one entitled to wear a tie and high boots, cavalry style. This callow youth looked on with a superior air, full of secret envy. It will be observed that I was a late developer. At sixteen I was not just innocent, I was ignorant.

On New Year's Eve the house was empty. I went to bed early and fell asleep. Suddenly I was startled by someone shaking me.

"Get up, get dressed."

It was my brother, James, and mother's nephew Armand, whom I always thought rather stupid. They were both in uniform.

"Come on, get a move on."

I fumbled for my clothes. I couldn't find my gray knitted tie.

"Where are we going?"

"Never mind, come on."

They bundled me out of the house into a waiting car. The hood was down and it was freezing cold. We drove along the Seine and pulled up at an apartment house on the cours la Reine, now cours Albert I. My teeth were chattering and my nose was a dripping icicle. They dived into the lift, leaving me shivering in the hall. "We'll send the lift back. It's the top floor." The lift came creaking down. I got in. It would be a New Year's party for sure. I pulled back the grille. The door opened straight into the apartment. I couldn't see the room, two lines of half-naked bosoms blinded me. I felt myself blushing to the roots of my hair. Their owners were smiling, winking, giving me that old come-hither look. At the far end of the line three awful hags, rouged to the temples, frizzled and mascara'd, beckoned to me with lewd gestures.

I couldn't move. I stood there, paralyzed.

"Allons-y, Philippe." Someone struck up the "Marseillaise," my brother's aviator friends saluted and I was pushed forward. The bosoms zoomed in on me, brushing my cheeks, trapping my poor cold nose. Those naughty ladies were kissing me, stroking my hair and not just my hair. I was stifled in a froth of feathers, lace and taffeta silk, sweet-smelling arms embraced me, perfumed with Mitsouko, Air Embaumé and L'Heure Bleue. I felt dizzy, my face and neck were covered with lip salve. An old one pinched my bum. I sat down, affronted. There was a roar of laughter and applause.

Of course they immediately forgot about me and started bunny hugging round the room to the tune of "Everybody's Doing It, Doing It, Doing It." I watched them for a while, a glass of tepid champagne balanced on my knee. I'd never tasted it before and I didn't like it. The gaslit chandeliers were burning low. I fell asleep.

My brother and his friends had assembled all the famous tarts of the time, Loulou Nanteuil, Clara Tambour, Pan-Pan Toussaint, Germaine Néris, Charlotte Neusillet and a host of others, as they say on the old playbills. The three old ones must have been reigning queens in my grandfather's time. They were the famous trio, Liane de Pougy, Fozane and Emilienne d'Alençon, doyenne of them all. Years after, when I next saw Pan-Pan, she was married to the Baron Hély d'Oissel and ran a jewelry shop, *le plus chic* in Paris. You've guessed it, Cartier's.

So as not to make fish of one and flesh of the other in these days of female liberation, I shall now name the gentlemen present, at least the ones I remember. They were all handsome heroes from the crack air squadron known as "The Storks." There was Raymond Bamberger, Pierre de Jumilhacq, Hély d'Oissel, André Dubonnet, Pierre Fouquet-Lemaitre, Fonck and others. When Pan-Pan married Hély he was in a highly successful line of business: glass making. He founded the St. Gobain factory, which makes all our Mouton bottles.

I should like to tell the story of my first romance in the style of Aucassin and Nicolette but, alas, I cannot. It's more of a droll story. Brother James again decided to take my education in hand. One afternoon he took me to a pretty apartment and left me with a lady called Lotty. As he sidled out of the room and closed the door, she approached me with slow snaky movements. I was transfixed. She touched me in my private place. I began to giggle; I thought she wanted to tickle me. She was taken aback, but she began again, her finger in my fly. I doubled up with laughter. At this she looked so cross that I took to my heels and ran. I never saw her again, I was too busy at school. To tell you the truth I once went back to that street on my way home. I wanted to find her, throw myself on her satin sofa and say, "Do what you like with me," but my courage failed me and Monsieur Salomé was waiting at home, polishing his pince-nez. I had three hours a day of that dryasdust, every day after school. The Lycée Condorcet was tough after Bordeaux, and my parents had no intention of letting me fail my baccalau-réat.

No, summer 1920 at the seaside was my first *lune de miel*. I teamed up with a lively crowd of friends who were going to Arcachon, then the most fashionable watering place on the Atlantic side. Luckily, some of the boys had brought a few good-looking females along with them, sisters, cousins and the like, so we spent the holidays swimming, flirting, careering around in our sports cars with the girls perched up above us, and sailing. I had a brand-new yacht, an eight-meter cutter built by the architect Fife. It was to be the first of many.

Arcachon. Even now the word rings bells over a summer haze of sea spray, wine and bouts of . . . She was so pretty, blonde and soft, with her hair in a large shining bun, and such a bosom under those loops of loose tulle. What would it be like. . . . She didn't look at me unkindly. At first it was sailing and oyster catching. Then swimming. My bathing costume, I'll have you know, was long-sleeved, dark blue and went down to my knees. Hers? Very fetching. We sunbathed, she got sand in her pants. Well, I got lost, but Henriette was a wonderful guide. She always knew the best way to get there.

And I had my first car, a Torpedo 8 cv Unic, present from my old man, a beaut. Well, after all, he owned the factory. She was a silver darling, torpedo shaped, open to the wind, fast, she could get up to seventy kilometers an hour on a good road. Liberty, roaring through the countryside, hens flying, dogs barking, country women running for their lives. We killed a lot of hens and quite a few dogs and sheep.

My Unic gave me great standing with the girls. Henriette was always ready to come for a spin, and I could make Mouton in 190 minutes. My enchanting Henriette was already made, so what with Merilda's cooking, the fabled wine and Henriette's charms, Philippe lost his virginity well and truly and developed his lifelong taste for the pretty girls—and good eating.

I knew we had made our love nest in a dilapidated wreck of a place, that the feather beds had fleas and the mosquito nets holes in them. It was as if we'd shacked up, bedded down in some raffish eighteenth-century inn and no one would ever find us. For me that was part of its charm. The state of the place did bother me, occasionally. Something would have to be done about it sometime, that was for sure.

At the end of the first summer of my manhood I arrived back in Paris two days late.

"Where is that boy? What does he think he's up to?" asked my father. I pulled on my gray winter trousers, my thighs felt like iron, my feet were on springs; I was sunburned, fit, ready for anything. I braved my old man in his den.

"Well? Where have you been spending your time lately, Monsieur Philippe, and what makes you so late?"

"I've been on holiday at Arcachon, papa. We missed the train, somehow."

"Staying at Mouton, I understand. What was the attraction there?"

I was embarrassed and stumbled over my words. "It's great, marvelous, but neglected of course. The people are splendid, very hardworking, but there's no direction. It's all go as you please, though they still manage to produce an amazing wine."

"And what do you know about wine, may I ask?"

"I drink it."

"I think you'd better forget about wine and women, my boy, and get on with your education."

Who had told him about Henriette?

"You are taking science at the Sorbonne?"

"Physics, papa."

"Then you've got some hard study ahead of you. Don't fail your degree, boy. One needs a degree in this world."

"Yes, sir."

And I began a daily grind, bent over my books at home, or trying to keep alert in the stuffy lecture hall. I could see Henriette everywhere. And there was that girl two desks ahead; a tiny ridge of fluff would appear right down the middle of her neck as she bent over her notes. She had a lot of hair, shiny blonde. How would it look . . . ? I closed my books and went for a walk.

The autumn term was cramming, dragging boredom, relieved only by mad flips round Paris in my Unic. Even then I had to have Maurice, one of my father's chauffeurs, beside me. I was not allowed to drive alone in Paris. Maurice wasn't too bad—he'd been driving during the war and wasn't all that struck on peace and parental authority. All the same, I longed to be rid of him.

Just before Christmas, when trunks and skis were being hauled out in preparation for the winter break, I came upon my sister, Nadine, sitting on her suitcase moping over her smart new skating boots.

"Now what?"

She turned a tear-stained face toward me.

"Blow your nose," I said, knowing exactly what the trouble was—a big handsome chap called Adrian.

"Hasn't he invited you for Christmas?"

"No."

More tears threatened.

"It's about time you two sorted yourselves out. This has been going on for yonks."

"But we're never, never alone together."

"Well, that's easily remedied."

"How?"

"I'll pick you up in the Place Vendôme at 14:30 prompt tomorrow, we'll call for Adrian—you fix that—and I'll provide you with the most private meeting place in Paris. The rest is up to you."

The next day I smuggled the car away, picked up the young lovers and off we went. Up the Champs Élysées, through the

Bois, along by the river and down by the Champ de Mars. As we passed the Eiffel Tower the sun came out, across the square by the Invalides we raised a cheer from a gang of road workers. Cars might be a novelty, my Torpedo was unique. Outside the parental palace we pulled up with a bang, and I sounded the horn. Adrian leaped out and lifted Nadine high in the air. As he set her down she threw her arms around me.

"We are engaged," she said.

"As good as," said Adrian.

And they set off to his parents' place for Christmas. James was taking my mother to Switzerland and pa was staying at home; he had a play in rehearsal. I was hanging around for a few days, hoping to fix up something with Henriette before leaving for the bobsleighing at Megève, so I asked my father if I could drop in on a rehearsal. He agreed without much enthusiasm.

Arriving at the theater, I found the normal entrance firmly shut; even the box office looked boarded up. It was the right theater, the Renaissance. I'd no idea which of his plays was in preparation—there was nothing on the billboards. All my life they'd been going on and coming off, sometimes rather rapidly. The family tended to turn a blind eye: playwriting was reckoned a queer sport for a Rothschild. My mother's sweet sister, Marie-Jeanne, was the only one who encouraged him. In gratitude, he dedicated one of his plays to her.

I'd never visited a theater during the day. How did one get in? I walked around the building and after trying several entrances, clearly wrong, located an *entrée des artistes* in a squalid back street. I pushed open a metal-covered door to come face to face with a fierce old man. To point up his instant dislike for me he gave a sycophantish smile as a perfumed creature wafted by.

"Bon appétit, Mademoiselle Léonie," he said, saluting her. She smiled back, faintly. I stepped aside. She brushed past me.

"Yes? And what can we do for you?"

"I am looking for Baron Henri de Rothschild."

"Well, he don't work here, this is a straight theater."

"He is a playwright."

"Not here. Our playwright is Monsieur Pascal."

I had completely forgotten that my father used a pseudonym for the theater.

"That's right, Monsieur Pascal, André. He's my father."

"You might have said so in the first place."

"I forgot."

He gave me a funny look. At that moment, Friendly Face appeared through some red baize doors and, wedging them open with his buttocks, presented us with a stuffed green macaw in a glass case.

"Don't like this one neither," he said.

"Still at it, are they?" said the doorman.

"Yip."

"Couldn't take this young fellow-me-lad through to 'em, could you?"

"Nope."

"Why not?"

"Still rehearsing."

Argus frowned at a wall clock, brought out his watch and chain. . . .

" 'Bout time they broke, ain't it, Props? They're going over. Won't do."

"Take this then," said Props, giving the macaw to the doorman. "It'll have to be changed." He nodded to me to follow him and paused at the red doors to put his finger to his lips. The doors were studded like a bridal chest, the cloth covering them was ragged, but they opened noiselessly. Beyond—a red votive light glowed above a dog-eared yellow card with "Silence. Rehearsal in Progress" on it, in black. What sort of holy place was this, smelling of pink powder, dust and sweat? Between two tall canvas screens I saw a brightly lit stretch of floorboarding, recently scrubbed. In the shadows where we stood, ropes cluttered our feet, mysterious swathes; feathered headdresses, swords and shimmering frocks hung on the bare brick walls, and in the gloom above us a gantry spanned the whole width of this fascinating place.

A man stepped into the lighted area; his face, turned toward me, looked enormous. I recognized him: Harry Baur, the great actor. Till this moment I had only seen him from the other side of the footlights. For a second he didn't seem real, but there he was, asking for something in an ordinary, everyday voice. Then he smiled and his face was seamed with laughter lines and crow's feet. He was telling a boy to fetch him a bottle of beer.

We tiptoed to a pass door which led to the auditorium, and slipped through. Behind us the door disappeared magically into the auditorium wall. And there, among the rows of seats draped in white dust cloths, sat my father, his eyes fixed on the stage.

Some intense-looking people were sitting all around him, passing notes and conferring in whispers. Best to wait quietly. On the stage Harry Baur was now being a doctor. The same old story—doctors, money, that was all my father ever wrote about. Acting with Baur was a sweet-voiced actress playing an American.

"Marthe Régnier," whispered my guide. He winked at me, smiling and nodded toward my father, who was in bliss as he watched his play unfolding.

"What's the play called?" I whispered back.

"*Le Caducée,* the symbol of medicine, that is."

He leaned over and picked up the proof of a program which had been lying among other papers on a board which covered two rows of seats.

"They've been arguing about it for days. There it is, looks like a torch, but Monsieur Pascal wants it to suggest big business as well."

"Is he attacking the medical profession again?"

"In a way, yes. Harry Baur is playing the successful doctor who makes money operating on rich women, only the women have nothing wrong with them. Mademoiselle Régnier dies in the third act."

"What a pity."

"Yes. There are lots of laughs in it too. Myself, I think they've got a winner, this time."

Suddenly the lights went up in the auditorium. The stage manager had called a halt, a break for a meal, after which they'd be rehearsing till midnight. Some of the actors and actresses had left handbags, brollies or outdoor shoes in the auditorium. To recover them they came scrambling over the temporary wooden steps which the producer had been using to get to the stage quickly.

There was a tremendous lot of kissing and hugging and joking. What a fuss, anyone would think they were parting for life, they were only going across the road to a restaurant. Pa was in his element. I'd never seen him so easy and relaxed. I hardly knew him.

"Ah, Monsieur Philippe, there you are."

He presented me to several of these affectionate people and I came in for my share of kisses and compliments. These characters certainly made you feel good.

Harry Baur went off with Marthe Régnier and papa asked me if I'd like a bite to eat. For a change I felt completely relaxed in his company. He was brimming over with enthusiasm for his actors and actresses and so optimistic. But then he always was, about everything, for a while. Even in the little restaurant, where the tousled beauty polishing glasses greeted him as Monsieur André, he seemed completely at home.

I made an excuse to call for my father the following day, and thereafter every day. I sat for hours in the darkened auditorium, watching my father's play come to life. The theme was very topical. At that time there was a vogue for expensive operations. There wasn't an appendix left in Paris and you were lucky if you didn't have one of your vertebrae whipped out to prevent backache.

At first nobody noticed me, except the doorman, then nobody bothered about me if they did notice me, but soon, as actors will, they began to ask my opinion, at least some of them, the most insecure, or the ones who hated the producer.

I had a job to get into the first dress rehearsal. No! Nerves would be frayed, time was getting short, the newspapers would be snooping around. I managed to slip through at last and sat discreetly on a corner of the stalls, waiting. Everybody was in the theater early but nothing seemed to happen for hours. The producer was somewhere in the dressing rooms. Suddenly he called for a complete costume parade. There were shrieks of horror, screams of laughter, tears, rage, hysterics as the girls appeared on stage and paraded by. Someone was going to have to console them. When I got to the girls' dressing rooms, they were busy tugging at their dresses, changing their hairstyles, buttoning and unbuttoning, drying each other's tears—they all hated their costumes. I made a few suggestions; one of the girls looked very angry. She handed me a pair of scissors. I took them and cut a bow off the back of her dress. She was delighted. I started snipping away right and left and center. Off with the folderols. Cheers from the girls. We were having a great time till the wardrobe mistress came in. She went white and began gathering up the mess of frills and ribbons. I said I would take full responsibility and told the girls to appear for the afternoon's run-through just as they were. I knew I was right. I could always choose a style to flatter a pretty woman.

Back on stage, more chaos. The set, a doctor's consulting room.

Well, he was supposed to be a rich doctor, but the designer had gone a little too far. Downstage, in the main acting area, he had arranged his very rococo Louis XV pieces all over the place, plus artificial trees in Sèvres pots, occasional tables covered in knickknacks and a rosy Fragonard on a taffeta-draped easel.

Upstage there were two enormous doors. Left, opening onto a library stacked with leather-bound books, right, to a green velvet salon, with chandelier. My friend Props was just entering this area with another stuffed macaw, blue this time.

As the afternoon wore on, the dress rehearsal degenerated into a series of slanging matches. Someone got hooked on a trailing plant, moves had to be changed or cut because there was furniture in the way. Marthe Régnier couldn't even make her sweeping entrance, for fear of two commodes, a statue of Aesculapius and a *jardinière*.

Papa was visibly wilting. I decided to help him out.

"Why don't you throw out 90 percent, father? They're never going to be able to move with all that stuff around. And how on earth will you light it?"

The producer and the designer glared in my direction. I didn't care.

"May I try something?"

"Go ahead," said my father.

I went on stage and started whipping away some of the more obstructive pieces.

"Now they can at least walk straight through," I said.

The stagehands carried away the discarded bits. All was silent in the stalls. I decided it might be more tactful to disappear for a while. As I left, the producer, looking rather supercilious, was giving a few notes, modifying moves and placating the designer. I skipped. The girls were arriving in the wings in their shingled costumes.

I stayed away for a while, took the air, looked at the shops. When I came back only the stagehands were there, busy on the brilliantly lighted stage.

"What's happening?" I asked Props.

"They're making cuts. The cast have gone out for coffee, the designer has gone home in a huff."

"How did the girls come across?"

"Very well. Everybody thought they looked 100 percent."

"I would like to scrap some more of this junk."

"What's stopping you?"

"Is there anywhere to store it?"

"Sure, there's plenty of space in the loading bay."

"I will have to convince the geniuses. Could we shift it all tonight when they've finished?"

"Any time. We'll be glad to see the back of it, load of old junk."

I was determined to win my father over and later that night when they were lighting, I did it. The advantage of growing up in a Rothschild household is the education it gives you in bad taste. You either spend the rest of your life surrounded by vulgar ostentation or you suit your own taste, whatever it may be. It can't be bad if it's absolutely your own and suits your particular needs. All the play needed was background. The company was marvelous and would provide the necessary life and atmosphere.

That night for the first time in my life I watched a lighting rehearsal. I had never known what a difference light could make. I wanted to learn all about it. I would too, but that would have to wait.

My father's play was a huge success.

4

The little foxes that spoil the vines.

SONG OF SOLOMON

THEY say you should never go back to the place where you have been most happy. The following summer, 1921, my visits to Mouton were spoiled by the disorder I noticed everywhere. Were things getting worse, or had I been oblivious last year? Henriette wasn't with me. She was having a baby. Not mine, I'm sorry to say. Her absence made me more observant. The place was going to rack and ruin; my father would have to take some action.

As soon as I arrived back in Paris I asked to see him. The message came that he was very busy but would give me five minutes. And there he was, as always, his desk covered with pages of scribble, the fume from his yellow Gauloises hanging in a mushroom cloud above his head. I went into the attack.

"It's about Mouton, father. Things can't go on the way they are."

"What things? What are you talking about?"

"Mouton. Something must be done, the place is falling apart."

"Monsieur Philippe, you do realize that you are interrupting my work. Since the success of *Le Caducée* I am very much in demand. I have two new plays on the stocks."

"I'm delighted with your success, father, but on the other hand Mouton is a disgrace to us. We Rothschilds are supposed to be good at running things."

"The place does not belong to me. It belongs to your grandmother."

"She isn't interested, she would make it over to you if you put it to her."

"I have quite enough responsibilities as it is. Surely there are people qualified to deal with such problems. Close the door as you go out."

And he disappeared into another cloud of smoke. Nevertheless something had got through. I heard that he had approached my grandmother but that the old lady was unwilling. She didn't want to part with any of her husband's property—it was God-given, she said—but there was a sudden change of heart when her lawyer told her that by giving Mouton to my father death duties would be avoided. It was an old story, I'd heard it all my life. All my relations seemed to be haunted by the amount of paperwork they had to get through before they could die. Instead of simply turning their toes up, while their troubles drifted away on the tide of time, they were busy altering wills, signing over their entire estate or salting away a good slice of their fortune in Switzerland. No wonder they were flaked out before their time.

In Dickens's time it was your nurse, or your nearest and dearest, who pulled the sheets from under your spotted carcass, now it was the government. If grandmother managed to die reasonably penniless, she'd save 90 percent of her death tax.

My father sent two of his management staff to investigate the situation at Mouton and report back to him. A private detective went with them.

*   *   *

Spring gave way to a marvelous summer in 1922 and my blonde was still my passion: lovely Henriette, more ardent than ever. Our flame had been fanned by her husband's jealousy and the rare Parisian matinées we had snatched when he was off guard. I forgot to mention him before, but you might have guessed I'd chosen a married woman. I always did. It was safer. Anyway there was no husband at Arcachon this year, they generally spent their summer holidays apart. We were very modern in the old days.

I meant to steal Henriette away to Mouton at the first opportunity. I kidnapped her as soon as she got off the train. We waved good-bye to all the cousins and friends and raced along the road to Pauillac, the vines nodding in their summer greenery, the sky an enormous vault of Médoc blue.

Into the yard, through a flurry of protesting hens, and not a soul in sight. Henriette went off to tidy up and I caught a glimpse of Merilda opening the door to greet her. Two chaps, lolling about in the stable, touched their berets when they saw me, and Monsieur Bonnefous, the maître de chai, emerged suddenly as if from nowhere.

Did I know that my father's advisers had appointed a new manager? No, he hadn't been seen yet. The old one? He was probably still around. He couldn't really see what all the stir was about. Everything was jogging along as usual. I couldn't see much jogging; an air of idleness hung over the whole place. Perhaps it was the heat.

My old man had never said a word to me about the new manager or the dire reports he had received. Just his way—he was secretive, he did things behind your back. In any case I intended to make my own investigation.

Henriette had decided to take a bath; the boy Roger was already working away at the pump. The *toilette* would be a lengthy business. . . . I might as well take a look round right away.

Émile Gerbaud was busy at his barrel making. A decent chap, not given to gossip. I passed the time of day with him. He gave me a cryptic look and when I asked how it was all going, he shrugged his shoulders, grunted and threw a dirty look at Bonnefous, who was hanging around the open door.

The evening passed merrily with Henriette in a naughty mood, and the night was divine, lost in our feather bed, swimming in the clouds.

The next morning I was up and about early and went poking my nose into every nook and cranny. I was staggered at the mess and neglect I found everywhere. The men loitered in twos and threes, eyeing me as I passed. Perhaps my smart new country outfit was putting them off. I'd had it made specially to impress Henriette: knee breeches, black and white check waistcoat and a Tyrolean hat.

Merilda had thrown out some dark hints last night but I couldn't pin her down, and there was Gerbaud's uneasy air; it could have been a half warning. This morning the atmosphere was positively surly. I decided that my father's detective had put everyone's back up. They all felt under suspicion. I tackled young Roger—boys don't have so many qualms about speaking out.

"Ah well," he said, "Do you want to take a walk?"

I followed him round the houses, along a narrow village street. He stood aside and pointed to a solidly built villa, with ornamental railings, quite a château in that street of humble dwellings.

"That's where your grandma's profits are going," he said. "My da reckons it's a shame, he says the old lady has always been good to the village." Then he pushed off before I could get another word out of him. I couldn't help feeling that we had somehow betrayed the good people of Mouton, and my grandmother.

Well, there was to be a dramatic turn of events at the end of summer when I got back to Paris. My bags were still in the hall when I was summoned to my father's study.

"Dammit," he said, butting the desk with his big belly. "You've seen this?"

He threw a few handwritten sheets at me.

"The new play?"

"No, not that! This!"

He had given me his play by mistake. He was trying to show me a police report.

"And take a look at that."

More sheets, written in beautiful copperplate, the year's returns pinned to them.

"The place is running into debt, heavily. What happened to the new manager?"

"He never appeared."

"What? And your grandmother's agent—what's his name?"

"De Miollis. He is getting on. . . ."

"On what?"

"On in years, father."

"So who's managing the sordid little place?"

"Well, no one at the moment."

"It's too much. This couldn't have come at a worse time. I don't even drink wine."

"No, father."

"On top of all that, I'm having trouble with my new play."

"I'm sorry to hear that. Can I help?"

"No, of course not. Well, perhaps you can. For a start, you'd better sit down and read it."

"I thought it was almost into production."

"It was. . . ."

"Going on at the Antoine . . ."

"Read it."

There was no getting out of it. I picked up the manuscript and retired to the corner of his large leather sofa. Meanwhile he was busy, fussing and phoning, occasionally padding across the room to see where I'd got to.

The play was amusing, a satire. A *nouveau riche* with social pretensions sets up a bogus company with the sole purpose of giving discreet handouts to penniless aristos. They repay him by bringing their titles to his table and adding a touch of class to his invitation cards. It was very funny and his characters quite recognizable: the old dowager prepared to sell her daughter for a box at the opera, everybody would know who she was, and the chorus of *pique-assiettes* rattling their coronets for the sake of a good meal. I could have named them all.

"Well?" he said, as I folded the last page away.

"It's good."

"Your mother won't have it."

I knew why at once. My mother collected just such burs at her skirts.

"What a pity, father. It's very good."

"We'll talk about that later. Meanwhile you have an appointment with Monsieur Jardot."

"I have?"

"Yes, and you'd better take that balance sheet along with you."

As I left, he picked up the play and lit another yellow Gauloise.

Monsieur Jardot was my father's lawyer. He was consulted about everything, every minute detail was turned over with him before any decision was made, and when it was, he would be left to cope with a mountain of notes, added by my father, to complicate the problem. I was sure he must have a swarm of little clerks hidden away in his back room, headed by his chief clerk, who was a nebulous character with parchment skin and shoe-button eyes which gleamed in the depths of his pebble glasses. Once my father's back was turned, I felt sure all those petty little jobs would be passed from Jardot, to chief clerk, to an army of little clerks.

I turned into the street where Jardot had his being, a street of lawyers, their names and degrees inscribed on black plaques in ornamental gold. Rue Mirabeau, a canyon between two tall cliffs of concrete, sufficiently close to prevent one ray of sunlight intruding on the scene, and topped by curly crests and scrolls which only the pigeons could enjoy. Monsieur Jardot nested at the foot of the darkest and steepest cliff.

I entered his outer office still a little mystified. Somebody punched a desk bell three times. Monsieur Jardot appeared.

There was the usual bony handshake and formal inquiry as

to my health and progress as he minced toward his mahogany desk—his button boots were too tight—and sat down to stare at the unblemished blotting pad.

"Working for your doctorate now, they tell me."

"Yes, monsieur. That is to say, I've begun work on my thesis. I think I know just about all there is to know about lenses and the effect of metals on glass."

"Splendid. Well, I have something rather important to put to you. You are now twenty."

"Yes, monsieur."

"Congratulations."

I didn't quite see why I was to be congratulated.

"It is not often a boy of twenty is given the chance to show his mettle."

"No, monsieur."

Monsieur Jardot bent forward to blow his nose. He had thin red hair, and long thin red mustaches.

"Bearing in mind your obvious attachment to the place and your . . . shall we call it instinct for leadership, your father has decided to entrust you with the management of Mouton."

I sat down. Monsieur Jardot pulled on his long mustaches. First the one on the right, then the one on the left.

"Rather a shock, what? Don't worry, we will be right behind you."

Well, I said to myself, a lot of help they'd be. There was a long pause. He must have noticed my expression.

"I can't believe you are hesitating," said the lawyer.

"I accept, conditionally," said I. "Is my father giving me full responsibility? If so, I need a letter to that effect, complete authority, the right to make decisions without consultation, and funds sufficient to cover the necessary expense."

Monsieur Jardot blew his nose again. "You have my complete confidence, Monsieur Philippe. Indeed, had it not been so, your father would never have . . ."

"Thank you, Monsieur Jardot."

"But we must go carefully on the money issue, otherwise . . ."

"There can be no otherwise about it, Monsieur Jardot. Either I have all that I ask or it's not on."

I was politely dismissed, but I thought I detected a slight touch of respect as he gave me his adieux. As I left, I heard him muttering into his speaking tube about an appointment with my father.

You would have thought my old man could have told me all this himself. Clever of him to unload the problem on to me. It remained to be seen whether he would give me enough money to find the solution, and rescue Mouton.

I waited every day, expecting some answer to my demands. None came. My father seemed to have disappeared. Was he at the theater? He wasn't in the house, nor was she. You could always tell by the servants' behavior: one heard laughter, doors were left open when mamma was away.

After a week I tore up the plans I'd been making. Ah well, if I'd lost Mouton, I'd gained a planet. One of my professors, Yves Rocard, had told me about a very gifted astronomer who was having to give up his research for lack of funds. I scraped together all I had and sent it to him. In return, he gave me a planet of his own discovery. He named it Planet Philippa. I never met my astronomer again, but Rocard and I were to meet many years later, in strange circumstances. He was stone deaf, but I'll tell you that story later, in its proper place.

As for my planet, I was very proud of it. When this world is a burned-out stub, I told everybody, I shall have somewhere to retire to. I could see myself sitting up there, alone in the galaxy, surveying the Milky Way from a tiny world of one. My friends pulled my leg. "If it's a nice place, don't forget to invite us."

I came back to earth with a bump one morning. An envelope arrived, on a silver salver. It contained a summons from my father. I went to his study at once. Was he going to give me all I needed? As soon as I saw him I knew that he'd forgotten all about Mouton.

"The contract was signed weeks ago, the casting is complete. The whole thing is held up."

"Why, father?"

"Your mother insists on changes."

He was almost in tears.

"I'll alter the names, modify some of the characters, soften it down. She says they are all instantly recognizable. You'll have to help me."

"She's afraid of a libel action?"

"No, it's not that."

"I see. Let's get to work then, papa."

We worked all day and all night, and a lot of fun went out of the play just to please my mother and her fatuous friends. In the morning, after we'd downed our final cup of black coffee, my father got up wearily and, taking the manuscript with him, made for the door. Now was the time to strike.

"You've forgotten Mouton, father."

His hand on the doorknob, he turned.

"No, I haven't," he said. "You shall have what you want."

"And you'll grant me full powers?"

"Yes, yes."

He was true to his word. A letter came that day, short and sweet; he gave me everything I'd asked for. I could hardly wait to pack. I raced to the station, found myself a wagon-lit.

Impossible to sleep, the train seemed slower than ever. All night, the wheels were saying, Hurry, hurry, here I come, life begins at twenty.

5

I come down dah wid my hat caved in,
Doodah! doodah!
I go back home wid a pocket full of tin,
Oh! doodah day!

STEPHEN COLLINS FOSTER

I arrived on October 22, 1922, the first Rothschild to move into the Médoc, the new manager, the boss. It was the fair weather that always follows the harvest. There was a dying fire in the courtyard. One or two of the men were standing looking at it. The boy Roger was with them.

"What's this?"

They stared at me, one of them raked over the ashes. I looked. Someone had been burning the books. I could see the remains of bills and accounts on blackened scraps of paper blowing all over the place.

"Who did this?"

The men said nothing for a long while. Finally Émile Gerbaud shook his head and looked towards the village.

"No names, no pack drill. Your man has gone anyway, vamoosed, vanished."

"It wasn't only the house he built for himself," said the boy Roger. "He bought land for a vineyard with your money, and used all your materials to work it, all your machines and tools, even the vines he planted were pinched."

The local police came. I said I wanted no prosecution. Let him go, forget it. We had been absentee landlords, no one had cared a damn about the place. He knew it and took advantage of our lack of interest. Well, from now on things would be different.

But first I had to win the confidence of the men who were left, they still looked at me suspiciously. At least he can't uproot the vines, I heard one of them say.

They knew I knew nothing. I'd have to watch my step. All the same, some decisions had to be made, without delay. The work team badly needed a boost; morale was very low. At some point I would have to be ruthless, and I've never been a ruthless person. All the same, the wastrels and idlers would have to go, but how was I to separate the wheat from the chaff? Over the years this small society had become a closed shop, and on top of that everybody seemed to be related to everyone else. I took the plunge, sacked people from every rank, and at once earned the respect of the rest. There was no resentment; a firm hand was welcome. I had not realized the importance of direction till then. These tough *vignerons* of Mouton had been making wine all their lives, and their fathers before them; they knew nothing beyond the little world of Pauillac; even their work isolated them. Tending the vines, lost in that lonely landscape, they hardly seemed to speak, even to each other, but among them there was enough skill and know-how to raise the whole standard of wine growing—if I could get it out of them. I invited a representative from each section of the work to my office, or what passed for my office. They sat uneasily on the edge of their chairs, caps on knees. I told them that we should share our problems and find solutions together. Nobody said a word. Of course I didn't realize that they'd never spoken to a boss in their whole lives. I tried a few jokes. There was a long silence, then somebody gave a grunt of approval.

I called them together every week and, slowly but surely, the ice was cracked. Someone would make a tentative suggestion, and they'd be surprised when I tried it out. Soon I found a title for them: my Commission Technique. They approved of that and the name stuck. That original band stayed with me all their lives, and it would be impossible to estimate how much Mouton owes to them. The commission still functions and, wherever I am, I receive their weekly report.

My father's new manager never did materialize. In fact I may have told him not to bother, I can't remember, probably I did. The doddery old gentleman at Bordeaux, the Baron de Miollis, who had been looking after the business since Moses was in the fire brigade, was on his way out anyway. He should have been retired years before. That side of things didn't bother me. I would sell the wine myself; two or three days in Bordeaux would fix that. I let it be known that I wouldn't be introducing any newcomers. There were some cagey looks—all the same I felt I was making some progress with the Moutonards. I wanted to win them over, I needed their devotion, but sometimes when I came out with a bright idea, they would listen, gazing over my shoulder into the distance, and say nothing. Then as I wandered off I'd hear them exchanging dry comments in that private language of theirs. I was still a foreigner, but they sensed that we had something in common. You see, I'm a peasant myself, a peasant in a silk nightshirt if you like, but I don't puke at the smell of steaming dung, or blench at the sight of a newborn calf; I can live without perfumed baths, pocket handkerchiefs and Bach on a harpsichord before breakfast. I like the smell of fresh woman, horseflesh and garlic, and my dogs sleep on my bed. So now you know why I liked Mouton.

Merilda spoiled me, preparing my favorite dishes, heaped with truffles and frogs' legs, and petite Odette put the hot brick wrapped in flannel in my bed on cold nights. All the same it was lonely. I read Ovid by the light of a spirit lamp, awakened at four in the morning by the schemozzle in the yard, oxen being yoked, horses harnessed. I began to savor the wine, to distinguish between the ordinary and the good; the exquisite was yet to come. I brooded over the state of the place. A lot of changes would have to be made, but it would take time and good planning: anything drastic would be disastrous in that eighteenth-century world where people went to bed with candles at nine o'clock, and deep silence descended on us all. If anyone owned a clock, it was a family heirloom, and I doubt whether they had ever seen a calendar. As for me I had only just learned that it takes five years for a vine root to blossom and give fruit. I decided to invest in a new racing car.

I stayed at Mouton long enough to be sure my team was pulling together. If I knew nothing about wine making, I'd had enough sense to winkle out the men who did and give them my confidence. At the same time I made it my business to study the methods of work, in field and shed, surveying the working areas, taking note of stumbling blocks, snags, time-wasting routines. I also bought myself a microscope and took a long look at the vine bugs.

Sometimes I'd listen to the old vignerons, who knew that land like the backs of their hands—a job getting them to talk but once started there was no stopping them. It was generally the taciturn old blokes who had pearls to scatter, if you caught them in the right mood at the right time, walking home at the end of the morning's work, or sheltering from a heavy rainstorm. . . .

> *Quand les hirondelles volent très bas,*
> *C'est signe qu'il va pleuvoir.*

Ah! And he'd give a great spit.

Or, looking over at the horizon, squinting at the sky before making his pronouncement, so often wrong, but still repeated like an old refrain. . . .

> *Quand le ciel est rouge*
> *Vent ou plouge.*

He speaks with a twang no one has ever tried to set down on paper. Imagine it round and rolling like broad Devonshire in

England, or a midwest burr if you know that one better. Occasionally he'll bend to pick up a handful of small pink and gray pebbles rounded by water, over a million years.

"You're standing on a great limb of land thrown up once, some while ago mind, by the fierce Atlantic Ocean. It's all stones, stones that give the soil its nature and hold the sun's warmth. Good for the grape, especially in this climate.

"You can't get good wine if the soil isn't right. The nature of the soil is the most important part of your wine growing, then comes good husbandry naturally, and the rest is heaven's work.

> *Il n'y a pas un samedi en France*
> *Sans que le soleil fasse sa révérence.*

"You want to know the seasons? Then start with St. Vincent in September.

> *Quand St. Vincent est beau,*
> *Il y a plus de vin que d'eau.*

"Then comes Toussaint, when the sun is almost gone. Toussaint, All Saints' or All-Hallows', call it what you will, it's known all over the world. We go to mass that day to pray for a good year and we're no sooner by our own fireside than winter is down on us. You reckon there's nothing to do in winter, the earth asleep, the vineyard all bare and empty? You're wrong. You're pruning for a start, forever pruning. And I'll tell you why—if you like old stories. For it was once upon a time, as the saying goes, that a certain donkey, a very intelligent beast, content with his lot grazing away up on a mountainside, strayed one day down to the lower slopes quite by chance. And there his blue eyes lighted on the vines and the tender shoots which sprout from the branches. He tasted one and he liked it and he went on to the next and the next, munching away till the owner of the vineyard happened to see him, ran out and beat him and chased him away. But, when the harvest came round, the owner found that the vines the donkey had pruned for him yielded grapes much richer and juicier than the rest. From that time on, we pruned, and that's how the main secret of fine wine was discovered, by a donkey. Donkeys wouldn't do that nowadays, mind you. Pruning has become an art. You have to know which shoot to cut and which to leave and you have to be right every time.

"Look at the vine in winter, all you see is two withered branches, two stretched-out arms. You can't believe that come July you'll be waist high in green leaves.

"Summer's a fine bustling time, but it's ordinary when you contrast it with the vine in winter, bare and elegant as she is.

> *Noël au balcon*
> *Pâques aux Tisons.*

"December's for muck spreading and in January the women are out gathering the bits fallen from the pruning, brown twigs now, fit for nothing but burning, though they make a sweet-scented fire. You never tasted anything so good as meat grilled on vine wood.

"February is men's work again and it's heavy. You don't need all your wrappings against the cold. The work will warm you. All those rows of stakes you see have to be repaired or renewed. They're there to support the lengths of wire, where the vines trail.

"March? Wrenching up the dead leaves. Vines last many a year, if they get the attention they should, up to a hundred sometimes, but like us they don't give much fruit in their old age. When they do, it's good still. They're at their prime when they're about twenty-five or thirty. And April?

> *Quand il tonne en avril*
> *Foncez cuves et barils.*

"Those vines beyond the Carruades have only just been planted, it'll be five or even seven years before they give us wine. You'll have to learn patience now you've come to Mouton.

"In April or thereabouts the vines begin to bud. It's a pretty sight, reminds you of nothing so much as a small bird alighted on a bough. That's when we have to watch out and do our best to protect them from the pests the Lord sends to try us. Oh yes, we've got a few treatments, but against naughty worms we can't do much.

"May's the time for following the plow, turning over the soil between the vine rows. Five or six plowings in the year there are. Used to be at the pace of oxen or sturdy horses, but in the last twenty years, tractors—faster and far more efficient, they say.

"June, and the women are back, tying up. July we're looking for grapes among green foliage, and August sees us cleaning the paths and ditches preparing for a good harvest. The grapes are turning red and we're weeding. Now come the critical days. Frost may kill everything. Sun and rain won't harm us, but with frost the grape can die on the branch.

"Autumn is here. It's October and every owner is wary, watching his neighbors. 'Well, she's just about ready. When do we start?'

"Decision time and everything depends on that decision. A day late and rain and frost may spoil the grapes, a day too soon and the fruit may not be ripe.

"They start calling round to see each other. 'Lafite has already started, when is Mouton going to begin?' 'Pedesclaux starts tomorrow.' 'Pantet Canet hasn't made up its mind.' And all the while the boss goes round sampling the grapes.

"It's a great time and a lively time, when you've been working on your own all year. The people come from far and near to gather grapes. The girls wear their kiss-me-nots, sun bonnets they wore when the British soldiers were here so their young faces wouldn't be seen."

I asked him which war that was in.

"Oh, the Hundred Years' War," he told me.

"When the harvest is done," he went on, "we go to the Big House with a handsome bouquet of flowers for the owner's wife. The Gerbaude of the harvest we call it. Mind you there's been no owner at Mouton for many a long year, let alone a wife."

Well, I knew a little more about the seasons after all that, but the ways he had learned were not eternal. The oxen with which he plowed, the beautiful shire horses you saw everywhere and the kiss-me-nots have disappeared long since. Now tractors plow and helicopters spray and soon the harvest will be brought in by machine. Nevertheless, Mouton will always be Mouton.

6

Le faux et le merveilleux sont plus humains que l'homme vrai.

PAUL VALÉRY

SOMETHING was happening to my father. Do men have a change of life at fifty? He no longer cared what my mother thought or said. I think he was very angry about his play, his satirical comedy. *Le Moulin de la galette* he'd called it, which is rather slangy; it means something like The Money Mill. He had agreed to her demands, made all the cuts she wanted, and then the maddening creature couldn't be bothered to go and see it. That, I believe, was the last straw.

Whatever had caused it, he was certainly a different man. He threw open his Parisian home to his theatrical friends, writers, painters, actors and actresses, and even bought himself some new clothes. Papa's soirées were, all of a sudden, the talk of the town.

One night, as I was leaving the house, I heard peals of laughter echoing along the corridor. There was light and the smell of cigars and booze coming from a large reception room, usually as dark and silent as a tomb. I looked in. Henri Bernstein was holding the floor and his audience was plainly theatrical. I had never thought much of his plays but outside the theater he was a great raconteur and very wicked. His anecdotes may have been apocryphal but his impersonations were superb: old Sarah Bernhardt, one legged, playing Napoleon's young son in *L'Aiglon;* Cécile Sorel doomed to live with eyes that never closed because she'd had one operation too many on her sagging lids.

Bernstein was the lion of the season and said to be the biggest rake in town. We became friends later, rivals perhaps, but he had his wings clipped. I never did. He fell in love with Eve Curie, Marie's *soignée* daughter, and that was enough. She was too clever for him and so very smart and good-looking. She still is.

My father was charmed with his new self and he even seemed to have taking a liking to me. He asked me to join the board of his Fondation Curie. I was amazed and I accepted. At the first meeting I attended I was thunderstruck. She was there, the great lady herself: Marie Curie, white haired, with a little black hat. She spoke rarely and then quietly and quickly, but she was deeply attentive. Cancer research, the continuation of her work, was all she lived for. I have never forgotten that. Today the Institut Curie flourishes and I am its vice-president for life.

Of course my mother kept away from papa's parties; she found his new friends vulgar and the theater sordid. I must add that little Marthe Régnier was always at his side nowadays and mamma could hardly have failed to notice that. Marthe had been in nearly all his plays and still looked the pretty ingénue, in the right light. She was a bit past it, but she was so sweet, really sweet. I adored her.

I took to drifting in and out of my father's soirées. One night I was there when he announced his intention of building a theater of his own, to general applause. I didn't for one moment believe he was serious, but then by chance I heard that he had actually engaged architects, chosen a site in Montmartre and was going ahead with his theater plans. He hadn't said a word about it to me. Why? I went and took a look at the site for myself. Just as I thought—dreadful, tucked away in a narrow street, way off the main road, hidden behind the boulevard de Clichy. He must have known that I'd disapprove.

I told him what I thought. He wouldn't have it. "There are lots of famous Paris theaters in side streets," he said. Anyway it was too late, he had already bought the site.

I made it my business to find out when he was having his first design session and invited myself to go along. There were three architects in the room when I got there. The youngest and brightest talked only in drawings, making charcoal sketches on huge sheets of paper. This must be the famous Charles Siclis. Papa was lolling back in his swivel chair, saying nothing. I asked what sort of theater it was going to be. That did it, ideas started flying round the room like paper darts. It should be a multi-purpose building. It must have a cyclorama: no one had seen one in Paris. A cyc would require a great deal of space, three times the depth of the stage. Germany was the place for new stage techniques. It would be worth going to have a look. Linnebach had invented giant lifts and mobile stages. Piscator was using moving walkways and multiscreen projection. Scene changing now could be as slick as film montage. We must make provision for projection.

At that time, the whole Paris theater was still drifting about in the nineteenth century. New ideas were rare. I liked the sound of the German theater. But, I said, we mustn't let machinery take over. Sets won't play the shows.

Charles Siclis gave me a look. After the meeting, I asked him if I might call and see him at his drawing office. "Come whenever you like," he said, I didn't only call, I practically moved in. I wanted to learn to read working drawings and understand scale. I would sit fascinated as he worked away at his drawing board throwing out ideas about space and light. For the first time in my life I felt I was getting some real education. I was learning to see.

Should I abandon everything and study architecture, spend my time with bright people like Siclis? I had a flair for design, I knew that, I just needed encouragement and stimulus. I was hardly going to find that at Mouton. The neighboring landlords were duller than my vignerons, much duller, they led such boring lives. My dear father had the only interesting job:

theater. Good, but if I was going to pull his chestnuts out of the fire for him at Mouton, I would need some reward. For a start a home of my own, on the seashore somewhere beautiful . . . Siclis-built. It could be near enough to Mouton, that uncivilized hole. If I could entertain my friends, go yachting and water-skiing, enjoy myself occasionally, Mouton might be bearable. I knew papa would provide the money, he was never mean to me. I decided to put him in the picture right away.

He was shut up in his study with his architectural trio when I got there. I don't know why he bothered: Siclis was the only one with any ideas. Along the passage quite a few people were waiting to see him. They looked like petitioners; one eccentric-looking gentleman had an automatic milking machine with him. By the door to the stairs a gentle-looking person stood waiting his turn. He knew me by sight but realized I had forgotten his name and helped me out.

"Édouard Marjary."

"Oh yes," I said, none the wiser. "Mustard?"

"Canned pheasant."

"How is it doing?"

"It isn't. And I just can't get to see your father."

"Give up," I said. "All he wants to talk about now is theater."

"So I hear, but his canning factory is not doing very well. It never has made a profit. The best thing would be to sell out at once before any more debts are incurred. I really have to see him."

I told him to go at once to Monsieur Jardot and not waste any more time in my father's anterooms. I offered to go with him. I didn't fancy waiting around for my father either. I might mention my house to old Bonychops, and he could work out a costing. En route I asked Marjary about himself. He was a rare bird, a country man who had studied bookkeeping and management; his mother owned a small shop somewhere in the Dordogne. The canning factory had been his first job. He had applied for work with my father, who had invited him to prepare a scheme for promoting canned pheasant with a complete

cost analysis and ideas for improving the efficiency of the factory, which was already in operation. Marjary went to work and
prepared a report, advising that the canning scheme was simply
not viable. Whereupon my father immediately gave him the job
of running it. Now he was out of a job, or soon would be.
Marjary was obviously a good-humored man and wise: before
we reached Monsieur Jardot's place I was asking him to work
with me.

"What as?"

"My personal assistant, private secretary."

He turned me down. "Out of the question I'm afraid. I have
to see your father through this business."

So he did, and I saw how tactfully he dealt with everything
and everybody, including my father. What's more, his books
were meticulous. He was my man. He'd make such a difference
at Mouton.

When I heard that he was off to the Dordogne to visit his
mother for the weekend, I told him he had to come to Mouton.
"It's next door," I said. We went together. I showed him round,
talked bravely of my plans for the future, then I asked him
straight if he would throw in his lot with me. "Yes," he said,
"I'll stay. This place suits me." He moved into a bare room
above the stables and stayed for forty-two years.

I've been lucky sometimes in my life, guardian angels have
appeared on the doorstep from time to time. I also have atten-
dant devils. Édouard was my unlikely angel.

In Mouton he grew rounder and rosier. He had a merry face
and a Charlie Chaplin mustache. The mustache was the key to
the mood. Ask him a question, the mustache would twitch, but
there would be no reply. One just had to wait for the twitching
to stop. It could drive you mad. Fling a bunch of brilliant ideas
at him, and all you'd get in reply would be a quizzical look and
a slight raising of the whiskers, starboard side.

"You are so conservative," I'd tell him. "After all, do you
really know any more than I do about wine growing? You've
only been a wet day in the place." That was true, but he had an

inherited wisdom which I lacked. He was quiet and modest, I was flamboyant and theatrical. If Mouton flourishes today it is very largely due to his spade work (and a bit to my flag waving, of course). He could talk with understanding to everyone from vigneron to wine merchant, knowing exactly what their problem was and where they stood. There was no fiddling in his day.

We shared the tip known as the office, and we traveled the highways and byways together. I don't think we ever had a harsh word. We were known as Don Quixote and Sancho Panza, though some of my windmills were real enemy giants, and I had not only to tilt at them but to bring them down.

It was a good partnership, only broken by the war years. In 1966, when he retired, it took three very bright young men to replace him. He chose them himself and trained them. His retirement didn't last very long; he died in 1967, and two hundred of us went from Mouton to Le Bugue in the Périgord for his funeral. His wisdom is still quoted by the men who worked with him.

I honor your memory, Édouard Marjary.

7

They all laughed at Rockefeller Center
Now they're fighting to get in.

IRA GERSHWIN

IN the early 1920s the fortunes of "My Lady Vine" were in eclipse. Wine drinking was not the smart business it has become. A new invention, the cocktail, was the thing. For "le six o'clock," the new girl with her Eton crop, long cigarette holder and tiny, straight skirt would demand gin or whisky and ——. People even drank whiskey with their meals. New concoctions were *à la mode* and wine was given away, *en carafe,* in the restaurants. It was a drink for the groundlings. Only a few connoisseurs seemed to care about the great old wines and there was nothing to attract the others. Labels were plain, old fashioned and dull, and often wine was badly treated—it could be "off" when you uncorked it. With gin or whiskey you knew where you were.

One fine day I was watching the barrels of new wine being loaded onto the drays. It was my second harvest at Mouton and I was disheartened. I had just driven from Paris, and every hoarding en route had been plastered with advertisements for the zazzy new drinks: "La Suze, l'amie de l'estomac"; "Picotin, apértif américain, honi soit qui mal y pense"; "St. Raphael, quinquina, c'est la santé."

The drays went lumbering down the road to Bordeaux.
They looked like an 1890s painting. Harvest home. Sunset on
the road to Pauillac. The picture needed touching up or maybe
scrapping altogether; it was dreary and old hat, what's more it
was all wrong. It came to me suddenly, the simple, obvious,
extraordinary idea which was to revolutionize the wine trade.
They could keep their hoardings and their slogans. I would
put wine right back at the top of the poll. I knew exactly how it
should be done.

They would call it revolution, but it would be a revolution
that had its roots in tradition. Always the peasant on his holding and the rich man on his estate had each cared for his own
wine in his own way, and every plot had yielded its own distinctive flavor. The old locals swore they could tell which side of
the railway line the wine came from.

Our *cuves*, the great wooden, iron-ringed vats in which the
grapes ferment, were works of art, built *in situ* by a master
craftsman. Wine for our own consumption was watched over
like an only child during its three-year sleep in the oak casks,
occasionally clarified with beaten white of egg, which Fleming,
the penicillin man, told me adds lysozyme which protects the
sight. Every year our store of oak casks was renewed, the wine
gently moved from barrel to barrel, and when its time came the
wine was bottled for us by our own maître de chai. At our table,
en carafe, it was labeled in his handwriting and its year of birth
given.

Why then, in the name of goodness, were we shipping the
wines we were selling to Bordeaux at the most critical period of
their lives? Anything might become of them in the wine merchants' sheds. Three years' maturation in a strange environ-
ment, the very time when we should be responsible for nursing
the precious juice. Had we ever known exactly what was going
into those bottles which carried our labels? It wasn't good
enough. That was my wine rolling down to Bordeaux in those
heavy barrels, and I wanted to be sure it was still mine when it
was labeled. Why not put my name on the bottle? That would

be an innovation—until now nobody had ever signed a bottle —but I, Philippe, intended to let the world and his wife know that my wine was the best. No criticism of the wine merchants intended: many of them were men of taste and integrity. (Not all of them, mind you, there's always somebody doing a bit of trafficking in the wine business, though they don't always get away with it; witness the Cruse affair a few years ago resulting in a disaster for a house which had reigned in Bordeaux for over a hundred years.) I believed that my idea would give the wine trade the boost it needed, put it back among the aristo-crats so that the good man in Manchester or Maryland would know where his wine was born and nurtured and who its par-ents were.

I couldn't wait to tell the world, but first I had to put it right with the neighbors: Haut Brion, Margaux, Latour and Lafite. I hoped to convert all four of them without too much trouble but I'd begin with Pierre Moreau, part owner of Margaux. He had taken a liking to me from the start; I knew I would be able to win him over easily. He was an old dear with a mop of white hair and splendid mustaches. I caught him in a good mood. Before I'd finished my sales talk he was bubbling over with enthusiasm. "A superb idea. It will give a whole new boost to the wine trade!" Monsieur Moreau was a merchant as well as a grower.

"We'll call it château-bottling," I said.

Together we went to see André Gibert, who owned Haut Brion, his beautiful French phrases slightly spoiled by the click-ing of his new false teeth. Then there was the Comte René de Beaumont at Latour. What a character—huge beaked nose, meerschaum pipe, a shabby shapeless jacket and spats, every inch the run-down aristocrat. They were both delighted with the idea, so there was only Lafite left, but Lafite, being so to speak, in the family, might prove difficult. Our two houses have a long and checkered history. I'm afraid I have to fill you in on part of it—I'll keep it short.

My English great-grandfather, Nathaniel, bought Mouton in

1853. In 1868 he was boasting of "extraordinarily good wine which I have sold at the fantastic price of 5,000 francs the barrel."

Baron James, his uncle and father-in-law, youngest of the original Frankfurt brothers, was jealous, having already tried to buy the neighboring estate, Lafite, and failed. He tried again, offering 4,140,000 gold francs, nearly four times as much as Nathaniel had paid for Mouton. It was accepted. A few weeks later he died, just as he was trying to get a better price than Nathaniel for the wine.

That was the beginning of the family rivalry, which has existed ever since, sometimes blowing hot, sometimes cold; and since the two estates border on each other, and here and there overlap, it can be inflamed from time to time by squabbling among the estate workers over a fallen tree or a shattered wall.

Since 1905 the Rothschild bank in Paris had been run, discreetly and unadventurously, by two cousins, Édouard, the elegant, and handsome Robert. They also owned Lafite, but they were never there. If you had a problem, you talked to Monsieur Mortier, their manager. Should he consider it of sufficient importance he would go to Paris to consult his two bosses, and await their instructions. On this occasion, having heard me out, he went to Paris.

I followed soon after, summoned to the Rothschild bank. Baron Édouard received me. He had a strange face, thin with a long, crooked nose. He was of my father's generation; they were distant cousins, but of very different stock. On my father's side, medicine, invention, art; on theirs, banking, politics, hunting. All the same, Baron Édouard had always been very kind to me; he seemed to have a soft spot for Henri's son, though not for Henri. I had been invited to Ferrières, his family home, several times—a monstrously ugly place, I must say.

"How now, my young friend," said he. "And what do you think you're playing at? How long have you been in the Médoc? You do realize, I suppose, that nobody has ever found fault with the way our wines are bottled. Very much to the contrary. In my opinion these merchant fellows do a first-rate job. Where would we be without them?"

"The wine passes through too many hands, Cousin Édouard—first it's offered to the brokers, then to the Bordeaux merchants, then to some wholesaler, who may be in the Antipodes, then to a retailer—then . . . We should be growers *and* merchants."

"Very commendable, all these bright ideas, young man, but the traditions which govern the wine trade have developed over centuries. You may have heard of Le Bureau de la Répression des Fraudes. It exists to put a stop to any mischief. There are laws to protect the consumer, my boy, the strictest control over quality. The large areas known as 'appellations' are carefully defined, so is the type of wine to be grown there and even the number of vines which may be planted therein."

"I do know about the wine laws, cousin. I also know that as things are it is the wine grower who carries the loss, the merchant who makes the profit, living off the backs of the growers, as he does."

"Now that is mere foolishness. Where would the poor producers be without the merchant's money? Most growers have no capital, they have to wait for the merchant to pay them before they can buy weed killer."

"Because he pays them in dribs and drabs, he hasn't much capital to fall back on either. The whole industry wants tuning up."

"I see. And I suppose you think your scheme is going to do the trick? Has it struck you that with your system the poor grower will be worse off? He'll have to wait three years before he sees any cash."

"No, the brokers will still buy the wine at harvest time. Only we will look after it for the next three years, instead of sending it to Bordeaux."

"But they're used to paying cash on delivery. Without the stock it's not going to be easy for them to raise the cash."

"They could pay by installments—three, let's say, spread over nine months."

"And have you asked yourself how many growers will be able to afford the necessary outlay? Have you worked out how much this wonderful idea of yours would cost?"

He seized his slim gold everlasting pencil and made calculations on the blotter.

He was right. It wouldn't be easy. Maybe it would drive some of the little men out of business. But they were going broke anyway. The main thing was to put some verve back into the wine trade, market the château wines for the aristocrats which they were, and produce more wines of quality.

Cousin Édouard was getting his figures right.

". . . Taking an average figure, say three harvests each of four hundred casks, allowing three by four meters for each cask, that's going to mean quite a large area. . . ."

My thoughts flew out of the window to our little old chai at Mouton. It was scarcely big enough to allow us to maneuver the dray horses when we were shifting the casks.

". . . Plus space for storing, for approximately 100,000 bottles, add the cost of installing bottling equipment at each château . . ."

"It would be a guarantee of quality, it will give the wine distinction. Each owner would be responsible for his own wine. You know, cousin, many of the so-called châteaux are now nothing but fronts, names. . . . "

I was repeating myself. Anyway, he wasn't listening, he was completing his calculations. He gave a flourish. "Reckon on a million francs, at least. And what for? Simply to make a break with tradition and upset our old friends the wine merchants. I'm going to give you a little advice, young friend, you go back home and hold your horses."

I was dismayed, but not discouraged, at least not till the storm broke. Christian Cruse, of the most famous merchant house in Bordeaux, led the attack with an article in *La Petite Gironde*. He laughed the idea to scorn. "In any case nothing will come of it, it would mean the ruination of the wine trade."

Letters even appeared in *The Times* of London. Berry Bros, the English importers, declared that their reputation was under attack. They are still cross with me, even today.

You cannot imagine how much the idea of château-bottling upset people, especially the old dodos. "Who is this young man? Is he questioning our capability or our honesty?"

Someone advised my father to take me away. "Why?" he said. "Let him cut his teeth."

I might have given up but my dear old gentlemen at Haut Brion, Latour and Margaux, backed me all along the line, especially Pierre Moreau. He was great. Through him, the best of the brokers, the Lawtons, were won over. Then I heard that Lafite was having second thoughts.

The time had come for a get-together. Nobody ever got together in the Médoc. Nobody ever ate well in the Médoc either. They still don't. I invited my converts to dinner at the famous Chapon Fin in Bordeaux. Would Lafite come? That was the question. I received a letter from the bank, informing me that Monsieur Mortier, the manager, would be instructed to attend; so I booked a table in the name of "The Five."

Monsieur Mortier turned out to be a rather severe man and a Freemason, but we all sat down in friendly style. Luckily the food was excellent and the wine impeccable. I talked about publicity; they winced. I changed the word, tried "glamour." Accepted. We came to the topic of the day, château-bottling. To my amazement they were all for it, even Lafite. I proposed that we sign a document committing ourselves to château-bottling and engaging to help each other in all matters, technical and commerical, and that we call ourselves the Association of Five.

Monsieur Mortier enlarged on Lafite's knowledge and experience, then with a superior air informed us that the barons Édouard and Robert never signed anything; it was not their custom. "Our word is enough," said he. The other four signed, Lafite never.

The storm began to die down as word of our agreement got about. We had already decided that our get-together should become a regular institution, as the first had been so pleasant and useful. So we met once a month, exchanged ideas and gossip, of course, mulled over problems and enjoyed a fabled cuisine under the Chapon Fin's spreading indoor tree.

Our club, if you could call it that, was the first of its kind in the Médoc. Everyone talked about the Association of Five—the name stuck.

I was worried about the storage problem at Mouton. I would have to patch up the old chai and extend it. I asked everybody if they knew of a good local architect. My progress report at the second dinner was a long moan about the chap who'd been recommended to me. I'd just received his plans for the extension of the chai, very 1910 art school, all shading and trees and suburban Tudor. I should have known: a rash of Swiss chalets and bizarre villas with bell towers and medieval windows had been appearing all over the Médoc.

I thought of Charles Siclis, busy on his pleasure space on the rue Pigalle, and wondered what he would have done with a chai. Imagine his ideas in poor old broken-down Mouton. Would any artist work in these backwoods? It was worth a try. I called to see him.

"It's the sticks," I told him. "There isn't one decent building in the place, but there's room to make something happen, and no restrictions."

He took a weekend off and we went to Mouton. One look at the old chai and, "It's no use tinkering about with that," he said. "Erase it, build a new one."

"Will you design it?"

"Yes."

And when you come to Mouton you will see, as two white doors roll back, a glorious piece of décor, the great chai that Siclis built. It is a hundred meters long and, as far as you can see, totally unsupported, the cool white length of its walls broken only by columns of light. At the far end, I have Mouton's coat of arms, two giant rams, rampant.

It took three years to build, from 1924 to 1927. The soil underneath was so hard it had to be dynamited.

I had no intention of waiting for the new chai before I started the whole process of château-bottling. I stored my wine anywhere I could find, the barrels stacked one on top of the other. Villages were scoured for disused chais. "Mouton 1924, mise en bouteille au château" was going to make its début in 1927, no matter what it cost.

"More money than sense," they said.

During the works, part of the old chai collapsed and went crashing down into the cellars. Nine-tenths of the 1925 vintage was destroyed.

"It's a judgment on him."

It was a nasty big hole. There was only one thing to do, speed up the tempo. Not only would my bottles be ready for 1927, but I would give them a new look. I was sick and tired of seeing Mouton go out into the world badly dressed, sporting that dreary nineteenth-century label with no design about it at all, and no color.

What would be right? It would have to be something special, my first label. Why not the latest thing, a cubist design? Jean Carlu was famous for introducing cubism into advertising, you could see his work on all the hoardings of Paris. Just the man. When he sent me his design I was thrilled with it.

"I'll keep it forever," I said.

In 1927 I stood and waited for the first château-bottles to appear. The old handlift came groaning to a halt. There they were. The Carlu label, red, gold, green, gray and black, made a dazzling, dancing border. They would catch the eye anywhere. They did.

Whether it was the label or not, château-bottling did the trick. Within a year, "Mise en bouteille au château" was a sign of quality, Médocain. Now it's universal.

8

Consider well the proportion of things. It is better to be a young June bug, than an old bird of Paradise.

MARK TWAIN

EACH time I returned to gay Paree from Mouton I felt an inch taller. I'd whizz through mad Montmartre, its colored lights making a bizarre ballet of the crowded boulevard, call by to see how the theater was coming on, rush on to the cocktail party of the day and make my entrance to its crazy chatter. "Where have you been? You missed Danny's first night. Colette turned up with bare legs and painted toenails. Of course now it's the *dernier cri*."

In that ephemeral world, a fashion could last all of a week. I may have built myself up a bit, even to you, my perspicacious reader, as a dedicated viticulturist, but you mustn't get the impression that I missed spending a misspent youth. You will have noticed, as you skimmed the pages of this book, that I'm no Adonis. I was never handsome, nor even a fine figure of a man, but I can't say that this put me at a disadvantage. I was young and eager, and I had staying power. The girls liked that.

You young emancipated ladies of today, don't be misled by all those sentimental cards with hands entwined, forget-me-not borders and wedding rings. Poor old things, you probably say, they can't have had much fun.

It may have been true, as John Marston said, that women feared to name that which they did not fear to handle. Wooing may have taken a little longer, and underclothes had more buttons and bows—but the wooing was all part of the game, and the underclothes were very pretty. Nowadays you've no sooner kissed a lady's hand than you're in bed with her, or worse, stuck in some uncomfortable corner of the house or garden. There's not enough comfort about and courtship seems very much out of favor. Pity, I like the preliminaries. Things shouldn't be hurried. It used to amuse me laying siege to impregnable fortresses, except when they were defended with girdles, those chastity belts. I learned to detect them, though, before any serious advance was made—a light preliminary touch would warn you as to what lay before, behind, above, below. I was also very good at the associated arts: quiet décor with a reserve of soft cushions, reflected light only, good wine, of course.

Don't imagine it all came to me naturally, by instinct as it were. I had to put in hours of practice every day and keep at it. The passionate lover, in full frontal attack, soon palled. I discovered the oblique approach, the nonchalant air, the telling gesture and sometimes hid my lechery behind a mask of tenderness, consoling young widows and deserted lovers, the ones who still loved on. Which reminds me—Henriette. She seems to have slipped out of the story. We had seen less and less of each other and there had been more sour looks than smiles last time we met. What could I do? Sad satiety had got me. We'd had four good years and I was in the mood for variety. You can't warm up a soufflé. She had gone back to her husband as far as I knew.

I was a tremendous success, and even amazed myself, leaping from bed to bed like a mountain goat. I certainly earned my reputation, the worst in Paris, and I think I may say without boasting that it hasn't faded yet. I have to confess the name helped. Now, for me, it was the top drawer. No slumming, like my father. I was always convinced that he had won his spurs riding my grandmother's chambermaids. No, mine were ancient titles, fashionable beauties, stars of stage and screen, salon queens and one mutinous lesbian, only one.

For six months I appeared at all diplomatic functions with the current Miss Europe on my arm. I came by her quite by chance; my car broke down beside the offices of *L'Intransigeant,* our most popular evening paper. There was a crowd outside. What was going on? I strolled in by the back door.

Amazing.

Young ladies at various stages of undressing were popping in and out of doorways. One, more ravishing than the rest, and more naked, smiled at me.

"What is your name, *mon chou?*"

"Aliki."

I sighed.

"Philippe!" cried a familiar voice. "Just the man. We're a hung jury. Come and give the casting vote."

And that was how I came to give the crown to Aliki.

We didn't go to bed. She was a virgin. Not my job.

It's amazing what a bad reputation will do for one. I had more ports of call than I could cover in a day's sailing. I needed a mooring. I decided to rent a *garçonnière.* . . . William, my sganarelle, found a minute apartment on the rue Cortambert, one room and a small kitchen. It was very difficult to locate without my explicit instructions. The essence of a garçonnière is its privacy. It must be the complete hideaway for the secret rendezvous.

William would go along first, arrange the cushions and close the shutters. It was all very discreet. Imagine my amazement, then, to discover a lady I hardly knew about to ring my bell only a few days after we'd finished redecorating. Where had I seen her before? At a wedding? Some formal reception? She bade me good day. I had it, she was the wife of a highly respectable diplomat; the only woman in Paris who wore pince-nez and patent leather boots. As soon as the door closed behind her, everything became clear: she had come to be ravished. I was rather cross. Who had given her the address? Why must women talk? I hadn't received more than two or three. Which one had betrayed me? I was so distracted trying to nail the culprit that I could not concentrate on what was demanded of me. Then William served tea, delicious orange pekoe, and I managed to provide the sympathy. Poor dear. She only wanted to know what it felt like to be unfaithful. It was a one-off. We never did it again.

And there was L——; that was rather a surprise too. She was the reigning wit: poet, author, renowned for her lovers and her love of the limelight. Going to bed with L—— was something to boast about, and of course we did. It was all one to L——, who believed in what used to be called free love. A dark-eyed girl, animated and attractive apart from that pathetic limp. What was wrong with her?

"A tubercular hip. She was in bed six years with it. Don't let it bother you, she's very good value. And don't be kidded by the ritzy style either, L—— is as poor as a church mouse. Mamma M—— disposed of the family fortune long ago."

I fixed myself an invitation to a vogue dinner party when I knew she would be present. Over the martinis, I contradicted everything she said—all through dinner we slanged each other across the table. We were very good. Dinner table slaughter is really the best theater in Paris.

A few hours later we were in bed together. I thought she was admiring my cock, but she was examining it. "Doesn't it trouble you to be a circumcised Jew?"

"On the contrary, it prolongs pleasure and is good for the health."

"Is that all that matters to you? Doesn't it worry you that you're not baptized?"

"Are you?"

"Oh yes."

"You are, I'm not, but we've just had a lovely time together."

She thought for a moment, twining my pubic hairs round her little finger.

"Was J.C. baptized and circumcised?"

"Yes, but don't let's talk religion. It's worse than politics."

This made her angry. We never could agree about anything. In fact, we were invited to dinner parties together simply because people found our quarreling amusing.

She was cross when I broke out. I took to driving fast when I passed the end of her street. She was on the lookout for me, and L—— of course might do anything. Rejection she found intolerable, though of course she always had standbys. I think she had us all filed.

In the end one of our most famous writers took her up, kept her out of mischief and became her full-time job. She finished her days with him and asked for two words to be placed on her tombstone: *"Au secours."*

Don't think women took up all my time. I had plenty to occupy me. The Théâtre Pigalle was going up and my father was leaving all the dirty work to me. My days were spent climbing the scaffolding at Pigalle with Charles Siclis, nosing into every detail as the building progressed. The nights were for the birds. Parties, first nights, restaurants—carefree and heart-whole.

I thought myself the cock of the walk until one sunny Sunday morning—it was spring, too, lilacs and horse chestnuts blossoming all over the place—when I decided to show off my new Hispano in the Bois de Boulogne: avenue des Acacias, the great place for the fashionable promenade in Paris. I was poodling along, among the Victorias and pony carts, curb-crawling, I think they call it nowadays—we used to call it collecting our parsley—when I spotted this piece of skirt strolling along the sidewalk. What a silhouette: a mauve parasol, a silver pekingese, long, long legs and high-heeled shoes with ankle straps. She was followed at a discreet distance by a chauffeur-driven Voisin, the very latest coupé, dark brown, highly polished, with chauffeur to match. Wow! I did a U-turn at speed, passed them again and took another look. She was oblivious, sniffing the air with her small retroussé nose. I slowed down. Through the mirror I saw her snap her parasol shut. The chauffeur stepped out, gathered up the snooty little dog, and away they went, fast. Well, I could hardly follow them, it wouldn't be very subtle. After that I made it my business to drive through the Bois almost every day. There were women disappearing through the trees, under the trees, into the trees: with dogs, without dogs, with coupé, on foot, on horseback, but never a sign of the one I sought. I inquired among my leary friends. My powers of description must have been weak. Nobody seemed to know who she was.

It must have been two or three weeks later, I was giving a rather strait-laced acquaintance a lift to a garden party at Neuilly, and of course decided to go by the Bois. There she was: cinnamon parasol, gold and brown shoes and a ginger dog. Smug-face nearly jumped out of his seat. "Oh la la, look who's taking the air. . . . You don't know? That's Charley Brighton. Her phone number? I think she's a bit outside your range, old chap. You know who has it, don't you?" And he named one of the richest whoremongers in Paris. "You might get it from Cartier's, or Ciro's, but I doubt it, they're very discreet."

Getting that phone number required some expertise, but it was a game I was very good at, still am. I had the number in my pocket book but getting through was another matter. One had first to establish diplomatic relations with the operator—dialing hadn't been thought of.

"Bonjour, m'selle."

"M'sieur."

"Could you put me through to Invalides 202 please?"

"One moment."

You held on while loud clickings and ratchety noises assaulted the eardrum, then—

"Invalides 201?"

I could hear her merrily contacting the wrong subscriber.

"M'selle! M'selle No! Allo! No not two zero one—two zero two. . . ."

"Sorry m'sieur, the line is occupied."

And you'd hang up and try again hoping for a more helpful operator. . . . Only to be told that the number was temporarily out of order.

When I finally got through and asked for Madame Brighton, a stern, very formal female replied.

"De la part de qui?" I gave my name.

"One moment please."

Short pause, utter silence.

"What is your business?"

"I would like a word with the lady."

"Impossible, monsieur. She is engaged."

"I'll call again."

She made me call three times. The fourth time, a rendezvous was arranged. The Bois de Boulogne, avenue of the Acacias, 11 A.M., Sunday. At last, a date with the queen of the cocottes.

She was sitting in the car when I found her. I introduced myself, bowing over her lightly gloved hand. There was a quizzical look, the slightest raising of the eyebrows, yet I had a distinct feeling that she knew all about me, had checked my antecedents, date of birth, blood group and state of bankbook.

Cleopatra winding in her line fixed her large, green cat's eyes on me. Who said that eyes were the windows of the soul, or mirrors was it? Whichever it was he was talking through his hat. Eyes tell you nothing. The voice gave nothing away either: high yet husky, diction precise.

"How do you do?" said she.

There is never any reply to that one.

"Would you care for a stroll by the lake?" said I.

I saw something that might pass for a smile as she handed me her silly little dog, which immediately began to snap at me. "Quiet, Pollux," she said as she slid gracefully from the Voisin. Chauffeur doing the honors. There followed a ridiculous dog dialogue, as she took him in her arms and we began walking.

Who was going to break the ice? We started together, but she took over, discussing cars and actually sounding as if she knew all about them—so she had been checking up on me. When she turned to the theater, I was given some crisp opinions on the week's new shows, not stupid and very snappy. So was her exit. She flounced into her coupé with a whisk of her short, pleated, beige silk skirt before I could say Jack Robinson.

I stood there like a statue in the Luxembourg, arm upraised, and felt a drop of rain on my face. So that was all? Except for a wave of her gloved hand as the rain came on, full tilt. Would I have to begin the whole damn telephone routine all over again? I would. But the next meeting was positively intimate. Same time, same place. And I was allowed to carry the dog. It still didn't like me. The lady sparkled. She had been to the races, she had run into one or two characters I might know. What was my opinion of this one and that one? She was sounding me out in her subtle way, but I could see through her devices, or thought I could.

At the third meeting she gave me a card. I turned it over; there was a date and time, as for a dental appointment. So I'd passed the preliminary test and I was to be given my audition.

As I stepped through the door of her apartment on the quai d'Orsay, I felt I was entering another world, the backstage of bourgeois society. It would be exciting, bizarre, different, something from the *Arabian Nights,* maybe. Dancing girls with rubies in their navels, an odalisque to take my hat and Pola Negri reclining on a leopard skin handing me the check. Well, if that was what I wanted I was sadly disappointed. My hat and umbrella were taken by a plain, angular woman called Blanche, obviously the keeper of the gate.

There was not a whiff of decadence in the air, no promise of voluptuous delights. I had simply stepped through the looking glass; it was exactly like the world I had left, maybe a little smarter. The interior decoration was certainly by Jansen, all svelte and white, the very latest thing in Paris.

Blanche, given some secret cue, left and the performance

began. Madame came to me, the perfect bourgeois lady, tastefully but fully clothed. That surprised me, so did the slow, modest disrobing. I followed suit. It was quite a pavane. And the climacteric? Beautifully well done, from the moment of occupation to the final flutter. Her bed linen, I noticed, was even finer than my mother's.

And so to dinner, excellent, served by Blanche, a woman without expression. The wines? Mouton's best. The chatter most amusing. What a very entertaining woman. With the port I longed for a repeat performance but was not given the chance to suggest it.

There was a creaking sound from the hall. "My sister winding the clock," she said. "The peasant. She goes to bed with the light."

"Your sister?"

She gave a tiny, suppressed yawn. I was being dismissed. The protocol worried me slightly. How did one pay such a rarefied creature?

I was shown out by Sister Blanche. There was a delicate white console in the hall, on it a Lalique bowl. Did one just throw down a diamond? I asked when I might call again. I was told to phone for an appointment. Ah, I said to myself, a long waiting list, but I was wrong; her clients were few and carefully chosen, she had no wish to fatigue herself: "It's bad for the . . . , " she said, patting her neat little bottom.

At the end of the month I was wondering how the devil to cope with pay day. Despite her delicate airs she was, after all, a working girl. Yet I knew the word money would be taboo, much too vulgar.

I made a check out for a tidy sum and put it in my pocket. After the delights, as I was leaving, I slipped it into the Lalique. At that moment Cleopatra drifted by, blowing me a kiss.

"Au revoir, Monsieur Mouton."

Her eyes lighted on the check. She lifted it lightly.

"Ah! For the cuisine, monsieur? Merci. Do forgive me but

you should try to do a little better next time. Don't forget that Charley attends to the *plat du jour* with her own hand."

It wasn't long before I was back between her sheets. It took much longer to wheedle some of her secrets out of her. I wanted to know about her other men.

"Why? You are much too curious. There is only my Polish Count Potocki, very old family. When he is tired of running after wild boar he comes to Paris to chase Charley, and dear Egmont, disgustingly rich and so old he doesn't count. . . . Like poor Porgy, he can't do anything, but his dear bald head between my legs reminds me that he is still alive."

"Any more?"

"Jean-Pierre, but he's only my boute d'entrain."

"Your what?"

"Haven't you heard of the stallion they bring in to excite the mare at mating time? I adore Jean-Pierre, he's witty, elegant, and he knows everything about everybody. If he brings me a very good client I give him one for free."

"Your pimp?"

"Oh no, my accountant."

"Any more?"

"Monsieur Cyrus B. Chicago millionaire. He married a French countess, but she doesn't care for it any more. And I nearly forgot my honey-sweet Khedive, he's been around for all eternity, ever since I was a *demi-vierge*. Now I come to think about it, he started me on the primrose path. Where? In Egypt. Oh really, you are much to obvious. It wasn't in a harem, it was at a *thé dansant* at Shepheard's. Last night? Oh, that was only my *jambon* d'York. He's a sweetie, he comes over from London just for me.

"No, of course he's not in love with me. It's just that I have to give him special treatment; he's frightfully distinguished, a real English aristo. No that's not the reason. How snobbish you are. It's because he's a little backward, retarded, but such a poppet. I blame the parents."

She told me I was her favorite. I know she made them all

believe that, she was an accomplished actress, but I was the only young one and she enjoyed my strength, though she could give me twenty years at least. She told me she didn't mind the others, but I gave her pleasure. In those days I could kill a woman. I was brilliant at it.

I loved taking her out. She knew how to make a star entrance, anywhere: a 24-carat Mistinguett, and her clothes were exquisite. The great couturiers of Paris—Worth, Callot, Lanvin, Patou, Chanel—competed for her patronage and furnished her wardrobe for nothing. Of course she wouldn't be accepted in a private house, but I took her to the races, first nights, and all the new restaurants. The top table at Ciro's was reserved for us every Friday night. She adored her Friday nights, they were her theater, she wouldn't have missed one for all the crowned heads in the *Almanach de Gotha*.

We would sit there in that elegant white room with its gilded frieze while loudly dressed Argentinians sambaed by and Charley gave me a running commentary on the proceedings.

"Everybody who's nobody is with us tonight, duckie. The thing with hair like a polished boot is an Etubi, richest family in the world. He goes too far. Just look at the way he tangos. . . . Does it too well, like a dago.

"The dwarf? An Esteban, the dark little woman you mean, with the heavy mustache? All the wealth of the Orinoco round her neck but no one will look at her. That thing she's dancing with is a paid-up gigolo.

"Gustave des Adrets has just arrived. Nine and a half million from army surplus and look what's stuck to his arm. Do look, it's his latest. I wouldn't give that dress to my charwoman."

But I was hiding my face in my table napkin. Charley had such a clear, penetrating voice.

The soup had to be negotiated carefully for fear of one of her bombshells.

"No! That is not the old Baron de Courtiade, it's his son. Yes, that's his petite Albertine. She has papa during the day and his son at night. Is it any wonder he looks older than his father?

Everybody gets them muddled these days. But here comes our *selle de chevreuil*."

"Who?"

"Food! I'm famished."

But she would only peck at her plate, like a supercilious flamingo, always lifting her prettily dyed head in time to catch the next entrance.

"Fanny de Saint Adresse, used to be Fanny Lafeuille, actress, very left bank, poor thing. Her marquis is trying to get rid of her, she's much too expensive for him but she's so stubbornly faithful. It's rather amusing. His wife does the beast with two backs all over Paris but he simply cannot get his sweet little mistress to be unfaithful. He's tried everything, except Spanish fly and that goat Gaston Rueff. You don't find it funny, Philippe? Well, you're not smiling. I find it a charming little comedy. If only the theater would give us such good entertainment. Nowadays it's all Freudian gloom in long underpants for highbrows or bouncing blacks, quite nude at Les Variétés. There's nothing in between.

"Quick! The marquise is smiling. You missed it. She was showing off her new false teeth, palest green and they slip."

It was the cheeky humor of the street urchin, but it amused me. She had a wicked tongue and only occasionally a touch of bitterness.

"You saw the Duchesse de Falaise cutting you dead? That's because you're with me. The two-faced, she —s like a rabbit but you'd think butter wouldn't melt in her —. Those dames will ruin the old profession. Who'll keep a cow when milk is cheap?"

I asked her if she knew any of the birds in my brother's aviary. "Oh no," she said. "I don't mix with trade."

Charley became a habit, no, a necessity. After an evening with her the next woman would seem insipid. She wiped away all memory of past adventures until one day, as I was dressing to go out with her, a note arrived, delivered by hand. It was from Henriette, my sweet first love, asking for a rendezvous.

"A final one if you so wish, but at least let's have a happy good-bye."

I couldn't face it. I would send William. I hastily wrote a note. "Yes, but when? Will write. Very occupied."

I was, for four years. How did that vixen Charley manage to keep her hold on me? She was quite frank about it.

"I've a nimble tongue, and I'm witty, I've a dab hand and I can cook. Since, as you know, the way to a man's heart lies through his belly we are halfway there.... But pleasure blooms first in the brain, my sweet, never forget that."

My mistress was very skilled in the art of pleasing a man and she was a brilliant businesswoman. She studied the Bourse with Monsieur Jean-Pierre, bought property, read the Court Circular in *The Times* and the gossip column in *Le Gaulois*, skimmed all the new novels and even dipped into the most fashionable philosophers—but most of all she made sure that her gossip was the latest and spiciest. Sometimes I wondered where she picked it up. Where did she get all those stories about my relations, and my own secret affairs with L—— and the rest? Who told her about Henriette? She'd taken some new lover of whom I knew nothing.

I had gotten to know her faithful quartet: the Khedive, the Porgy, Potocki and Cyrus. Indeed we occasionally went out to dine *en famille* when we were all in town together—Charley and her circus act, one of the sights of Paris. It was remarkable how that woman kept all her men as friends long after they were through with the sport.

"Jealousy is so petit bourgeois," she told me. "One cannot take love too seriously these days."

I had to learn to swallow her pills, without pulling a face.

"I can't see you tonight, there is someone else."

"Oh really." I said I would phone her the following morning. I waited till noon.

"She had rather a tiring night," said Blanche. "She is resting."

"I'll call later."

"I wouldn't do that, she may be busy. It's a . . . ."

"I'll call later."

I did.

"What's going on?"

"I'm afraid she's tied up. It's a new gentleman. You under-stand the position, I'm sure."

Yes, I understood, only too well. My imagination was on fire, my skin burning, blistering.

The next morning, instead of phoning, I went straight to the house. Too early. The man was still there. I could tell at once by her sister's attitude.

"She's not available, monsieur."

"Why not?"

I brushed her aside and strode into the hall. I could hear a rustling in the bedroom. Blanche gave a signal. Did she take me for a fool? I threw open the bedroom door. Madame stood there unruffled, pulling on her negligée. I saw the open sheets, the rumpled pillows . . . and more. . . .

"Where is he?"

"He? Where? What is this, pray?"

"Don't play with me. Do you want me to kill you?"

"Monsieur Mouton, please. I have to earn my bread. Do you think you provide for all my needs?"

I heard a sound from the bathroom. I moved toward the door. She threw herself in front of me.

"Philippe! Really, this is getting more and more like a bed-room farce."

"Get out of my way or it will be a bedroom tragedy."

"Supposing there is someone there. Is it your affair?"

"Your business is yours but don't give me lies."

"I didn't lie, I tried to disguise the truth."

She half smiled at me. I turned and fled, calling her sister a filthy name, hating, loathing the place and her and her absurd yapping half-breed of a dog. Most of all that naked male thing skulking in her bathroom, probably laughing at me.

Jealousy? I've only known it once in my life. Jealousy over a woman, that is. That once was more than enough. I was consumed by a fierce, uncontrollable passion, blinding me, clouding my judgment. I couldn't think. What was the matter with me? Was it hurt pride, the old animal, possessiveness? I was disgusted with myself, with her, with everything, and I couldn't control my feelings. Murder seemed easy.

I tried another woman. It didn't work. I couldn't do it. Wait, wait. Be cool. Try some distractions, the cinema. . . . No, tire yourself out.

Had my feelings much to do with love? Could you love such a woman, a brazen, cold-hearted whore? Of course I did, loved and hated her. Isn't that how it goes?

We did not meet until our regular Friday night at Ciro's. Neither of us was at our best, perhaps because we were avoiding any discussion of our little contretemps. There was a ravishing young thing, very beaumonde, sitting at the table opposite with three men. She caught my eye. I smiled, she smiled back. . . . With a sudden crash, our table was overturned, plates, cutlery, glasses, champagne bucket went flying. Charley stepped over the debris and walked cooly out of the restaurant. Julien and Maurice, the two maîtres d'hôtel, came to help; I was covered with *boeuf bourguignon*. I brushed them aside and rushed out. The doorman pointed to her taxi disappearing down the street. I jumped into my new Delage, stepped on the gas, and arrived at her apartment just as she was closing the door. I put my foot in and shoved it open. She had never given me a key.

"I forbid you to enter," she said.

I entered and closed the door.

"Stay where you are." I moved toward her. In a flash, she had opened a little drawer in the console and brought out a revolver.

"Don't move."

I seized her fur coat, which was lying on a chair, and using it as a shield advanced toward her. I didn't think she would put a hole in her mink. She didn't. It was becoming a comedy, but she wasn't laughing. Suddenly she threw the revolver across the parquet floor, bolted into the bedroom and turned the key.

At Ciro's at the end of the week, she was with someone else. I was dining elsewhere but the message reached me soon enough. "Philippe! There you are! How funny, I've only just left Charley and Gaston."

"Who?"

"Your friend, Gaston Rueff. They were dancing at Ciro's."

Back it came, the jealousy, choking me, shattering my savoir faire.

"Why not?" I said. "Charley and I are all washed up, anyway."

The abominable bitch, I said to myself, the unspeakable cow. Gaston was one of my closest friends, very rich. Did that explain it? How long had they known each other? I started trying to figure it out, checking on the days she'd turned me down. I was back in the pit, calculating, hating, ready for knives. Luckily I was with a friend who always laughed at all my love affairs. We drank and talked racing cars.

I knew one thing. If Gaston was in I wanted nothing more to do with it. He had gone to school with me and even then he'd been jealous of me. I wouldn't dream of sharing Charley with him. Let them get on with it. They did. They were inseparable.

I thought of my long-suffering Henriette, how she had stayed faithful to me no matter what I did. A few days after I'd decided to quit Charley forever I called Henriette and invited myself to tea. Her sitting room was pleasant, pretty actually, and she herself had more than a glint of girlhood left, especially when she smiled. But as she handed me a ratafia biscuit and a second cup I heard the first rumble of reproach.

"No, Philippe, that's not fair. Don't accuse me of misunderstanding, I knew it was all over, only too well, but I thought it would have been nicer if you'd told me so yourself."

"Quite right."

"It was not, of course, all over for me."

I stroked her hand. "Poor Henriette."

"I walked by the river all night. I wanted to do away with myself. . . ."

I squeezed her dimpled elbow.

". . . If it hadn't been for my child."

She turned her head away. Then suddenly she faced me.

"I think what hurt me most was that you should have taken her to Arcachon."

"Did I?"

"To our place. The place where . . . that woman."

"Which woman are we speaking of now?"

"Madame Brighton or whatever she calls herself."

"But I didn't take her to Arcachon. . . ."

Did I? I couldn't remember. Perhaps I did. I wasn't listening any more. I was trying to recall that summer, after Henriette, when the new house at Arcachon was being built. I remembered inviting Charley to Mouton. "Too many mosquitoes," she'd said. I could see her now wrinkling her nose, giving me that snooty look. She had never wanted to enter my life, at all events she never tried to do so. Could I have been wrong? Perhaps she would have liked to be accepted in my world. I had always taken her for a back-room girl; I thought she preferred it that way. I saw my other life as real. And you, Charley . . . ? Not altogether. The only time you dropped the act completely was when you talked about your family, your father's brothers and sisters—their poverty. Then you'd cross your hands like an old woman. "You never had to struggle," you said to me, "which means you will never take life too seriously. So much the better for you."

"Philippe, are you listening to me?"

It was Henriette. "Where was I?"

"Where were we?"

"I was asking if I'd ever taken anything from you."

"No, of course not."

"She did."

"Henriette, this is a happy room."

"Why shouldn't it be? I have my husband, who is devoted to me. . . ."

"And you have children now."

"Only one."

She showed me a photograph, madonna and son. Henriette looking softly attractive. I kissed her good-bye and left.

With both my flames snuffed out, I felt a little lost. Between them I had burned out eight years of my life. Tomorrow looked empty.

I saw Charley one night on her way to the Casino de Paris. She was on his arm and slightly too bright with diamonds. Obviously she liked what she'd picked up. I have never wooed women with trinkets. My gifts have been eccentric, unique but not necessarily expensive. I have been known to buy a pretty bauble and give it to some bubblehead in a Cartier jewel box just to see if she knew the difference; generally she didn't. Charley would, I guess.

She used to tell me that when her mirror gave her a third warning she would disappear. Four wrinkles would be too much.

"Where will you go?"

"It's all prepared. To a house with many shutters, venetian blinds and lace curtains so that no one will ever see me and everyone will know that my time is done."

"It sounds lonely."

"No, I shall enjoy my old age. The best time is always the present time."

When the Germans came, she retired to Cannes. Sister Blanche went with her, bony, pale-faced Blanche who had cooked, cleaned, slaved for her all her life and kept her secrets. I often wondered what she did for her pleasure. They were the daughters of the doorman at Les Trois Dauphins in Grenoble and grew up in the back streets of Stendhal's town, hating it as much as he had.

Charley Brighton, née Charlotte Bouquet, finished her days a rich old lady, promenading with her sunshade when the weather was fair, always veiled.

She lived in a pink villa with white shutters in a very respectable district. She and her sister had been reared in a strictly respectable home.

9

*All good times have to come to an end, and ours is over now.
Come now and bid me farewell.*

STANLEY HOUGHTON

UGUST, a hot dry day. Walking through the woods at
Auffargis, near L'Abbaye des Vaulx de Cernay. My
father, my brother James, and I. Thick foliage hides
the sun. This is the sandy soil of my childhood. A country boy
opens a wicket gate and the rabbi walks through into the small
cemetery. We are following my mother's simple, elegant coffin.

Glancing over my shoulder, I catch sight of Cousin Armand
and my friend André Wisner, among a small group of males,
friends and close relatives. Today it is a private affair, there
won't be much of a ceremony. The proper memorial service
will be in Paris when the holiday season is over. We shall have
prayers for Mathilde, beloved wife of Henri, that's about all.
She was fifty-two. Leukemia, incurable.

She died at a clinic in Luchon, high up in the Pyrenees.
Unbelievably, only the day before the day before yesterday. A
week ago I was yachting at Arcachon, a sudden call from my
father and I was in my Hispano, speeding to Paris to fetch two
more doctors and another nurse for her. I drove like the clap-
pers though I knew it was a wasted journey.

We pass . . . an open grave, artificial grass, enormous wreaths of crushed flowers, tricolor bandoliers stamped with gilt paper letters, someone of importance. The mourners, all men in black coats, are shaking hands at the gate.

Long life.

For my mother there are no flowers by request. She made her last wishes very clear. "I want a Lalique glass tomb, like a hothouse, then I'll blossom in the spring," she said.

My father is moving to the graveside. He too is paying his respects to a stranger. It must be a long time since they were man and wife. Divorce was out of the question, frowned on in the family as among orthodox Jews generally.

He was faithful to her for a long time, but I don't think she returned the compliment. When I was five he was still dedicating books to his "dear Mathilde." Later it was to us, his dear sons, or his dear children. I wonder if any of her lovers are here today.

Who was my father? Is he? You have taken the secret with you.

The rabbi begins mutterings. Grandmother Thérèse thrust a prayer book into my hands before I left the house and kissed me. What hypocrisy! She hates me and my mother. "That boy Philippe is a bastard. Henri was never his father," she told someone in strictest confidence. It came to my ears at once. I didn't mind, I was bitter against my father at the time. I didn't want to be his son.

Let's hope you were happy with your lovers, Mother—

> The grave's a fine and private place,
> But none I think do there embrace.

The rabbi is going at it, nineteen to the dozen, perhaps there's a queue? I didn't care for either of you when I was young. When people said how pretty you were as you went your way, flattered and feted everywhere, I wanted to tell them that you were cruel and hard. I didn't think you good-looking. You were too small, tiny; a woman has to be tall to be beautiful.

Papa moves forward. The gravediggers take a step. Ah yes, they're going to lower her now. Who's going to tip those chaps? They're doing it all very decently, sufficiently solemn. I glance at my friend André, standing beside me.

"Don't worry, it's all taken care of," he says.

My father wanted her to rest, as he put it, here at Auffargis, near our country home.

> They throw in dirt and they throw in rocks.
> And they don't give a damn if they break the box.

At last we're moving away. I have to pinch myself to be sure I'm here. Hope I have enough gas to get me straight to Paris. Forty kilometers! Should make it in half an hour. James looks stricken, but then he was the only one who meant anything to her, poor old James, her hero, her brave son.

I hated that woman. Why pretend? She came back from the 1914–18 war sharp tongued and overbearing. I felt sorry for the soldiers who'd been in her care, but then perhaps she was nicer to them.

I left home because of her. I'd been studying at home one day, and I was hungry. I went downstairs and suddenly found myself in the middle of one of her glittering luncheon parties. She obviously didn't much care to have me there. Perhaps I made her look too old in front of her boyfriends. I sat down and ate solidly. During a lull in the tittle-tattle, she took it into her head to make fun of me, my shape, my clothes, my manners. Her stupid friends sniggered and smiled, turning to look at me. I felt myself blushing. I dropped food onto my trousers. This delighted her, she went on, playing for laughs. An old woman in a turban who sat next to me patted my head sympathetically. That was too much. I jumped up, my chair fell.

"I am leaving this house," I said. "And I shall never darken your doors again."

I went to my room, packed a small case and left.

My father's sister took me in—Tante Jeanne, plump, plain and kindly. She was so ugly that her husband had abandoned her a week after they were married. She was left with her one love, a scruffy little dog, Kitou. She was kind to me, my first friend and confidante, the first person who ever listened to me for that matter. I lived with her for a long time. Eventually I had to return to my father's house, he wanted me back. I avoided my mother. I never even spoke to her until that day in May 1926 when Élise, her maid, came to fetch me. My mother had to see me, she said. I went. It was a shock, she was so shrunken.

"We must make it up, we must be friends," she said. As she turned to me I could see the tears coursing through her makeup.

I should have been moved. I was not. I just couldn't think of anything to say. I lifted her to her feet and sat her in her chair. I remember inviting her to stay at my new house at Arcachon. She seemed pleased. I left the room quickly. I only saw her once again, when I got to Luchon with the two doctors, and she was almost dead.

They are getting into the cars. I kiss my father and run for it.

1926. A dead mother and plague over the vineyards, not a good year.

10

*I'll put a girdle round about the earth
In forty minutes.*

PUCK

AFTER the memorial service at the Central Synagogue, rue de la Victoire, with anybody who was anybody in attendance, I motored down to Pauillac, fast. I wanted to see how the new chai was coming along. We'd lost last year's harvest when the old chai collapsed, and the insurance had barely covered us. The buyers who'd paid for their wine in advance had all had to be given their money back.

On the other hand, replanning for château-bottling having proved more difficult than I'd foreseen, the accident had given me a little respite, but I certainly didn't need another disaster.

The place looked as if we were transferring the pharaohs. There were builders and diggers all over the place. The Mouton hands could be picked out a mile away by their long mournful faces.

"Who's dead?"

"The harvest."

"What's wrong?"

"There isn't going to be one."

"Why?"

"Cochylis."

"What the hell is that?"

"Take a look."

I looked. Grapes were withered on their stalks, marked with black spots which told you they were rotten within; a white grub was nesting there, feeding on the pulp.

I'd never seen such a pest before—all over the vines, everywhere.

"Where does it come from?"

"Butterflies, very small ones. They arrive in swarms and settle, the caterpillar thrives on the grape and kills it."

"Something must be done about it. Isn't there a spray?"

"No, and if there were it might harm the grape."

"That attitude'll get us nowhere."

"You tell us what is to be done then."

Well, I would. I couldn't bring myself to write off the entire harvest. I walked off on my own, trudging up and down between the rows of blighted vines. Here and there a whole bunch of grapes had escaped, and there were some healthy grapes even on infected branches.

I could perhaps save some. But how? The women might do it, with their careful fingers. Extra work, and not very pleasant, but they would be earning. I called my village *belles* together, the ladies who prepare the meals for the harvesters, prepare the village fetes and help in the vineyards sometimes. I showed them the problem.

"You will have to go carefully through each bunch and pluck off the grapes which bear a black spot."

They tackled the unpleasant job in their practical, easygoing way. Slowly barrel after barrel was filled with wriggling white grubs, and 25 percent of the harvest was saved. It was pathetically little, but all our neighbors lost the lot; their entire year's work went for nothing. Surprisingly, that 25 percent produced the most delicious wine. It was snapped up at once. You'll never find a bottle of '26.

Nevertheless for me it was a bad year. I'd had enough of

grubs and vineyards. I got into my car and escaped. Marjary could deal with Mouton and its problems. I was going racing.

I needed speed and danger, the kick you get as you drive her over the top . . . 200 . . . 220 . . . 230 . . . wow!

I am a great driver, a born driver, my buttocks were designed to fit a driving seat. When I was ten I sat on the chauffeur's lap and held the wheel.

My Torpedo Unic was long gone, obsolete. No more pumping up tires by hand, acetylene headlamps lit with a cigarette lighter, starting handles, the tank refilled every two hundred kilometers. I had moved on to the Hispano-Suiza, a marvelous car, the Rolls Royce of France. Burkight and Lacoste, the engineers, used to let me test each new model. I made the Paris-Nice run in twelve hours in a Hispano—that was before the days of motorways, of course. Many of the roads were narrow and scarred with deep ruts. There were level crossings, always shut, cows lumbering along, dogs barking, hay wagons blocking the way, and all manner of horses and carts on their way to the markets which flourish in every town in France. It was crazy driving.

For racing it was the Bugatti. I entered all the big races, competing with the world's top names. I only pulled off a first once, the Grand Prix de Bourgogne, top speed 230 kilometers an hour. Mostly I came in second. I thought I was going to win the Grand Prix d'Espagne. It was raining heavily. I was leading till mid-race, at least four minutes ahead of the rest, when the steering went. I lost ten minutes getting it fixed, but I picked up and again came in second. My performance in the German Grand Prix was rather brilliant too. The track still exists in the Eiffel Forest, mountainous country and difficult driving, 23 kilometers up and down steep hills, hairpin bends . . . the last lap flat out, a long straight run. I was competing against the crack drivers of the time: Louis Chiron also in a Bugatti, Caraciolla leading the Mercedes team. The cars were narrow, bullet shaped. We were doing some trial runs one day when a racing journalist asked to be taken over part of the course. When he got out he collapsed. For that scenic road you needed strong nerves; at every bend you could dive into the next world.

The race itself lasted four hours. At half time I was three and a half minutes ahead, not bad going—but I had to stop to refuel and change the tires. Starting up again with a heavy, full tank, I made a slight miscalculation, and the car grazed a railing. I had to drive more carefully, and, in the second half, Chiron overtook me. I still managed to arrive second, well ahead of Caraciolla and the Mercedes pack. At the finish I relaxed, slumped at the wheel. The mechanics pounced on me. "Up, up." They pulled me out and got me to my feet. "What's wrong?" I couldn't hear a word they said. I'd gone completely deaf. "They're playing the 'Marseillaise,'" they shouted. And so they were, in Germany. True, the war had been over for eight years, but we hadn't yet played the German national hymn in France.

Five years ago some wine-loving friends presented me with a model of my first racing car. How could you jump from slow-going oxen to Bugattis? Ah well, that's the secret of long life— variety. Besides, you may discover that swift can mean slow and slow seem swift.

I didn't tell you how I came to invent the very first windscreen wiper. It was all because of one of my little darlings. I've forgotten her name, I only remember that she was extremely pretty about the head. I would call for her, she'd look very alluring, her coiffure *bouffante,* a jeweled butterfly or a flower above her ear; I'd whisk her off in my smart new sports car and she'd arrive looking like a wind-blown witch, and just as bad tempered. Even an interminable sojourn in the ladies' room didn't really restore matters. Something would have to be done, she was rather a sweetie. So I designed a closed car, a charming little blue velour boudoir of a thing, the first *conduite intérieure* with a closed, fixed windscreen and a wiper. Until then the windscreen had to be tilted open when it rained so that you could see out, and if you wanted to keep dry you had to jump out, unfold the hood of the car, tighten its straps, hook 'em to the wings and jump in again, feeling rather damp. It didn't make for *l'amour*. How can you murmur sweet nothings or try a little preliminary grope with the girl hanging on to her ruined hairdo?

I worked hard on the design of that car. The wiper proved annoyingly difficult. The first one had to be operated by hand, then I found how to move it by depression from the carburetor. Later, from the batteries. I'm pretty good at gadgets but it took a while to perfect this one. By the time it was right I'd lost the girl. And of course I completely forgot to patent it.

11

The viol, the violet and the vine.

ERNEST DOWSON

THERE I was, a small, sulky-looking fellow, five foot eight in his socks, never able, apparently, to lift his head and look the world in the face, yet boss of a large estate, several women and two racing cups; also, by that time, a discriminating boozer.

Here I am now, after sixty years of trying to grow the best wine, smaller, paunchier, bald and really not much the wiser.

"Never mind all those confidences about love and life," I hear you saying. "What we want is a little inside info on wine; let's have a few indiscretions on that score, if you please." I know; I am simply Monsieur Mouton for you, as I was for Charley B.

The only trouble is that I don't talk about wine, at any rate not in company. I learned early in life to be discreet, never to let slip the name of a favorite for fear of hurting the other charmer. I can't write about wine either; has anybody else succeeded? When I see the slush spilled over the newspapers by wine critics I wonder who's paying them, and what for.

It's not easy, in fact I think it's impossible to describe wine. I remember years ago Monsieur Marjary decided to keep a golden book of wine. In France we call our visitors' book a *livre d'or*. He wanted all the poets, writers and distinguished wine bibbers who visited us to describe the wine they had tasted. It was a dead loss. "Divine." "Crushed violets." "Nectar." "Raspberries." "Mmmmmm!" "Black currants." And so on. He abandoned his book. Better to have put, "I have drunk Mouton '56 or '68," or whatever. A good bottle is what it is, incomparable, unique. Can you describe the taste of roast chicken, a ripe peach, fresh bread and butter, let alone Mouton Rothschild?

How far do you get with "rondeur," "corps," "tenue," "souplesse," "oaky on nose," "bottle sick," "fruit on the nose"? I could go on. Frankly, now that wine drinking has become so popular, and much that is popular is also good, simple indications such as those given in the supermarkets are good enough to start with—"full-bodied red," "dry white," "sweet." You find out the rest for yourself. Developing your taste is one of the pleasures of the game and if you finish up drinking Mouton with Irish stew and champagne with spaghetti it seems to me entirely your own affair.

I can't write a wine book for you. I only drink my own wines: though I see no reason why a popular wine should not be very good. Mine is; I drink it regularly, and keep my exquisites for the occasions. I'm a Bordeaux man, because our wines are incomparable. I'll go further, I'm a man of the Gironde. "The best wines are grown within sight of the Gironde." It's an old saying and still true. Let the wide, gray river run softly past my Mouton till I end my song.

We Girondins are still a club, we appreciate each other and we're courteous to each other—sometimes. If I dine at Latour, they will serve a Mouton at the first course, then a Latour and so on, and I naturally return the compliment when they dine with me. We all pay homage to each other's achievements, at least nowadays. There was a time . . . but that's another story.

I don't believe anybody can identify wine from more than

two or three vineyards, and those vineyards would have to be his, or vineyards he'd worked for a long time. Recently some jokers in the wine trade organized a wine tasting and invited the critics to taste the wines, blindfolded. Many refused, of course. Quite right, they have to make a living. Take off the labels and most of them would be lost.

Wine is a woman—uncertain, coy and hard to please. Every time you draw her cork you risk disappointment, but when she's on form—and because she's a professional she mostly is —what bliss! (Stupid word. Find me a better one.) Mauriac, the novelist, at our table one night: "The sound of the cork reminds me of the curtain going up on a first night, when God only knows what's in store for us."

Only a poet can capture the flavor of wine, and when at the end of this chapter you find that I have failed you, as you will and I will surely, don't worry, there is a small reward. You shall have some of my "Gems from the Classics." You could set them to music if you're that way inclined; if not, crack a good bottle in memory of the man or woman who first invented wine.

I wonder what it tasted like, cooled with dirty snow, or spiced like a pudding? We might not have recognized it.

For hundreds of years it was drunk very young: maturing wine is a comparatively recent idea. Now we seem to be returning to older, more primitive ways. "Le beaujolais nouveau vient d'arriver." You can see the announcement chalked up outside every popular wine shop in Paris. A plane load flies to London, where fast cars are waiting to carry it to the smartest tables in town. To someone of my persuasion, it sounds crazy; the thought of it gives me a headache. Is it because I'm old that I love old wines? I don't think so. Young people come from all over the world to help with the harvest at Mouton, and when it's in, young and old, gods, goddesses and mortals, join in the bacchanalia, good food, good wine, then singing, dancing and making merry, as they used to call it.

"Ah, the pagans!" the Puritans said, frowning on May games and wine festivals.

"Man's job on earth is to work, there'll be pie in the sky by and by."

They couldn't win. Someone remembered how Yeshua, J.C., had turned the water into wine when the party ran dry.

The conscious water saw its God and blushed.

Didn't he give us bread and wine to represent his flesh and blood? Among his people, the Jews, he had drunk ritual wine ever since he'd been bar mitzvahed.

And when he died a strange thing happened: the country people all over the classic world got muddled up and mixed the stories of J.C. with the tales of the old god Dionysus. There are pictures, carvings and stained-glass windows all over Europe showing J.C. treading the wine press *Le Pressoir mystique*. In some the cross beam of the press is placed across his shoulders to look like the cross he was made to carry. In all of them the cross is the press, and J.C. treads the grapes while young lambs drink the wine which gushes from his wounds. So wine became a part of the mysteries as well as a very pleasant way of improving our meat and our conversation.

The nearer the altar the less respect for the chalice. For example, that dignified acolyte, with his silver cup and chain, cork sniffing above his victim—the chap who will have to foot the bill—he knows perfectly well that the wine is corked. He knew the moment he opened the bottle. He should have taken it away at once, it should never have come to the table, but of course there's always the chance that the drinkers won't notice, and the restaurant will be so much to the good. They have to replace corked wine.

The corking problem cannot be avoided. It comes from using a natural product instead of plastic. In fact the invention of the cork in the eighteenth century was considered an enormous advance on waxed stone stoppers, but in the cellars the bottle is slightly inclined so the cork spends its long life lapped in wine. If it holds the slightest speck of infection, a sharp taste will impregnate the whole bottle. It happens rarely but it's one of the risks you take. You have to choose—oakwood barrels and corks, or cement vats and plastic screwtops. The latter are more efficient, but are you prepared to sacrifice that wonderful plop when the cork leaves the bottle and the faintest odor of oak which a sharp nose detects in the wine?

The thing that annoys me most is the basket, putting young wines in old baskets, a silly pretentious habit. Why not a velvet cushion, if it's ritual we're after and we want to make believe that our wine is 100 years old? If it is, it will indeed be fragile and must be treated like a very old lady. Madame Simone, for example, who is 106, the oldest actress in France, you could hardly get her into the basket. No, each bottle is as individual as each one of us, and as difficult.

I have some very old bottles in my cellar, seventeenth century, eighteenth century. When de Gaulle went to Italy in 1959 for the centenary of the Franco-Italian victory at Solferino, I gave him a couple of bottles of 1859 to take with him. Pierre Blondin, then maître de chai, opened one of the same year to see if they were drinkable. "Lively," he said. For victory 1945 I sent Winston Churchill a bottle of 1874, the year of his birth. He never acknowledged it, perhaps it was no good. If by chance you acquire such a treasure and manage to draw the work, give it a little air, not too much, then gently pour it into a clean decanter; be sure it's very clean. If you use crushed ice it will shine like stars. If the wine is good, drink it all at the one sitting. It won't last long; the wonderful taste soon goes after its encounter with the air.

If you have a good wine, not quite so old perhaps, you can finish it at the next meal, so long as you don't forget to put the cork back between whiles. It may have lost a little of its taste, but not much. Personally I never serve a wine previously opened to guests but that is just my old-world courtesy. Wine, you must know, likes good manners, don't just slosh it around. I had to rebuke the dignified-looking wine waiter at the Savoy Hotel in London one evening for giving a great wine rough treatment. Everyone should know by now that after a wine has lain in the cellar for a long time, it collects sediment, which if it is allowed to spread will cloud your drink. At Mouton we shine an electric light bulb through the wine bottle to be sure it's clear. In expensive restaurants they use a candle; but then at Mouton our wine has been carefully decanted, passing through a glass funnel with a nylon filter into carafes with long, long necks. The carafes wear a small, wine-colored bow beneath their chins to prevent the drips, a memory of wartime when we couldn't get soap to wash them white.

The carafes I have made at Lalique, copies of an original found in an antique shop in the Quartier Latin.

There is a lot of cant talked about wine, yet even cant is better than total ignorance and too much respect better than none at all. Would we want to see all courtesy, all charm, all grace banished from the world? Then wine would go with them.

To tell the truth and shame the devil for once, the best wine I ever tasted was in a snow-bound chalet in the Pyrenees in a large double bed in a room with a blazing log fire. Yes, there was a pretty gal beside me. Oh, sweet mystery of life, of wine, of time. I don't remember the name of the wine.

As with the round-shouldered bottle, so with the little dwarf of a tree that we plant in March with high hopes for its future. Our vines stretch their withered arms in winter, poor crucified things, pleading for attention, and they have to have it. From birth to death they are subject to as many maladies as man. Until a couple of decades ago we knew very little about the bugs and illnesses which attacked the vines and what we did know was mostly wrong. Now, thank God, we have made such progress one can be sure of a healthy harvest every year. Before the tractors and the new sprays the year's work was often lost and many a wine grower went broke over a bad autumn; even fully established growers were usually deeply in debt. I'd like to say those days are done but it's not so: there are still empty châteaus and vineyards recently abandoned within walking distance of Mouton.

In 1927 my own enthusiasm for wine growing was quite dampened as I motored down to Mouton for the harvest. I'd heard nothing but moans from Marjary and the team all year, and it had been rain, rain all the way. When I got there the clouds were low lying, dour. Still, maybe it would clear up. There's one thing about Médoc weather, it is changeable.

The new chai was finished. It looked magnificent; don't let's talk about the cost. I walked the long aisle between ranks of new casks, awaiting their complement of wine. The echo of my footsteps made the splendid place sound even emptier. How many casks would we manage to fill this year?

The rain was still beating down. I went out to take a look at my domain. The slow-going oxen were plowing their way through rivers of mud; it was warm, the air was thick, a soup of insects.

Goddamn Bordeaux and its filthy climate. Why hadn't I settled in Burgundy, Beaujolais? Anywhere but here. Anywhere but this flat, dull, faceless dump of a place. Why couldn't nature have given us pleasant hills and fertile valleys, orchards and flowers, like the valleys of the Loire and the Rhône? What had Beaujolais done to deserve her parkland of a landscape? Nothing. Nothing but a pleasing name, a fortunate location, good weather. . . . The rain was coursing down my neck.

Last year cochylis, the year before the collapse of the diggings.

I had to make some money this year or go bust.

Behind me the splendid new chai, in front of me the grapes moldering on the branch. My feet were sinking in sludge. I looked round, a gloomy chorus stood watching me. What was I supposed to do? Break into a lament?

"Don't just stand there," I shouted. "Let's get cracking."

"Monsieur?"

"I said, let's go."

The harvest was brought in, damp and flat, like us. There'll be no great wine this year.

I ordered a bottle of Alsace with my supper. It didn't help. One had prayed for a good harvest after the lean years. It was not to be. Did anybody ever make money out of wine?

A lemon yellow sun rose timidly the following morning. The harvest wasn't quite as meager as we'd feared. The wine would be passable, but you couldn't call it Mouton, it would be a disservice to the great years. Should we sell it as *ordinaire?*

No, we agreed, it merits a name, at least. Everyone knows the importance of a name, and everyone knows how difficult it is to find the right one. It was like the hassle over a new baby— nobody was very bright.

Marjary said, "What about Carruades?"

"What does that mean?"

"It's the name of a stretch of land on the road to Loubeyre; comes from an old dialect word *charroi*."

"And what does that mean?"

"A farm cart. Why not a good local word for a good rough wine?"

Well, whatever about carts and local words, that name lasted one year only, the wine longer. We couldn't sell it at any price. We lost 90 percent of the value of that harvest. It was a shame because, as I said, it wasn't a bad wine. I just didn't know enough about promotion.

"Good wine needs no bush," said Will Shakespeare. Which shows you how much he knew about advertising. Carruades de Mouton Rothschild was a useless name. The bush, in case you don't know, was the Elizabethan wine seller's way of letting the people know he had the good stuff. He hung a green bush up outside his shop.

Well, ours was good stuff. In fact the two following years, 1928 and 1929, were great. I began to put money in my purse, the luck of the game. You can't bank on wine when each year it's totally different, no two years ever the same. The taste, the color, the perfume, call it the bouquet if you prefer the word, its very composition varies, and so of course does the quantity. The wine grower must be a philosopher, like the farmer.

I was luckier than most. When things got too depressing, I had an escape route. From Mouton I could motor to the ocean and sail my eight meter clipper in the teeth of the wind.

*   *   *

Here are your wine quotes, the "Gems from the Classics," as promised:

> Bring water, bring wine, boy!
> Bring flowering garlands to me!
> Yes bring them.
> So that I may try a bout with Love.
> ANACREON

> Use a little wine for thy stomach's sake
> and thine often infirmities.
> PAUL'S FIRST EPISTLE TO TIMOTHY

> Come quickly, brother, I am drinking stars.
> THE BLIND MONK DOM PERIGNON ON
THE DAY HE INVENTED CHAMPAGNE

> And Noah he often said to his wife
> when he sat down to dine,
> "I don't care where the water goes
> if it doesn't get into the wine."
> G. K. CHESTERTON

Give me books, drink, French wine and fine weather and a little music out of doors, played by somebody I do not know.
JOHN KEATS

When men drink, then they are rich and successful and win law suits and are happy and help their friends. Quickly bring me a beaker of wine that I may wet my mind and say something clever.
ARISTOPHANES

Drinking is almost the last pleasure that the years steal from us.
MONTAIGNE

12

This theater is a voyage and when the curtain is flown away the scene that meets your eye is profound, surprising. Today's techniques give us the perfect illusion of drifting April skies. We are offered a choice, man-made beauty or nature's beautiful terrors.

JEAN COCTEAU

THE walls of Théâtre Pigalle were up, the roof would soon be finished, the wide, deep stage was already marked out. We were entering the most exciting phase, the installation of the stage machinery. And most important of all, the program planning. I had taken over a good deal of the organization work. My father was enjoying himself as the successful playwright, *homme de théâtre*, taking his theatrical friends round the Mediterranean on his yacht *Eros* and planning a trip to Hollywood.

I felt rather important. I was twenty-six and had just about everything a young man could want. The house Charles Siclis had built for me, in the pine woods above Arcachon, was paradise. I called it Doncupi. Cupidon is the French translation of Cupid, and I'd called all my yachts *Cupidon* since I was eighteen.

My lovely house, with its white terraces, looked out over the Atlantic Ocean, so I was never short of friends, sunbathing, surfing, sailing and listening to me talking theater and films, my new craze. To a privileged few I would read my poems.

In Paris I played the young man about town, only to be seen at smart houses when the company was very amusing; disap-

pearing on mysterious trips to Berlin, New York and Hollywood, reappearing with blueprints for unheard-of gadgets
medical and theatrical, and giving reluctant interviews to the
press.

How sweet to be reluctant when one finds oneself in demand.
I've just turned up an old cutting from a gossip column of the
period:

> I ran him to earth, M. Philippe de Rothschild, the young
> man of the moment, as he was leaving his office, a tempo-
> rary set up amongst the wild activity which appears to be
> shaping a most extraordinary building, the new Théâtre
> Pigalle. He tried to brush me off, so I asked him if his twin
> brother, Georges Philippe, might give me a few words.
> That stopped him in his tracks.
>
> "How did you blow my cover?"
>
> Didn't he know that his picture was all over the papers?
> German Grand Prix, Louis Chiron wins, Georges Philippe
> a close second. He thanked me charmingly, pointed out
> that at the moment he was more interested in a machine
> that cured paralysis, which his father was installing at his
> hospital.
>
> I asked him about his theater, but he turned back to ask
> the stenographer what time he was due at the Poetry Soci-
> ety. Apparently he was giving a lecture on *vers libre*.
>
> I couldn't help marveling at the drive and vigor of this
> young Rothschild. He looks a nice boy, with his round face,
> rosy cheeks, eyes beaming with intelligence and mockery,
> and his small nose, not in the least Israelite. I inquired
> which side he was on in the Breton-Cocteau fight. . . .
>
> "Fifty laps in three hours thirty-seven minutes," he
> shouted, and vanished.

If he'd looked outside the theater that very night, he would
have seen the lights go up on a tower above the scaffolding,
ouverture octobre. It was spring 1929.

What a show-off I was. I became friends with that young reporter afterwards. There was more swank on my desk but he didn't even notice it. I had asked my friend André to design a crest for my new notepaper. I wanted two rams rampant. When he'd done, they looked rather arty but the idea was right. I fancied having my crest everywhere—on the labels, in the chai, on the menus, all over the place.

All the old wine growers ever put on their bottles were drawings of their châteaus, which looked like smudged fingerprints. The rams had them puzzled.

"What are they supposed to mean?"

"It's a fertility rite."

"No, it's part of the Rothschild coat of arms, there are a lot of animals and mythical birds on that."

"It may have something to do with Mouton—sheep. Ram, the male sheep, sheep equals Mouton. Simple."

They were all wrong. If you want to know the secret, the ram is my birth sign. Nobody guessed. In any case, Mouton has nothing to do with sheep: it's a corruption of "mothon," which in Old French meant a height. Lafite and Cos d'Estournel are similar derivations. Lafite, from "hite," height, Cos from "côte," slope. Or so they tell me.

Rumors of my activities, artistic and otherwise, buzzed round stuffy old Bordeaux.

"They say he's going into the cinematograph business."

"Good. Perhaps it'll stop him making a show of the wine business. That cubist horror of his is a disgrace."

Cubism was by this time nearly twenty years old. Léger, Braque, Picasso, Gris, had offered the world a new vision in pre-1914 Paris. Nowadays you could buy them on your bath mats. The mustache on the Mona Lisa, dadaisme, surréalisme, vorticism had come and gone since Cubism. Not in Bordeaux. I withdrew my zazzy label, Jean Carlu himself persuaded me. "After all," he said, "you are trying to sell your wine." We fashionable ones did not realize that our exhilarating world only stretched from Montparnasse to St. Germain des Prés,

but what a world it was. Giraudoux's *Amphitryon 38* to set the
scene, lighthearted sex, witty chat, Cocteau guiding us through
his garden of androgynous fairy tales and Gide, the ambigu-
ous, knocking us for our cruel imperialism. We were self-criti-
cal, cynical, emancipated, tolerant. There were no taboos.

I remember a lady accosting me one night. "Come with me,"
she said, "You'll have such a surprise." I went. She was a perfect
hermaphrodite.

I didn't miss a trick. I could dot an i on the latest manifesto
with the best of them and spent long hours analyzing the effect
of the cinema on art, and vice versa, with Cocteau. He was in
love with me. I was not interested.

Even if I had been, my spare time was fully occupied—with
Nicole. I had only just taken her in hand. Blonde, clear-eyed,
with strong muscles and steady nerves, she merited every attention, and repaid it. Nicole was brilliant at all sports except the
one that really matters, so I decided to give her a course of
training. Awakening, rousing, exploring, it was my specialty.
Not all men are good at it, obviously, or there wouldn't be so
many unsatisfied wives. Nicole came into my sights skimming
across the bay of Arcachon upright on a tilted surfboard. What
a figure! As soon as her husband was out of the way, I pounced.
He was a shipping magnate in La Rochelle, and had to be at his
office early on Mondays.

It may have been this story which was upsetting gossips
rather than my rams and my Paris escapades. So what!

I didn't care what they said so long as they talked. My wine
was selling, Mouton's star was in the ascendant—'28 and '29
were brilliant years. My balance sheet looked happy at last, and
I had persuaded Cousin Édouard to give a banquet for the
Association of Five at Lafite. As yet, there was no accommoda-
tion for receptions or banquets at Mouton.

Baron Robert agreed to come from Paris to preside, an un-
precedented event. I invited the world's press. They came, and
we did them proud. The tables groaned, fine wines went the
rounds. Fine? They were superb, unique. We even drank a
Lafite 1811, the year of the comet which was said to have her-

alded the birth of Napoleon's son, and a particularly good wine harvest. Everyone sang the praises of château-bottling, especially the foreigners, which impressed the Bordelais. That was the night, at Lafite, when the owner of Château Yquem, Count, later Marquis, Bertrand de Lur Saluces, said he would like to join the Five. We were all delighted. He was a solitary untouchable; a brilliant linguist, philosopher and mathematician, isolated in his studies and his passion for his exquisite Yquem.

October 10, 1929. Théâtre Pigalle, grand opening night. Architecturally it made history. Outside, white light cascaded over the streamlined building, completely transforming the ordinary little street. Inside, the box office area led to a spacious foyer where you could choose between theater, art gallery or night club. The ceiling glowed with indirect light and a curving wall of chromium-plated tubes reflected the human parade as it sashayed around. There were areas for promenading, lounging, quizzing your neighbors, gossiping or just boozing. Then, when you arrived at the entrance to the auditorium, there was enough space for you to make your own star entry.

Everything was designed for comfort and convenience; that it was good looking appeared to be accidental.

The first night was an extraordinary affair. The local concierges and shopkeepers had installed stools on the pavements and hired them to the crowds who turned up to watch the arrival of the mobs. Policemen blowing on their shrill whistles were vainly trying to disperse the traffic jam outside, while dragoons in white pantaloons and black-plumed helmets formed a decorative, useless frieze within.

Getting the guest list to work must have taken a month. What a mixture. And they were all there, maharajas and marquises, archdukes and actresses, the famous and the infamous. The list of titled folk filled two columns in the classy papers. The geniuses came too. In the foyer I had made a light show—waves of color played over the well-coifed heads.

"How pretty."

"Yes dear, but when are the acrobats coming on?"

Well, if I'd made a circus parade of the opening, all fashionable Paris was performing. They'd flocked to see what the theatrical Rothschilds were doing; one simply had to be there or die. The show, or rather the sideshow, was merely an added attraction. It was a patriotic revue, *L'Histoire de la France* composed by Monsieur Sacha Guitry—fourteen tableaux, beginning with our remote ancestors and finishing with Marshal Foch. It featured François Ier, Louis XI, XIII and XVIII, Richelieu, Molière, Talleyrand, Napoleon, Thiers, anybody who took Monsieur Guitry's fancy. It lasted four and a quarter hours. The highlights were Louis XIV's Versailles with ballet, and Napoleon III's court with songs. Monsieur Guitry played all the best parts, including Napoleon III, with Yvonne Printemps as his Empress Eugènie. They were the stars of the show, the biggest box office draw in Paris at that time, and for a long time after.

As the Printemps moved downstage through a frou-frou of crinolines, singing Offenbach's "Dites lui," she stole my heart away. I went into the same box every night to listen to her and she would look up at me and wink. What an adorable creature. We had the most delightful affair, unlike any other I ever had before or since. It lasted four months, and only ended with the run of the play.

The show itself was expensive window dressing. There was never an empty seat but we ran at a loss. It was a very costly production. What a waste when France had so much to offer, when Jean Giraudoux, Henri-René Lenormand, Jules Romains and Armand Salacrou were writing their plays, and Copeau's *Compagnie des quinze* was influencing the whole of Europe. The new school of actor-directors—Gaston Baty, Charles Dullin, Louis Jouvet and the Pitoeffs—were soon to become world famous, and Antoine, the father of twentieth-century French theater, was still alive, still alert. The standard of acting, production and décor was higher than France had ever known, or has ever seen since.

I wanted the new wave at Pigalle. "Let's open with something startling, something contemporary, try the new techniques. Have you seen what Gaston Baty is achieving with his cinematic style?" Like everybody else in the swim, I was thrilled with the new direction in the theater. My father, on the other hand, backed up by his hammy old theatrical friends, favored the well-made play; perhaps, secretly, his own plays—he had written three that year. As a director of Pigalle I wouldn't hear of such old stuff. All the same I lost out over the Guitry.

My father had dedicated *Circe,* one of his three plays, to Antoine, and at the same time asked him to be artistic director of Pigalle.

When the argument about the opening play seemed to be going against me, I decided to go and see Antoine at his house on the place Dauphine, to try and win him over to my side. He received me graciously and I told him what I thought. "No, no," he said, "you will have to open with something that will please your father and display his theater, then you can introduce new ideas and give the theater style."

"So what do you suggest we open with?"

"The Guitry," said the old man, gathering up his three chins. "That would be best."

I couldn't believe my ears. This from the man who had sacrificed everything to create a new style of acting and production, used all his meager savings to support his Théâtre Libre and managed to accumulate one million francs of debt in the pursuit of a theatrical ideal. I went away quite shattered.

After the excitement of the opening I took my father aside and spoke to him like a Dutch uncle. I told him the direction would have to be more inspiring and proposed a cartel of four, to choose the plays and produce them.

Who would they be?

Baty, Jouvet, Pitoeff, Dullin.

The names were impressive. He agreed, and I said it might mean changing his program. It did. With Baty, I chose *Le Feu du ciel* for the second production. It was marvelous, brilliant and a complete flop. It had to come off, there was no one in the house. My father took it all philosophically, but I knew my programing had been wrong. I should never have put the tough Baty immediately after Guitry's *Crême Chantilly*. Jouvet would have brought them in. Baty threw in a revival of one of his box office successes, *Simoun*. That went well. Giraudoux's *Judith* followed, a wonderful play, but it didn't raise the roof. The third play, *Donogoo-Tonka* by Jules Romains, swept the boards. Well, of course, it was directed by Louis Jouvet. *La Patissière du village* by Alfred Savior? *Comme çi, comme ça.*

Wild applause, silence or two or three tepid curtain calls—it was impossible to predict the first-night response. The empty seats depressed me, especially when I knew the show was good. I found the critics destructive, more interested in developing a savage prose style than discovering theater, but the public slavishly followed them. Can you judge a painting at the first view? You notice I haven't mentioned star performers. The idea was to have a company in which everybody gave a star performance, but we didn't have a company; each play was cast ad lib and that was costly. The box office returns didn't cover the running costs, let alone pay for new productions or compensate my father for his initial outlay. I noticed none of his rich friends, those wise counselors, dipping their hands into their pockets to invest in theater. There we were, putting ourselves at the mercy of public taste, hoping to change it, as Jean Vilar did later with his Théâtre National Populaire, and we were out on a limb. There were no government grants for new theaters and new plays in those days—added to which we were divided among ourselves. The theater kept going for two years. My father lost a fortune in the Wall Street crash. Monsieur Jardot insisted on economies. He nearly had apoplexy when he saw the theater's balance sheets.

My father's old hams blamed my management. "Philippe is far too avant garde," they said. To them it was a dirty word. I was bitterly resentful.

I had made a huge success of the nightclub, the fabulous

New Orleans jazz band I'd discovered at the Moulin Rouge was a must for every smart Parisian. I'd organized magnificent exhibitions in the art gallery—Chardin, African sculpture from Nigeria and Senegal—and I'd presented th Kabuki for the first time in Paris, bringing them from Tokyo. I was also showing banned Soviet films in the newly formed cinema club: *We from Kronstadt; Nana; The Battleship Potemkin; Turk-Sib*. I had asked Marcel Pagnol, Louis Aragon and Princess Bibesco to write plays for me, and they'd all promised to do so. True, I hadn't seen anything yet, but the cartel of four hadn't folded. Dullin and the Pitoeffs were still ready to come to us, but my father told me he had had enough. He wasn't prepared to bankrupt himself for art. He let the place and went off to Hollywood.

After he'd sat Shirley Temple on his knee and kissed Anna May Wong, he went on to Boston and acquired another miraculous machine for his Hôpital Marcadet.

He left me in the depths. I felt betrayed. It seemed that Pigalle had been just another of his expensive whims, but perhaps it meant more to him than I could have known at the time. After 1931 he never wrote another play. Had I stolen the theater from my father? It looks like it now, but I'm afraid she was too tough an old whore for either of us to handle. For the few nights of pleasure she'd given us, she'd emptied our pockets and shown us the door.

Yes, I am prepared to admit now that I was not skilled enough, or experienced enough, to handle that theater. I loved the place but that was not enough. I hadn't the patience to stay and conquer it. My only consolation has been that everything I learned there influenced my whole life. It all went into Mouton, but for many years I avoided the rue Pigalle . . . I didn't want even to glimpse that costly building.

During the occupation it was in the hands of the Commissariat des Affaires Juives, the organization set up by Pétain to manage the Jewish property he had confiscated. Nobody used it. When the war was over, during the long wait for restitution, the theater remained empty. When my father died, I sold the place.

In 1957, I heard it was to be demolished to make way for a garage. I took my wife and daughter to see it—they'd heard all about it and seen the playbills and programs, which I still keep.

Unbelievably the old concierge who had taken care of us in the hectic years was still there, not much altered. "You, Monsieur Philippe? It can't be true. Come in. Oh yes, they're here. They've started at the rear. You're just in time to take a last look."

We went in. I didn't know what to expect—crumbling plaster, rats, fallen roof timbers? No, the place was alive, as if waiting for the musicians to start tuning up, for light to move over the gray cyclorama.

A tall figure appeared on the stage, and walked slowly toward us. It was a little unnerving.

"I know who you are," said a working man's voice, "though you don't know me. You put her up. I'm pulling her down. But believe me or believe me not, monsieur, I'm sorry to be the one to do it. Whoever built her knew what he was doing."

We went with him and watched the heavy stone ball crashing into the back wall. Pigalle should have been standing today. There is no theater like it.

II

How Many Miles to Babylon?

13

How many miles to Babylon?
Three score and ten,
Can I get there by candlelight?
Yes, and back again.

ANON.

NINETEEN THIRTY-ONE. No more Pigalle. I found myself suffering from withdrawal symptoms and there was no exciting woman in my life to help me out.

From time to time I had persuaded la belle Nicole to come to Paris for an afternoon's fun. I mentioned finding her at Arcachon, didn't I? She was a wonderfully healthy specimen, no makeup, good teeth, well-brushed hair and a charming light fluff over her entire body. What's more, her technique had improved considerably.

I would meet her at the station, we'd rush to the rue Cortambert, strip off our clothes and dive into bed like two channel swimmers. She wouldn't even want to take the snack with orange juice William had prepared for her. A few hours' good sport, after which we'd stagger out to eat a hearty meal, and that was it. She didn't care for theater or cinema. She agreed to come to a party in Paris once, and there she fell asleep, stretched along the only divan in the room. I had heard someone mention her provincial accent, and guessed, quite rightly, that she was pretending to be asleep. That night I was told, in no uncertain terms, that she didn't care for Paris or Parisians. So then I only saw her when I was staying at Arcachon, and we would go sailing. She adored yachting, and so did I. In fact my feeling for Nicole was so mixed up with my passion for the sea that, apart from her intimate attractions she might have been my favorite cutter . . . hand on helm, head close to the bosom of the waves, foam whipping one cheek, the caress of the wind on the other, surging through swift thighs of water, the gull's screech, the groan of wood . . . whee-e-e-e-e!

But it hadn't worked on the boating pond in the Bois de Boulogne.

For a while I had this little actress, sweet as a nut, and did it all very prettily. We used to go ice-skating together, but actresses are not my scene. All they think about are their performances and their notices. On top of that, their hours are ridiculous. I needed a break, a change from Paris, Mouton, everything and everybody. I would be off, see the world before somebody decided to blow it up. My father had a yacht the size of a corvette, with every luxury and a crew of twenty-five. I'd had enough of all that. I wanted my own "tall ship and a star to steer her by." I sent one of the footmen out for some navigational charts and told William to gather my yachting gear. Round the world in eighty days? A cinch. After all, I'd done very well in the six-meter class in the Bay of Arcachon.

Perhaps I should build my own boat. Was there time? I'd need a shipmate. Well there was always André, my sparring partner and lifelong friend. No, he would have to take care of Mouton if I was going to be away for any length of time. What about Bertrand? His family were close friends of ours. His father, Dr. Zadoc-Kahn, was the family doctor; his grandfather had been chief rabbi of France. Bertrand was studying medicine, but he could easily give that up for a few months.

They were both agreeable. I abandoned the idea of forestalling the tall ships round-the-world race, and booked two berths on *La Malle des Indes*, Marseilles to Singapore.

We almost missed the boat. I'd never seen Marseilles. We got lost in the Arab quarter, through following a crowd of foreign legionnaires and Senegalese soldiers down a narrow alley. What was the attraction? Veiled beauties in doorways, eyes dark with kohl. We made the boat by the skin of our teeth. Then three weeks of *dolce far niente* while the world drifted by: Djibouti, Ceylon, flying fish, dolphins, sweltering heat—new smells, new colors, unknown tongues.

At Singapore we found there was a three-engined Ford biplane that flew to Java. From Java across the narrow sea to Bali, where we were received with grave and princely hospitality. Yet we must have been a funny sight, two stiff young Frenchmen surrounded by nude-breasted girls, trying to join in those shimmering Balinese dances while exotic boys beckoned us into the bushes. Well, I will try anything once, and I did, but naked boys are not to my taste.

So on to Siam, now Thailand, by train. We were surprised that the duke of Brabant, future King Leopold II of Belgium, and Princess Astrid of Sweden, his wife, were on the same train, and even more surprised when we were invited to join their party. We felt highly honored. It turned out that the duke was bored with the journey and fancied a game of cards. We were all going to Bangkok. He was paying a state visit to the king of Siam.

When we stepped down from the train there were a clash of cymbals, the pounding of giant drums, and we found ourselves swept along with the royal party past an exotic guard of honor, almost into the arms of the king's emissary. It was very embarrassing but we couldn't escape. In fact, we were immediately invited to a grand reception at the royal palace that very night. The duke and his lady pressed us to go so we accepted, with a thousand thanks, only to realize a few minutes later that we had no formal clothes whatsoever. Rolling round Bangkok in a rickshaw, scouring the place for a tailor, we found the only one, "Anglish Tailer Late Bond Streat" said the shop sign. The traveled tailor whipped up two black tailcoats for us, plus two white ties. Unfortunately as I bowed to His Royal Majesty, there was a nasty rending sound—it was the middle seam at the back of my coat splitting open from top to tail. With the coat mended on the royal sewing machine, I managed to get through five days of Siamese celebrations taking care not to bow too low.

Impossible to leave Siam, we were told, without visiting the source of the mighty Mekong. You mustn't miss it, said the king, for there the lands of China, Laos, Siam and Burma meet, and en route you will pause to watch the elephants working on the teak plantations.

The duke and his princess thought they ought to see the teak and we all set off together. The plantations were very boring and the journey impossible. A rickety train deposited us all in the middle of nowhere. Two ramshackle old bangers belonging to the plantation managers took us from there and when Bertrand and I finally reached the source on foot, we found that we'd mislaid our royal party. As we stood gazing at the empty landscape and dreading the return journey, the duke suddenly appeared on the skyline escorted by the prince, Tiao Petsarath, brother of the king of Laos, with all his train behind him. He had been looking for the duke, who had got lost among the teak, to announce the arrangements for the return journey by the river route. They advised us to join them; we didn't need to be asked twice. The canoes were waiting on a broad stretch of river. They were dugout trees, piraguas, with those natty little shelters in the middle of them, the kind you see in Japanese prints. The smiling boys who were to steer us brought cushions and helped us tuck ourselves in. At the last moment on each canoe a flag appeared: Belgian, French and a red one with a white elephant, Laotian. We pushed off, to applause. All we lacked were Hollywood tom-toms offstage.

The days passed speeding over swift waters or gliding slowly under tangled ropes of greenery, accompanied by the never-ending cacophony of the jungle. Each evening we landed at a pleasant spot and bivouacked. Before we had even tied up, a string of villagers would arrive carrying baskets of freshly baked fish, rice, fruit and gourds of spring water. We felt very safe and cared for.

On the first morning Princess Astrid kept to her tent and the duke organized Olympian games. It was very hot and they were very competitive. First we had to see who could pee the farthest. The winner was congratulated. "Urine attracts butterflies," said the duke, brandishing his butterfly net. No butterflies appeared, so he set us to work collecting those small flat stones which ricochet across water. Mine sank. Then we had a race.

Prize for the fastest up a palm tree.

Nobody made it, too hard on the shins. The locals watched in respectful silence.

On the third morning a deputation arrived. They begged us to stay and kill a tiger which had picked off two or three of the villagers. None of us knew anything about big-game hunting, but we were assured that only tigers which were old and beat took to man eating. Nevertheless we moved rather gingerly into the shady undergrowth. We stopped in our tracks as a big brindled cat started up. It looked rather attractive, its large eyes full of fear.

"Don't touch. Dangerous wild cats," shouted a guide.

After a morning scratched by vicious branches and eaten by mosquitoes, we gave up. We saw neither hilt nor hair of the man eater. I dreamed of him all night though, his eyes gleaming through a curtain of dark green fronds.

> Tyger! tyger! burning bright
> In the forests of the night,
>   What immortal hand or eye
> Could frame thy fearful symmetry?

The image haunted me. It went on haunting me till later, in Annam, I banished him. I made my first and last kill, a tigress. If I must tell the truth, I killed two, the tigress and her cub, they both went in the same round. I know what you are thinking, you preservationists. Well, now we all know better and it's probably too late.

At the time I was proud of my marksmanship and took the skins back to Mouton, where nobody liked them. They finished up in my Paris flat, and later the Germans pinched them.

Where were we before my confession? Still on the Mekong. Well, at Luang Prabang the king of Laos was waiting to receive the royal party. After the usual feasting and dancing, the time had come to part. The royal party was going on to Hanoi and we were heading for Saigon. It had been an extraordinary encounter. These honored royal people accepting two unknown young men. They embraced us. "A bientôt," said the duke. "We shall surely meet again."

We did, but it took over fifty years, and then there were only two of us. This summer, in the little French provincial town of Brignoles, I dined with ex-King Leopold. His lovely Princess Astrid met her tragic death long ago, before the war, and my dear Bertrand did not survive the Nazis.

We sat together on a pleasant summer evening, exchanging old men's tales of hairbreadth escapes and enemies outwitted. I hadn't known that he too had been imprisoned during the war. Then we talked of happier days and the great times we had on our famous Oriental tour.

God be with the youth of us.

Bertrand and I did all the things that a young man should on his first world tour, and many that he shouldn't. We visited the temples at Angkor, stood on the Great Wall of China, spent three nights in a lamasery, first cousin to a monastery, sipped tea with the geishas in the red-light district of Tokyo. We didn't get very far with these ladies, though I promise you it wasn't for want of trying; it was just that it took them so long to untie their obis that by the time they were ready, all desire was spent. To complete our round trip, we crossed the Pacific Ocean and Canada, and landed up in New York, where we couldn't understand a word of the native language, but there was a song in the air and long lines everywhere. The song was "Buddy, Can You Spare a Dime?," the lines were for soup kitchens.

And so home to France, where we landed in the spring of 1932, rather thinner and not very sun-tanned. We headed for Paris, gray skies, rain and hunger marches, unemployed men at every street corner. In the early 1930s, the world scene was very gloomy, and nature followed suit. We had bad weather and bad harvests. André was delighted to hand me back the baton.

Oh for the great years, and Mouton acclaimed. As in 1927, the wines we were producing were good and hearty, but they were not aristocrats. I had always believed there could be a world market for reasonably priced, palatable wines, though in the United Kingdom and the United States at this time wine was still not a popular drink. Well, it could be and would be. I'd learned a thing or two since Carruades. The name was of paramount importance. No more dialect words. Monsieur Marjary and I put our heads together. After many fanciful excursions we returned to the basic truth.

"It's actually a new Mouton. Why not call it that?"

"No, they'll think it's a Mouton Rothschild."

"Junior Mouton? Too childish."

"Cadet Mouton? It's the youngest member of the family, like me. Let's call it the cadet, Mouton Cadet."

And we did, with the usual roar from the opposition.

"What the devil is he doing now? He'll cause irreparable harm to Mouton Rothschild." But of course it didn't. I took great care to avoid any confusion.

The 1928 and 1929 Mouton Rothschilds had broken all records. When Mouton Cadet was launched it was billed as a first-class blended wine. Mouton Rothschild, a luxury name for the great occasion; Mouton Cadet, a popular wine produced with all the care for which Mouton was renowned, and in reach of everyone's pocket.

The success of the Mouton Cadet was instantaneous. It even surprised me. The demand grew year by year. How could I increase the output without impairing the quality? The best harvests were purchased from neighboring vineyards. Cadet became a blend of wines from the immediate locality. And so

Chateau Mouton Rothschild and Mouton Cadet flourished side by side, distinctive, different, yet strangely enough each enhanced the reputation of the other. There was even a touch of jealousy, always good for the competitive spirit.

14

If I had a talking picture of you
I would run it every time I felt blue.

BUDDY DE SYLVA

IN 1932 I needed Paris and new contacts. I was going to be a film director. Well, half a film director—Marc Allegret would be the other half. He had walked into my life during the Pigalle period, a film fanatic. He took me to see films, every day. We raved about Fritz Lang's *Metropolis* and René Clair's *Italian Straw Hat*. We met only to talk film. Then came the shock of *The Singing Fool*. . . . Couldn't talkies have exciting music like the silent movies and marvelous words? Maybe we could show the world. I didn't think I had the talent to write a play, or even a screenplay, which I imagined would be easier, but I rather fancied myself as a director—there again, not on my own. Marc knew the ropes, he had already made films and I liked him. We talked happily of making a film together, with wonderful ideas for lighting and camera angles, but we had no story. We'd just started kicking storylines around when I decided to go off on my world tour. I took a few books with me, and when I came back I was sure I had the right one in my pocket. It was *Hell in Frauensee* by Vicki Baum—romance in the Austrian Tyrol, tender love scenes in funny hats; just the thing for the harsh days we were living through. Marc Allegret was wild about it. "Tremendous film possibilities," he said. "Let's get down to the screenplay." We did. It took far more work than I'd anticipated, and when we paused to take stock I was doubtful, thought we should show it to a third party.

"There's my uncle André," said Marc.

"André?"

"André Gide, one of my lovers."

That seemed a good idea, especially as I was anxious to get on with the practical side, choosing actors and locations. Marc found a production manager and I approached Georges Auric to do the music and Colette for the dialogue. Both accepted, largely for the novelty of working on a talkie, I think.

One couldn't say that Gide was wildly enthusiastic. Indeed he was no help at all. He explained that he really wasn't a film man and told us to change the title. "Call it *Lac aux dames*," he said. So we did.

The best thing, we thought, would be to employ a professional scenario writer to lick our script into shape, while we got on with the casting. I enjoyed that part. We had a cast of beautiful people, headed by the *doux* Jean-Pierre Aumont, who still charms the public, and feline Simone Simon, *la vierge sensuelle*.

For rather a small part we managed to secure that magnificent actor Michel Simon, who'd just finished filming Jean Vigo's *L'Atalante*. I was surprised—I hadn't realized that a really great actor would accept a minor role, if it pleased him.

Jean-Pierre was to play Simone's swimming instructor but unfortunately he couldn't swim, and his muscles were terribly frail. We sent him to a gymnasium every day to do a little body building, then to a swimming coach at Antibes who worked on him for four months. This held us up a little but we banked on Jean-Pierre being good box office, not that he'd ever made a film before in his life.

We had the best cameraman, Jules Kruger, the best dress designer, Marcel Rochas, and for continuity a Turkish girl, Françoise Gourdji, who later became Françoise Giroud, secrétaire d'état à la culture for Président Giscard d'Estaing. We were, in fact, a fish farm of talent.

France has some of the oldest studios in the world and it was in such a one that we started filming. Each morning we would drive out to a distant Paris suburb where we would try and create our magic in a barnlike building that not long before had witnessed the earliest efforts of the film making pioneers. The walls were now covered with thick layers of straw—sound-proofing.

As is often the case just before shooting starts, the script had been somewhat neglected. Not to put too fine a point on it, Colette's dialogue was a little thin on the ground. So each evening, having told the cast it was all going splendidly, I would shoot across town to Colette's apartment in the Palais-Royal. Sitting by her bed, I would describe what we had just done and outline tomorrow's rather desperate needs. As I talked she would draw some sheets of her blue paper toward her and start making beautiful scribbles.

By the time we left the studios we were running late. Luckily when we got to Austria we found that our liaison officer, a most elegant young man, Prince Tassilo Fürstenberg, was also highly efficient. He was a member of the café society of the day, knew everything about everybody and proved invaluable.

For the main location we had decided on the Wolfgangsee, heaven in fine weather, but because we got there so late, a washout. It was pouring with rain and had been raining for weeks, but so that we wouldn't be completely balked by the weather, clever Tassilo had already built a temporary studio. It looked like a lakeside—leisure center, I think we would call it nowadays—and there we could go ahead shooting a few interiors: swimming pool, bar, drinks terrace, with ever in the background the rainswept Wolfgangsee. We appeared to have a tremendous lot of haughty-looking extras hanging around, all ready to take part in any crowd scene, as required.

"Who are they, Tassilo?"

"Friends—Metternichs, Schwarzenbergs, one or two of my own relatives."

There were members of almost every distinguished family in the Tyrol, all very happy to be earning a few ha'pence.

I would never have believed that so many things could go wrong, but they told me it was the same on every film and I wasn't the first to want to make the film of making the film.

The weather was disastrous. Simone Simon's Great Dane, which was in the film, snuffled an ant's nest and got so many ants up his nose he went mad and had to be taken away. My current number, a big Rumanian blonde, fell in the lake and lost her specially designed Parisian frock. She looked rather better naked, but Françoise said it would spoil the continuity. We would have to send to Paris for a reproduction—of the dress, not the blonde.

The film had to end on a gentle autumnal note with Simone Simon singing a sad song as she rowed across the deserted lake, words by Colette, music by Auric. All very well, but even they wouldn't be able to save the ending if we had to shoot in that endless, relentless, downpour. We waited and waited, till finally during a break in the clouds we uncovered the cameras, dashed out and got it—Simone's sodden dress didn't show up too badly in the rushes.

It took a long, long time back in Paris, and many pick-up shots, before the fruits of our labors bore any resemblance to the original concept, thanks largely to Marcel and Anna Tortet, two of my father's devoted staff, who prepared delicious meals each day for all of us: actors, actresses, technicians, condemned to pick-up scenes and dubbing sessions.

At last it was ready and we rushed to show it to the distributors. They turned us down. So we hired the only cinema on the Champs Élysées, the Colisée, erected a huge billboard façade boosting our film, which upset everybody, and opened to an invited audience of our best friends and enemies. My father came, my new wife, Lilli, Colette, all the cast and the team of course. We had a super party and our film ran for a year. It was the first French talkie to receive worldwide distribution.

*   *   *

I trust I haven't shocked you, throwing in my wife like that. I was a little shocked myself at the time. When I first met her she was the comtesse de Chambure, and she told me she could never make love to a poor man. I ran into her again, fresh from my trip round the world, and she looked very beautiful. She was married to a bold and jealous Belgian baron. This did not deter me, but when she told me she was carrying my child it was a different matter. There would have to be a divorce.

Monsieur le Baron swore he would not let her go and threatened murder. On November 22, 1933, the baby was born in Paris, a bouncing daughter, and Lili named her after me, Philippine. The husband declared that the child was legitimately his and he intended to kidnap her, so I whisked her off to Mouton, where my stalwart vignerons kept a lookout night and day. They were a team to be reckoned with.

Monsieur evidently didn't relish a baronial tourney; he relinquished his claims on my daughter and her mother, and a year later Lili and I were legally spliced in the Mairie of the 16th arrondissement. I was thirty-two, she was twenty-seven, a fashionable young woman-about-town, a confirmed Parisienne. She wasn't attracted to Mouton and the rural life, and indeed you could not blame her. The house my grandfather built was ugly, inside and out. The long lines of the chai gave a touch of elegance to the courtyard, but for the rest it was still an untidy dump. There was simply nowhere else to put all the paraphernalia of the vineyard.

Inside, the rooms were small, the wallpaper had been chosen by my grandmother and the tiled basement looked exactly like the local workhouse; and there was still no running water. The smart young Parisienne was not tempted to try her hand at redesigning the place; in any case, who could carry out her orders? No one in the Médoc had heard of interior decorating.

There was nowhere to take a pleasant walk and no social life whatsoever. She was delighted whenever the time came to leave Mouton. She liked Arcachon; and she loved Paris, so that was where we spent most of our time together.

15

'Course I don't like dictators none
But the whole country it ought to be run
By Ee-lec-tric-it-ee!!!

WOODY GUTHRIE

MARRIAGE and Philippine and, at Mouton, the biggest revolution since the invention of full frontal copulation—central heating, water pressure, telephones, electric motors. As the cables were being laid, we took advantage of the works to make another revolution: we dug drains. Nineteen hundred thirty-three, and we were catching up with the Romans.

It is difficult to realize how much electrification meant to these isolated villages where babies were borne by candlelight, and even oil lamps were rare. It was a miracle, light at the touch of a switch. I had reveled in the magnificent switchboard we had installed at Pigalle. In the end I was a very good lighting man. Now I could light all Mouton.

Our cellars had always been unusual—lit by thousands of candles, set in iron candelabra made from barrel rims. Lighting them was quite a performance, but as we only had visitors once in a blue moon, it didn't matter. A mile of cotton fuse had to be wound round all the candles and looped from chandelier to chandelier. Once lit, the spark would travel the whole length of the cellar, leaving loop after loop of lighted candles. It was the system used in local churches. Nothing can reproduce candlelight, so I had some tiny bulbs made, to give a suggestion of starlight. The design, my own, is still in use.

On the other hand, I introduced good clear lighting, well angled, in the working areas and made an attractive atmosphere in the lay-bys. Work might as well be as pleasant as possible, and I've always found that people will respect a place that is elegant and tidy.

One day all Mouton will be beautifully lit, I said to myself—the vines, the distant woods, statues, stones and trees. It took a long time to get round to it, but when you come by now, at night, you will see the whole place shining, like gold on black velvet. Too much moon spoils it.

Come by tonight, and you will find me in my woolly hat and hairy coat, relighting the garden and a newly acquired statue of Pan; my numerous assistants—recruited among the houseguests and any members of the staff silly enough to go home that way—will be perched on ladders, adjusting lamps and receiving instructions, while Rajah, my Labrador, with me as always, watches every move. These sessions have been known to go on until morning.

In 1933, lighting the dark corners made me more and more dissatisfied with the state of the rest of the place. We had no drive-in, no entrance, just that cluttered courtyard opening onto the village street. All the traffic between Le Pouyalet and the neighboring villages passed by my window. If I could clear that yard, it would be a start.

I cast my eye over the fences which marked the boundary of d'Armailhacq, the neighboring property, and its border of bush and brier, dead and dying trees. I knew that beyond the trees there was a large estate. I had been there once, long ago. It was during my first visit to Mouton, when I was at school in Bordeaux at the end of the war; the fences, fallen in here and there, tempted me to slip through and explore, but I was told it was forbidden territory. That fixed it. One afternoon when nobody was about I decided to visit d'Armailhacq.

The woods were almost impenetrable. I had to find a good stout stave and beat my way through the dense brush. The sun had gone in, the light was somber. When I stopped to look around, I heard the undergrowth humming with life. I was scared. What of? Snakes. And you wouldn't even see them till they curled themselves round your ankle or your arm or your neck. I walked into a spider's web, hastily brushed it off my face. By now I was really frightened. Remember I was a town boy. I'd never been in such a jungle in my whole life. I was even scared of the ivy strangling every tree. If I stood still much longer, it might strangle me. I tried to push on, first this way, then that. The place smelt rank, my feet were sinking in slime, giant fungi broke softly into my hand as I plunged on toward what looked like a clearing. It was. With great relief I reached a grove, where the grass was lush, vivid green under a nave of ancient plane trees. They had been planted, Lord knows when, to define what must have once been a carriage way. I followed it until I came upon a very strange sight. So strange that at first I thought it an illusion. No, there it was, a half château, so neatly sliced that you were left with half a door, half a pediment, half a window, the other half seemingly blotted out by a giant backdrop of sky and woodland. It was bizarre. Had the original owners fled from some sudden catastrophe, plague or revolution?

There was no sign of human activity, but I felt I was being watched, someone's eyes were on me. I hadn't the temerity to go nearer. Then a shutter moved and I turned and fled, climbed a gate, tore my trousers and found myself on the normal, everyday road which crosses the Carruades.

Back at Mouton I asked Merilda about our fairy tale neighbors.

The Armailhacqs had moved in more than two hundred years ago, she said, about the time when old Ségur, the marquis, who'd been lord of all the land hereabouts since time immemorial, had been forced to break up his estate. Baron de Brane had bought Mouton at the same time, she told me. He had been known as the Napoleon of the Vines.

"But why was the place left like that, half built?"

There had been stories about the old half-of-a-place, that the builder had run off with the owner's daughter, that the revolutionaries had occupied the d'Armailhacq house—but as she had never heard of any revolutionaries in Pauillac, nor any lovelorn builders for that matter, she thought the plain truth was that the family had gone broke when it was half built.

"When was that?"

"Lord knows, Master Philippe, I only know it was long before my time."

I would have to open up my grandmother's fusty histories of the Médoc if I wanted any more. Neither Merilda nor anybody else around here was interested in olden days.

Merilda's story was correct, as far as it went. In 1744, the Marquis de Ségur, overwhelmed with taxes, had to sell off wide tracts of his land. Lafite had been his country seat. At Mouton he stabled his horses and stored his farm implements. The estate of the half-built château had no name till the Bordeaux family d'Armailhacq bought it. With the Baron de Brane, they introduced the famous cabernet sauvignon grape to this region. "The grape which gives the great wines of the Médoc their distinction," wrote Armand d'Armailhacq.

I was beginning to learn the history of the plot of land my great-great-grandfather had bought in 1853, knowing no more about it than I did.

I still didn't know why the work on that early nineteenth-century château had stopped so abruptly. I skipped through the chapter headings till I came to Charles X, the bigoted old king who was a bit soft in the head. He made such a hash of things that in 1830 he had to run away to England, borrowing his fare from a Rothschild, of course—Baron James. The country was going broke, so was Mouton; even so the Baron de Brane managed to sell the place to his rich Paris banker, Monsieur Thuret. In 1832 the d'Armailhacqs, similarly embarrassed, tried to interest Monsieur Thuret in their property. Their new house in the park was half built and they couldn't afford to finish it.

So there it was. Merilda was right.

Monsieur Thuret was not interested. Mouton was not proving profitable: a deadly white fungus, oidium, was ravaging the vines. The d'Armailhacqs was left with their half-a-house on their hands, a curiosity—as you see it today—and a monument to the hazards of wine growing.

The family probably thought things were looking up when the Comte de Ferrand married the granddaughter of the original owner. He might have been the man behind the shutters when I had trespassed there in 1918. Even then, he must have been on his last legs. All his ventures had come to naught. When his wine making didn't pay, he tried making aperitifs and that did no good either. He created the Société Vinicole de Pauillac in an attempt to organize the winegrowers. He thought they were being menaced by the vignerons, who were demanding higher wages. Serious trouble was brewing when the 1914 war intervened and the local lads were called to the colors. Afterwards, when his wife died, he lived alone in his half-a-house with one old serving man for company, practically penniless. He was still there in 1933.

Behind that house there were forty hectares of vineyard plus chais, cellars and outhouses. I wondered if he'd sell. There was no harm in trying. I called round one day; this very frail, very old gentleman received me. When he managed to grasp my name and work out who I was, he invited me to dine with him on the following Sunday. I went. The meal was frugal, the wine very good, the white gloves of the manservant carefully darned. I felt sure he stood in for butler, cook, bottle washer, male nurse, gardener and maître de chai as well. When I broached the subject of the property, the old man hedged. I suggested that the château itself should remain his till the end of his days. No one would dream of asking him to leave his home. He sighed. He had not many days to dispose of, he said.

Was he relieved at the thought of selling up? I thought so, but he was much too proud to mention money. We agreed that the price should be discussed by an independent party.

The deal was concluded without delay and to the satisfaction of both parties. I owned d'Armailhacq, its park and vineyards —at the last moment, the count threw in his Société Vinicole de Pauillac, which was to become my first marketing house. To my great joy, there was an ample yard behind the chai at d'Armailhacq, where the oxen, horses, washing lines and farm implements, which occupied the courtyard at Mouton, could be installed at once.

The old gentleman actually walked out into the sunshine to watch all the hustle and bustle when we moved in.

It was a relief to have the yard cleared, but it also meant that one saw even more of the ramshackle sheds and empty stables, woodwork painted a dried blood color, typical of the Médoc. I knew that sometime I would have to change the whole aspect of the place, and dreamed of the day when wine lovers from all over the world would visit a new, elegant Mouton, but for the moment I had other fish to fry: forty hectares of vineyard added to our estate, the old chais and *cuviers* at d'Armailhacq to be completely renovated.

The wine had been highly esteemed even in the historic classification of 1855, and it figured in the earliest catalogue of Médoc wines.

> Among the eleven excellent wines for which Pauillac is famous, Mouton d'Armailhacq has received honorable distinction. The black sauvignon grape is cultivated here, with a skill which can only lead to perfection. As with the wines of Brane Mouton, its royal neighbor, Armailhacq gives forth a delicate perfume.
>
> ALFRED DANFLOU, 1867

Today this wine is so delicate one might almost call it feminine. You may know it as Château Mouton Baronne Philippe.

Nineteen hundred thirty-three brought light to Mouton, but to those of us who have lived to tell the tale, it meant one thing only—Hitler, chancellor of Germany.

"Thank God for the French army," said Winston Churchill, but few in France believed there would be another war. Few wanted to believe it. All the same, the construction of the impregnable Maginot Line slowly proceeded, at enormous cost to our country.

Hitler withdrew from the League of Nations. France was divided against itself. One had no heart for great schemes, there was no money for them anyway. Best to concentrate on improving the property, getting rid of the disused allotments, chicken runs and empty pigeon lofts scattered round the vineyards, and that meant first of all locating their owners—elusive birds. We weren't helped by the fact that nobody anywhere round here ever uses an address. They've no interest in street names, let alone numbers. "It's by Big Marie's place, second gate," and, "Round by where Jean-Paul's father had his forge," that forge having been demolished in my grandfather's time.

Monsieur Marjary would go knocking at doors, trying to trace owners on the strength of local gossip, only to be told, in the death, that a certain minute patch belonged to four or five different people. A hen run, with an empty rabbit hutch and dog kennel attached, was a family heirloom, but the family were not on speaking terms. Nobody seemed to have heard of title deeds. There is nothing the country people enjoy more than a long, drawn out squabble about property.

Endless negotiation is going on now, as I write, over a hovel no bigger than a pigsty on the land at the back of the chai. The surrounding land is ours and we want to plant vines there, but the owner of the hovel, a one-armed old man, says it is his winter residence. He spends his summers somewhere in the Pyrenees. When he's in the mood he sends a message informing us that he is prepared to negotiate, but only with me personally.

So I call by, maneuver my way through the planks that serve him as a door, take the seat he offers me on an old barrel, reply politely to his inquiries about my health, then wait every time for a detailed description of the pains he feels in his lost arm. Each time I have to remind him of the object of my visit, then

—as if it's of no importance—he casually names his price. It is very high, but before I can comment, we are back in the Resistance, he's a commanding officer, and it's the fatal night when his arm was blown off.

A year later, at his invitation, I call again. At once he picks up the story where he left off. A Nazi troop train is approaching, the boys have retreated to the ridge, the detonator is in his hand . . .

Again I have to remind him that I've come on business. He bows his head. He is very sorry to tell me that his second wife, defunct, left the property to her son-in-law, who is nothing to do with him. He is not sure that the son-in-law will sell, he's a hard man. Nevertheless, for a certain sum he might be persuaded to part. How much? He quotes a price twice as high as last year's.

Another year passes. This time he's in a sorrowful mood. Life isn't what it used to be, everybody out for themselves. His wife's daughter, nothing to do with him, has gone off with a lorry driver. The son-in-law is very bitter. Women! The wife had no right to will the property away in the first place. It was rightfully his. But of course he was away, in the navy at the time. Had I ever met Admiral Darlan? No? An inspiring man. I got up to leave as we were being moved into battle line and managed to squeeze through the planks just as the first salvo was fired.

I can't help liking the old romancer but I would also like to have that land. We offered him a smart little cottage on the estate and a generous price for his property. He said he would think about it. But now if anyone calls when he is there, he hides. Do you think he will sell? Never.

In those far-off, unhappy days with Hitler biting the carpet, French prime ministers whizzing across the political scene like demented ballet dancers, and Fascist colonels waiting in the wings, these country people simply went their own sweet way, oblivious to the outside world, their plots of land the only things bothering them.

I was not so different. Apart from my daughter's birth, all I thought about in 1933 was selling wine. It was the tenth anniversary of the Association of Five, a good occasion for going to town with spotlights and fanfares. So we went the whole hog, hired the best restaurant in Paris and invited a couple of the more personable and useful of the politicians: Tardieu, who'd been président du Counseil three times and looked like staying the course, and Barthou, flashy and patriotic. They were both included in Doumergue's "Peace, Truce and Justice" government the following year. Shortly after, Barthou was killed in Marseilles. He was trying to shield King Alexander of Yugoslavia from the bullet fired by Ante Pavelitch, a Croat nationalist. He didn't succeed.

Our dinner at the Pré Catelan in the Bois de Boulogne was a great success. As you know the Parisians never trouble themselves about anything that goes on outside Paris, but we were a sensation. It may have been our quaint clothes. Comte René was wearing what looked like his oldest suit and his white spats; Lur Saluces was with us, elegant as a skeleton, and I was playing the English country gent, in green tweeds. Whatever it was, we made the headlines; there were pictures of us on all the front pages, standing shoulder to shoulder. "The Médoc moves." "The men of the Gironde."

I had brought a display of Moutons with me and my labels came in for more than their share of attention. They now carried a list of the number of jeroboams, magnums, bottles and half bottles produced each year, in the style of a rare edition, which caused a lot of amazement and some admiration. There was no longer any doubt about it—the Médoc was on the map, and so was Mouton Rothschild.

In 1935 I put my signature on the label for the first time, and racked my brains to think of a way to attract people to Mouton. Next to the chai there was an area used for cleaning barrels. It was really much too attractive to be used as a washhouse; Siclis had designed it. Cleared and refitted, it would make a superb banqueting hall. It did, with oak shields on the walls bearing the coat of arms of every Bordeaux wine merchant, two white doors opening onto the grand chai, and *oeil-de-boeuf* windows offering a view over the vines.

A banqueting hall? No one had ever heard of such a thing, but once it was there, it created a new breed in the Médoc, the banquet goer and the after-dinner speaker. The lawyers decided that they would enjoy a get-together, then the architects, then the boiler makers, candlestick makers, paper makers or what you will; every club, society or fellowship in the district turned up, and if you didn't have a club in your neck of the woods, you invented one on purpose. We invented one ourselves: the Commanderie du Bontemps. I pinched the idea from Burgundy's Chevaliers du Tastevin.

No one had ever dreamed of visiting Mouton before, but now the village was amazed to see so many cars arriving, so many pretty ladies and their escorts, all dressed up with somewhere to go.

16

Guns will make us powerful, butter will only make us fat.

HERMANN GOERING

DRAMA on the world scene, but if I try to recall my own life in the years before the Second World War my memory plays tricks with "if" and "if only" or leaves me with blank pages. I should follow the example of Jeff Bernard, the English columnist who put an ad in the paper when he was writing his autobiography—"Can anyone remember what I was doing between 1960 and 1974?" He got some funny answers.

As usual there were wine and women. Of wine I remember only two great years, '34 and '37.

And women? Well, there was my wife and inevitably, after a lull, others. I think it was at this time that I earned the title of "womanizer." I would have preferred "woman lover," but there it is, seducers can't be choosers, and I didn't really care a damn what they said—I loved the game. By now I had broken all the rules and it didn't matter if the satisfaction lasted a minute, a day, a week, a year—few lasted longer. The only thing I found impossible was living with someone. I have never yet spent a whole night with a woman. It's the thought of waking up in the morning to find her beside me; I wouldn't care for it. My advice to philanderers is: meet occasionally, have separate establishments if you can, and the affair may last for years. I should know, I come from a philandering country. We Frenchmen have a reputation to keep up.

Of all the girls who came and went at this time I can remember only one. Her name was Anne Marie. Red-haired, green-eyed, she was the Rumanian wife of a French doctor, a sedentary type and bookish. At first I mistook her for a lesbian —she liked women. She was elusive, a bit of a mystery; she would disappear for weeks, months. Then suddenly she'd burst in on me, kiss me, bite me and tear my clothes off. She was a tigress. It might have been too much if she'd always been around, but she wasn't; so I grew rather fond of her, and in the end I had her eating out of my hand.

Do you disapprove of my goings on, or only of my owning up to them? Either way, I hope you have had as much fun as I have. I guess the women will disapprove more than the men. Women are like that, most of them—difficult. Lili was. She was jealous, hurt, as if the others could possibly interfere with my feeling for her.

I still admired her elegance, the brilliant makeup, gossamer stockings, her poise and the way she wore her jewels. As she moved into a drawing room full of well-dressed people, she could still take my breath away.

We had one thing in common: Philippine. We adored her and she knew it, the perky, bright little thing. We were so proud of her.

In 1938, a son was born to us. When my father heard the news he was delighted—his first grandson. We named him Charles Henri.

I did not know at first, neither did she, that our second baby was born horribly deformed. He was twisted and crooked and had no fundament. It was not a sight for a newly delivered mother. They operated twice, I think, possibly three times, before he died. At the time it had a curious effect on me, as if a dog in pain had been put down. Now, after all these years, the thought of it hits me more than it did then. One day I shall build a mausoleum in the park here, go to Auffargis, where he lies next to my mother, and bring the tiny coffin home.

At the time I was sad for Lili, very sad, because she thought I was to blame. She had taken pills to make her sleep all through the pregnancy and she couldn't sleep, she said, because of me.

So the truth is no longer disguised and, however hurtful it may prove, it can only hurt me.

I prefer to leave the subject. I would like to talk of pleasant things, but unfortunately at this point in my story the world was drifting into a bank of storm clouds. Some say war was not inevitable. Maybe they are right; I am no politician and facts only speak for themselves after the event. Here are a few such facts.

At the end of the First World War France had thirty-nine million men, Germany fifty-nine million. "This is no peace, only a twenty-year truce," said Foch, but France needed peace. "Plus jamais la guerre." On Bastille Day and May Day two million men and women would march all day through the streets of Paris, trundling giant statues of Peace. Peace at any price? It seemed so. French forces were withdrawn from the Rhineland five years before the agreed date.

In 1935, Henri Barbusse, the great apostle of peace, died, and three hundred fifty thousand people followed his coffin to Père-Lachaise. And in May of that same year France made a pact with Russia and Czechoslovakia. Czechoslovakia was the link between them, a strong link on which they might both depend. If Czechoslovakia was attacked, the two countries would go to her assistance.

In 1936, Hitler moved into the Rhineland. Civil war broke out in Spain, and Hitler and Mussolini moved in to try out their weaponry for the war they were preparing. "No intervention," said the French and British governments.

In March 1938, Hitler moved into Austria and stationed

himself along the borders of Czechoslovakia. From Prague, President Beneš called on France and Russia to stand by the 1935 treaty. France turned a deaf ear, and in September 1938 —sellout, Munich. France and England made a pact with Hitler and agreed to disarm and dismember Czechoslovakia in exchange for a promise of peace.

From this betrayal the world has never fully recovered, and never will. At the time there were fools who cheered. "Now we can all sit back and watch Russia tearing the lights out of Hitler," said one British sage, who should have known better.

On August 28, 1939, we were on holiday at Arcachon, Lili and Philippine and I. They were on the beach. I was out in the bay, sailing. Suddenly Lili came speeding past me in a launch. She shouted something——

"What?"

"General mobilization. It's just been announced on the radio."

Oh no! Why have they let it come to this? I am too old for such nonsense.

"You have to report to your unit straight away."

I had done my national service in the Armée de l'Air, donkeys' years ago. We would have to return to Paris as soon as possible and locate my unit. We threw our things together and made for the railway station. It was jammed with people all desperately trying to get home. We went by car, made Paris in record time.

On September 2 the Germans marched into Poland; on the 3rd France and England declared war on Germany. The announcement was hardly over when we heard the first air-raid siren. One's heart stood still. There were people running toward the air-raid shelters; but it wasn't a raid, merely a demonstration.

For a few days nobody moved without a gas mask. There was an atmosphere of suppressed panic, but as people got used to the blackout and the sandbags in the streets, panic gave way to suspense. We just waited. There was a long lull. Someone christened it the phony war. Across the channel the British were cheerfully optimistic: "We're going to hang out the washing on the Siegfried Line. Have you any dirty washing, mother dear?"

They felt safer on their island. France had been invaded twice in living memory.

October, and the phony war continues. Hitler makes no move. It's uncanny. We are fined for having an imperfect blackout on our windows. It's a joke. After all, the horror is a thousand miles away. Too bad for the Poles, but not really surprising: you would hardly compare the Polish army with the French army.

November 30, 1939. The Russians invade Finland. General Weygand wants us to attack on the Finnish front, take on the Russians and the Germans at the same time. How old is he now, seventy-three? The ski brigades go into practice and France wins the first round—against the Reds. Thirty-five Communist deputies are put in prison and the French Communist Party dissolved. Weygand, Gamelin, Daladier and Chamberlain are all for intervention in Finland; the only snag, Norway and Sweden are not at all keen on the idea. It isn't long before the situation is resolved:

1940: March 13: Finland makes peace with Russia.
March 21: Reynaud ousts Daladier.
April   4: Chamberlain says Hitler has missed the bus.
April   9: Hitler occupies Denmark.

The air force had sent me to Évreux in Normandy, on a re-fresher course, and Lili had sent Philippine back to school in Paris. In Évreux I fell sick—pains in my stomach, fever, and my ears killing me. The beginning of the tinnitus which has persecuted me ever since. They put me to bed; I was there for three weeks, my recovery pleasantly retarded by the appear-ance of a darling friend, Madame F—g. She came upon me by chance in the army hospital and whisked me away to her home to nurse me herself. It was a charming place and she was a

ministering angel, her cool, lovely hands so helpful. The
weather was divine in that fatal spring and we spent a few
halcyon days lying together out of doors.

Then the air force decided I must convalesce at Chamonix.
Good, I would get myself fighting fit on the ski runs, and be
ready for anything.. . . . On the very first day out, on a steep
slope I went arse over tit and broke my shinbone. I'll not forget
the joyride in a ramshackle ambulance, down the bumpy road
to Annecy, till my dying day.

As soon as Lili heard where I was, she arranged for me to be
transferred to the American hospital in Paris, where I heard
the announcement of May 10.

> Today at 4:30 A.M. the Wehrmacht launched an offensive
> against Luxembourg and the Low Countries.

They crossed the Luxembourg frontier by way of the Eiffel
Forest, that same Eiffel where I had raced against German
drivers not so very long ago.

Hitler cut through Holland like a knife through butter. On
May 15 the Dutch surrendered, and the enemy entered France.
The Germans hadn't bothered with our famous Maginot Line,
they had broken through on the Meuse, entered our country
by way of the Ardennes. Belgium gave up on May 28.

It was unbelievable. Where was our army? What the hell had
gone wrong? No one knew, no one knows yet. No official history of the debacle has ever been published and all the memoirs
contradict each other. For the majority it was every man for
himself. I was still in the hospital but beginning to get around
on crutches. I had only one thought—to get to Mouton.

Lili said there was no need for drama, she still had the car
and enough gas to get us there, Philippine would have to come
with us, of course.

Surprisingly, the road was empty. The world looked calm
and ordinary but in every little roadside café the radio was
blaring out news of the German advance, and people stood in

silent groups, listening. Were they hoping for a counteroffensive, or for peace? Nobody knew what was happening to our government and nobody seemed to care.

Our arrival at Mouton was like a dream, everything still and quiet, as if nothing was happening. There was nobody about. Lili took Philippine and went to find out what was wrong. She found them all, the entire staff, in Monsieur Marjary's office, listening to the radio. When they came out to meet us there was fear on every face.

We heard that the British Expeditionary Force, which had been with us from the outset, was now packing up and leaving. People spoke bitterly against Belgium, against Great Britain, but the mood did not last. The situation was too desperate. The war was lost. If France did not want to see her army wiped out she must bend the knee and sue for peace.

Many had prayed for it, others had taken the law into their own hands and thrown down their arms, and some had resisted to the death. The British who were left, hopelessly encircled in the north, were evacuating as many men as possible, British, French and Polish troops—it took them nine days, from Dunkirk and St. Malo, one hundred thousand men. We felt abandoned; for the first time the two nations, Britain and France, were divided. Some felt angry, but mostly people were silent, crushed and desperately sad.

I asked Monsieur Marjary to take my wife and child to the Dordogne, to my friends Jane and Pierre de Fleurieu. They would be safer there. There wasn't much time. The radio announced the incredible news that the Germans had crossed the Loire. They were in the center of France, they could be here at any moment. I called my people together, told them what they already knew, that my presence would make it worse for them. The maître de chai, Albert Blondin, spoke:

"We'll take care of the wine, monsieur. Let's hope that God will do as much for you and all our absent ones." His son, Raoul, was a prisoner of war in Germany.

"What have we done," cried Merilda, "that he should punish us with Germans?"

"Who do you mean, Merilda?"

"Why, God!"

I had no answer to that one. Eusèbe, the smart young carpenter who had recently arrived with his father and mother, refugees from Franco's Spain, smiled at me: "Adiós, monsieur, I wish you a beautiful journey."

"Adieu." I turned away. The sooner I went the better. What more was there to say?

"Good-bye, my friends. I believe that Mouton will protect you. They will not want any harm to come to the wine."

"What is going to happen about money, monsieur?" It was Blondin who spoke.

"There is enough in the kitty to pay you till Christmas. If by then there is no more forthcoming, Messieurs Cruse and Eschenauer at Bordeaux will take care of you. Let's hope it doesn't last that long."

Personally I was not too sure about that.

"Good luck, monsieur. Come back soon."

While they waved good-bye to me, their eyes were scanning the road for the first sight of a German. It was three days later when the tanks arrived. They drove into the courtyard and hoisted the swastika flag above the gate. Then they went looking for me, turned the place upside down, and when they couldn't find me, took potshots at my portrait hanging over the mantelpiece in the drawing room. Merilda marched in, daring them to harm her, took down the portrait, tucked it under her arm and left, taking her daughter Odette with her. She'd come back, she said, when the Germans had gone. When the Resistance was organized some of my team at Mouton joined them. The village lost its quota to forced labor in Germany or the concentration camps.

Édouard Marjary would have no truck with the occupying forces from the start. After he had seen Lili and Philippine safely installed in the de Fleurieu home, he disappeared into the Dordogne. It was a long time before I had news of him. He had been working with the Resistance. So had Jane and Pierre de Fleurieu and their cousin Tania.

I turned my back on Mouton to face an empty road, and a
future completely blank. I couldn't bring myself to look back
as I walked away; I didn't want to see the relief on their faces.
I had just had an unpleasant scene with my driver who flatly
refused to put me on my way. He offered to take me to the
station but that was as far as he would go. I sent him to hell. I
preferred to walk. In any case I doubted whether I'd find any
trains running and I didn't fancy hanging around that pokey
little station, where everybody would know me.

I wanted to get to Morocco and that was some hitchhike. I
was still in my air force uniform, which could help, and I was
still on crutches, which was ridiculous, but I am not one for
sitting down and weeping. I waste as little time as possible on
emotions. If there is something to be done I like to get on with
it. . . . On the other hand there is a very trying emotion called
frustration, and that had me in its grip as I stood by the roadside waiting for a lift on the long road south.

The rumor was that Mendès-France was in Casablanca trying
to set up an alternative government. If so, that was exactly
where I wanted to be. Meanwhile I was two kilometers from
Mouton. I got a lift at last, from a neighbor on his way to
Bordeaux, but after that it was army trucks, farm carts, a motorbike and sidecar.

Sometimes one couldn't pass for a flock of frightened human
beings moving slowly ahead, pushing prams, wheelbarrows, improvised carts, humping whatever they could carry on their
backs, the women with children and the aged trailing behind.
Once it looked as if a whole village was moving together, their
priest, schoolmaster and village policeman with them. I had
seen the pictures of Badajoz, Guernica, Madrid, but never
thought to see such sights in my own country. Now it seems the
world has grown accustomed to them.

On June 16 Marshal Pétain, age eighty-four, hero of Verdun, father of his people, agreed to form a new government.
On the 17th he was asking for an armistice. On the 18th
de Gaulle was on the air from London, refusing to accept defeat and trying to rally France. Few heard him. On the 21st,

France, or rather Pétain, capitulated, and the next day at 18:42 hours, in the railway carriage at Rethondes where Germany had signed the 1918 armistice, a separate peace was signed with Hitler. I was in the harbor at Bayonne. The officer in charge of the port was standing by a cargo boat loading up for departure. He saluted, glancing at my officer's pips. Some American civilians were bargaining with the ship's captain for a passage to . . . I thought I heard the word Morocco. I asked the officer. "Correct," he said, "and I need someone to take charge of the cargo."

"I'm your man. What is it?"

"Armaments."

On the 23rd, the good ship *Hébé* set her course for Casablanca, Lieutenant Rothschild on the bridge beside the captain. It was the day Hitler arrived in Paris after a tour of 1914–18 German war graves and a glance at the Maginot Line. He visited Napoleon's tomb and paraded along the Champs Élysées. Enough French men and women turned out to make a crowd for the German cameras, hands raised in the Nazi salute.

As we steamed through the Gulf of Gascony I had a wild thought. Why not seize the boat and deliver it to the English at Gibraltar? Could I bring it off? I had no revolver and I was none too active on that damned leg. I thought better of it. Later I regretted that change of heart. I should at least have had a try.

As soon as we docked at Casablanca I reported to the commandant's office.

"Mon colonel, I am here," said I, waving my crutch, "Lieutenant Rothschild at your disposition."

"May I see your papers, lieutenant? Thank you. Where did you get your wound?"

I explained.

"So you are on sick leave? May I see your *congé de convalescence?*"

I gave it to him and he turned it over, like a suspicious shopkeeper on the lookout for forgeries.

Two or three days later I was shocked and amazed to find

that my wife had arrived, with Philippine. She must have had great difficulty in getting to Morocco. Now she was walking into a rather dangerous situation. Pétain, installed in Vichy, had ordered us to demobilize. There could be trouble. I told Lili she should return to France at once, and she, having satisfied herself that I was still alive, was more than willing. Casablanca was not a comfortable city at the best of times, and with twenty-five thousand men and fifteen officers stationed here, ready for anything except dispersal, it was a place to leave behind you, fast.

I told her she should be sure to stay in the Non-O. France was now divided into two zones: "O," occupied, and "Non-O."

I was relieved to see them go. There could be no comfort in their staying. Our camp was divided against itself. Many of the officers were reluctant to obey Pétain's order. The demob didn't seem to be getting started. There was a lot of subdued talk in corner but nothing happened.

The men were in mutinous mood, but there was no leadership. Then our C.O. got a rocket from North Africa H.Q., Algiers. It was from General Pennes and he wanted to know what in hell was happening. Why hadn't the demob got under way? The Vichyites moved. In fact, they jumped about like fleas. We'd missed the right moment and our little army, which might have thrown in its weight against Hitler, was rapidly liquidated. I had the thankless task of dismissing the men on the military airfield. I was surprised how meekly they took it.

"Sergeant Martin?"

"Sir."

"Your demob papers and travel chit."

"Sir."

With a salute he left. He was the last of them. It was a hangdog exodus. Now what would happen to the rest of us?

The job done, on August 15 I was told to report to the C.O.

"Step into the colonel's office, lieutenant."

The colonel was the friendly type. We passed the time of day, then . . .

"Sorry to have to break it to you, lieutenant, but you're under arrest."

"How's that?"

"Orders from Vichy. I have it from General Noguès."

Noguès, Auguste, was governor general of Morocco, and like most of the French generals in North Africa, anti-British, anti-American and anti-Semitic. I looked round. A captain of the gendarmerie, accompanied by an N.C.O. carrying handcuffs, stood behind me.

"A French officer does not submit to handcuffs," I said.

"Quite right," said the colonel. "Do excuse me, Lieutenant Rothschild. On the other hand you are not thinking of resisting arrest, I trust?"

I couldn't speak. For the first time in my life I was being treated as a criminal. For the first time I was not free to do exactly as I pleased.

I followed my captors. They took me to prison, where I was kept in solitary confinement for two weeks. When I was let out to a sunbaked courtyard, surrounded by cells, I was amazed to see nearly all my fellow officers there, among them Captain Biche, who had been particularly keen on forming a Resistance unit, and Pierre Mendès-France. Somebody introduced us. His eyes nearly popped out of his head. "I thought this was all a bit silly, but with Philippe de Rothschild here it becomes ridiculous."

"Why are you here?" I asked him.

"I'm accused of desertion. I was vainly trying to locate my unit. The rest of these gentlemen, as you probably know, don't care particularly for Monsieur Pétain's New Order."

"New Order?"

"His Tra-Fa-Pa. *Travail, Famille, Patrie.* True fraternity is possible only within natural groups, the family, the village, the nation, says our leader."

"And Liberty? Equality? Fraternity?"

"Abolished."

"It is not possible. He would have to change the constitution."

"He's take advantage of the Occupation to do so. Everything he's doing is illegal. He hadn't been in power two weeks before he set up a commission to review all naturalizations granted in the last twenty years. Undesirables are to be stripped of their French citizenship."

"If he'd waited, the Germans would have done that for him."

"They're too busy enjoying their first summer in France, behaving decently on the streets, showing politeness to old ladies. We are asked to reciprocate, to be peaceful, friendly and work with them. Roosevelt and Churchill are the enemies—they deserted us in our hour of need."

Vichy's policy was soon given a name, the dirtiest word in the French language: collaboration.

But words change color as the years pass. "It was so much more chic to collaborate," declared a smart Parisienne in the year of grace, 1981.

17

Don't get around much any more.

DUKE ELLINGTON

WE were kept in prison for eight months. It took that long for them to prepare a case against us. One by one we would be summoned to face interminable interrogation. One day, after being questioned for the umpteenth time about my voyage to Casablanca, the juge d'instruction militaire asked me what sports I had practiced in my youth.

"What's that got to do with it?"

"Answer the question."

"Yachting, bobsleighing, motor racing."

"Ah, the pastimes of the rich."

"Well, I *was* rich. Is that a crime?"

It was all very boring and it was insufferably hot. The days dragged by. . . . Anyone fancy a game of *belote*? The eternal *belote*.

Sometimes, driven mad by the stinging flies, we'd throw down our cards and break into a frenzied fly-swatting competition. In the evenings I made them all write poems: it took their minds off their troubles, searching for *le mot juste*, though

I can't say the results were anything to write home about. Then we tried inventing crosswords. I sent mine to Philippine.

The nights were the worst, turning and turning on the thin *paillasse,* tortured by my need for sex but repulsed by the thought of contact with myself or my fellows. As soon as morning broke I would be out in the yard, exercising, jumping, stretching, sweating. One by one the others joined me. Not Mendès-France; his escape was talking politics. He never stopped. If I talked it was wine, women and Mouton. The only light relief was our man Aissa, who brought us food and water. He was coal black and made wonderfully bad jokes in bad French. He was very fond of prison. He was a trusty and had been inside all his adult life, but he would never tell us what for. "If they ever throw me out," he told us, "I shall have to do it again and that would be a pity."

In October we heard that the Pétain government had begun its legislative assault on the Jews of France with the Statut des Juifs. It was October 3, 1940, a black day for me and for the France I loved.

If the Jew had served in the French army, during 1914 to 1918, or distinguished himself in the defense of France from 1939 to 1940, he might still be regarded as a French citizen. If not, he was excluded from the teaching profession, the officer corps, theater, cinema and radio. So we were moving back to the ghetto from which my forefathers had escaped two hundred years ago, even to the wearing of a yellow star, the size of the palm of your hand, to be stitched to an outer garment over the left breast. This measure, introduced in the O-zone in 1942, proved so unpopular with the French people that it was difficult to enforce it. Travelers on the métro gave up their seats to star bearers, and students wore yellow stars inscribed with the name of a Jewish friend or sweetheart.

In jail our only race problem was prisoners and screws.

One day I was immensely cheered by the arrival of Maître Feillet, a lawyer sent by Lili to see what he could do for me. After he left, there was a long, resounding silence.

The advent of Christmas was marked by the sharp scent of citrus fruits, carried on the breeze from groves we had never seen. Then one morning I was separated from the rest, put under escort and marched to the railway station. As I sat half asleep, between two silent guards, watching the arid landscape drifting past, I felt I must have committed some unspeakable crime, and wondered what it might be—a new law in the New Order which I had broken, a sin of my father's visited on me? When I woke up I was amazed to find we were at the Algerian border and that night I found myself in yet another army jail. This time I was alone, but not for long.

"You are being sent back to France."

"Which part of France?"

To be taken back to the occupied zone would mean curtains for Philippe de Rothschild. They refused to tell me and the following morning I was put on a passenger steamer by two more grim-faced guards and locked in a cabin. I found it very pleasant and slept the morning away. When meal time came around I was escorted to the dining room. Some French citizens objected to the presence of a prisoner so I was marched back and had my meal brought to me on a tray. Luxury.

That evening, I recognized the stony hills above Marseilles. Non-O. Before nightfall I was to see the inside of my first French jail, Fort St. Nicholas, very grim, much more unfriendly than Casablanca or my Algerian cell. I was locked up with an elderly French officer; he too had been imprisoned by Vichy. He was pretty sick, crying and raving all night. I could do little to help, words being Job's comforters, but I did my best. It was a relief in the morning when they came to take him away.

Then I heard that my dossier had been lost in transit. I told them how sorry I was, because I'd been so much looking forward to hearing a complete account of my crimes, and in that setting too.

"Setting? Setting?"

"Well, it is rather like getting a small part in a provincial tour of *The Count of Monte Cristo*, even to the noises off."

The screech of the gulls could be heard, and even the lashing of the sea against the rocks below.

Questioning was about to begin, and I'd had it up to the neck with questioning. So, armed with the army's legal jargon, newly acquired, I decided to confuse the issue from the outset. It wasn't difficult, especially as I myself hadn't the slightest idea what I was doing there. The session didn't last long. My interrogator gave up, he had decided that I was a complete lunatic and cancelled our second engagement.

"You're for Clermont-Ferrand," said my guard.

"Town or gown?" I asked innocently.

"Nick," said the guard, who wasn't a bad sort. I wheedled the time of departure out of him and the means of transport—train. I'd had an idea. Sister Nadine lived not far away, in Grasse. If I could get a letter to her she might manage to see me en route. It was a long time since I'd had any news of the family.

The friendly guard obliged and I smuggled a letter out. On the morning of departure, we arrived at the station much earlier than the schedule time. I wondered if she'd make it. She was already there, waiting for me, looking pretty, very civilized, and prewar. I asked the gendarmes, my guards, if I could have a private talk with her.

"No nonsense now," they said. "Okay."

She gave me the worst first: all the family property had been confiscated by Pétain, and we had lost our French nationality.

I asked her how my father had taken it. He was now seventy.

"Calmly, he seemed more upset about his yacht than anything else."

"Is Marthe Régnier still with him?"

"Oh yes, that's the best of it."

"Where is he?"

"We sent him to Portugal, it seemed the safest place, poor papa."

She talked fast, family news of relatives surviving in England or the United States, cousins Guy, Alain and Élie prisoners of war in Germany.

The doors were being slammed, the train was about to leave. I asked her if she could let Monsieur Marjary know where I would be.

She said she would try, and it was good-bye, the train carrying me to a world of yesterday, as we steamed through the fragrant valleys of Provence, so civilized, so peaceful, the familiar red-roofed villages, that the horror of last year and this faded, receding like the plume of smoke we left in the sunny sky.

At the military prison in Clermont I was brought back to earth—keys, giant locks, salutes. But then, all locked up in the one barracks of a room, who should I find but my comrades from Casablanca, all except Mendès-France—he had been taken away to stand trial.

I was delighted to see my friends again. We embraced like long-lost brothers. There is nothing like prison for creating close bonds of love as well as hate. Where had I been? Why had I been separated from them? I told them I just didn't know and they believed me. We were all getting used to the army's peculiar ways.

We settled to the old routine: belote, exercise, writing poetry, inventing crosswords, waiting . . . and our fits of deep depression. One by one we had the black dog on our back . . . the flies had followed us too.

One morning I was told that I had visitors. I thought they were pulling my leg. Nobody had a visitor in that place. I entered the small guard room at the bottom of the yard and who do you think was there? Édouard Marjary. Behind him a good-looking young man I didn't recognize at first. It was Gérard de Chambure, my wife's younger brother, her favorite. They both looked thinner, quieter than the chaps I used to know, but that was long ago, before the flood.

Nadine had managed to find Monsieur Marjary and Gérard had been with Lili. Where?

"With your friends Jane and Pierre de Fleurieu in the Dordogne."

"And Philippine?"

Gérard had a small photo of my wife and daughter; they both looked well and happy, smiling at me, or rather at the camera.

Monsieur Marjary presented me with a food parcel—roast chicken, hard-boiled eggs, homemade bread.

"How did you manage to rustle up such a feast?"

"I live on a farm now, ten kilometers from your friends and your lady wife."

"That sounds good."

"It's better than that," said my friend Marjary. "I am now what you might call hitched."

"Hitched?"

"Settled, married, wed."

"I don't believe it."

"Well, it's true."

"Who is the lucky girl?"

It seemed that he had been sheltering refugees from the occupied north. One night he had taken in an elderly lady and her daughter. They stayed, he had taken a liking to the daughter, Hélène, and she was more than willing. Naughty old Édouard, the confirmed bachelor.

"And she's a big strapping girl," he told me.

"Young?"

"Ripe."

Monsieur Marjary was still carrying a large parcel: "Your clothes," he said. "Lili was quite convinced we would manage to get you released. You know she's had Maître Feillet, our family lawyer, working on your case."

"Yes, he came to Casablanca, but I heard no more."

I was overwhelmed by Lili's solicitude, the kindness of Gérard and Marjary. In prison one is often near to tears. I asked for news of Mouton. They had none. Inevitably we turned to the war. Gérard told me how Pétain was toadying to Hitler, sending forces to fight the British and the Free French at Dakar, interning refugees from Eastern Europe without waiting for the Nazis to give him his orders. Xavier Vallat, who had led the racist campaign against Leon Blum in 1936, was now commissioner for Jewish affairs.

The sad recital was cut short by the arrival of the guards: "Time's up."

Promising to shift heaven and earth to get me out of there and with messages of love and hope exchanged, we parted.

The day after my friends' visit I was taken for an outing, in a prison van. We pulled up at a dour barracks of a building where I was ushered into the ferocious presence of Colonel Leprêtre, local juge d'instruction militaire. We were to play out several black-comedy scenes together, each one more cat-and-mouse than the last, as the dossier on his desk grew fatter with his researches into my war.

As I entered for the fifth session and we exchanged salutes, he was scowling heavily. He took a deep breath, puffing out his chest like a pouter pigeon. "I have examined your case very thoroughly. There is no doubt in my mind that you have been guilty of grave dereliction of duty. I will go further, you are in my opinion nothing more nor less than a deserter." His paper knife was pointing at my left tit. "In the first place, how else can one account for your presence in Casablanca? Furthermore, it is my candid opinion that your motive in taking charge of the S.S. *Hébé* was treachery. You intended to deliver that ship and her cargo to the enemy."

I hadn't mentioned that story to anyone. I hadn't opened my mouth, or had I? Perhaps in prison, but to whom? Who would . . . ? What was he saying?

". . . the military code, from end to end, and I can find no parallel case, but you may depend on it, Rothschild, yours will be inserted, in time for the next world war. I shall see to it personally. Meanwhile, since I cannot, or rather, I have to admit it, since I have failed to pin a charge on you, pending further evidence, I have no alternative but to grant you provisional liberty."

"I thank you, mon colonel," I said, saluting and clicking my heels. "And I have no alternative but to refuse. Total liberty or nothing. I shall return to my cell." And I set off down the corridor with the guards chasing me. I have a flair for the dramatic moment and an excellent memory for dialogue, as you will have noticed.

Two days later, it was seven in the morning and we were all asleep in our communal cell, when the door was banged open. A sergeant barked out: "Lieutenant Rothschild!"

"Shut up, he's asleep."

"Too bad, I've brought his discharge."

Four of my friends jumped on the man, brought him down, sat on him, pinched the discharge paper and read it out loud.

"I don't care," I said. "I'm not going."

"Are you coming or not?" said the guard, as he searched for his cap.

"No."

He went, slamming the door. A few minutes later, two sergeants arrived.

"Rothschild?"

"I'd like to take coffee with my friends," I told them. "After all, I'm a free man now and can do what I like."

"You either go, or we'll have you back."

"How can you have me back, if I don't go?"

There was a noticeable pause.

"Why don't you go, man?" said one of my friends. "You might win the war for us."

"Let's have a game of cards," I said, and shuffled the pack. The two sergeants sloped off, not sure how to deal with me. In fact I was experiencing a touch of Aissa's malady. In prison I was safe. I had been with these men for nearly a year and they were good company. Together we had managed to stay cheerful. Whenever the guards came by, grinning with news of yet another Nazi victory, they'd let them have it: "On the winning side, are we? Don't be too sure about that. Our time is coming, and when it does, you quislings had better look out."

Meanwhile, our time had not yet arrived. My tormentors came back, five of them, and this time they picked me up bodily, and threw me out.

I needed money, a good meal, friends, and I had to know what was happening to our country. France seemed to be turning a terrible face to the world.

I asked the army for a railway voucher to Lyon, the capital of the Non-O zone. I knew my friend Hervé Mille was there. He had been one of the editors of *Paris Soir* and *Paris Match* before the war, the newspaper and color mag started by Jean Prouvost. The Nazis had taken them over, and Hervé got away, to Lyon. He would certainly have all the latest news. He was now bringing out a journal called *Sept Jours*. Jean Prouvost was behind it, working with Hervé by phone from some hideaway in the south.

The pleasure of seeing Hervé and other friends soon evaporated as I learned the truth about the state of the nation. Pétain was convinced that Germany had won the war and Britain was in her death throes. He didn't believe the United States would be ready in time to save her. Vichy was willing to join the war against England, and Fernand de Brinon, Vichy's ambassador in Paris, had told the Germans Marshal Pétain realized that anti-Jewish activity must be accelerated throughout France. Such protection as the Non-O had offered us would soon be no more.

Did I know that my friend Bertrand Zadoc-Kahn had committed suicide? Yes, the day Hitler marched through Paris. He left a note: "This is the end of us." Hervé said that Mendès-France had been found guilty of desertion and sentenced to seven years in jail, but by some miracle he'd escaped and was on the run.

Lyon seemed to be a divided city of divided people. Its Archbishop Gerlier venerated Pétain—"La France, c'est Pétain"—yet protested at the terrible conditions in the concentration camp at Gurs, where Spanish refugees and Jews were held. He approved of the Statut des Juifs, yet intervened on behalf of Jewish internees. Some professors were trying to organize a petition against racial persecution, while at the same time there were outbreaks of racist violence on the streets.

Times were bad, but friends were good and courageous and

freedom, however limited, was sweet. The simplest things were enjoyable: the private lavatory, light clothes and the meals we shared—frugal and makeshift, but they tasted like manna from heaven after the prison scoff.

And I was delighted to find that I could still draw on a little money. After some hesitation I tried a local bank. I couldn't believe my eyes when the cash slid over the counter in exchange for the check. Better go easy, it might be the last, but it was wonderful to see money again. After money, the next best thing about Lyon was the presence of women. For me the worst of jail had been my need for them. Now, I fell in love eight times a day. If a fairly pretty woman went by in her skimpy wartime dress and wooden-soled shoes, my hair stood on end.

> The time that is to come is not,
> How can it then be mine?
> The present moment's all my lot;
> And that, as fast as it is got,
> Phillis, is only thine.
>
> John Wilmot, earl of Rochester

Inevitably I was ensnared. She was very young, a lovely, frail thing. Her name was Marie Edmée. I called her Freckles. Her hair was the color of her freckles, her eyes dark amber. She seemed to live on air and she hated wearing clothes. A strange sprite, she hardly belonged to this world. She didn't stay in it long.

In that grim time, how I loved and needed her. Innocent Marie Edmée, if I close my eyes I can see your child face so clearly. My very dearest one.

It may seem strange to you, distanced as we are from those dark days, that we could make love and laugh or find any joy in life, but of course we did. Even in the concentration camps babies were born.

Everybody tried to lead what we began to call a normal life, to move slowly, smiling slightly, to the shelters when the bombs dropped, spend every spare minute bartering or hunting for food in the surrounding countryside—an egg, maybe, or a rabbit—and most of all to keep your eyes closed and your mouth shut. A popular tune whistled on the street might carry a message as people hurried by. Few stopped to gossip. Fear and suspicion kept us isolated; you never saw a crowd. We lived behind locked doors, because nobody could be sure of their neighbors. Everybody was scared of denunciation, even the ones who accepted the fate which had befallen France, or went further and embraced the alien creed. As for arrests and disappearances, it's easy to look the other way when the axe falls.

In Paris, on the grand boulevards, or in the smart restaurants frequented by the good collaborators, the German officer was the soul of politeness, while only a few hundred yards away, a young man was being shot against a wall.

Ici est tombé
Gérard Danvers
17 ans
Fusillé par les Allemands
mort
pour
La France

You can see these little blue plaques in every town and village in France.

Behind the elegant façade of the Hotel Lutetia, boulevard Raspail, victims of the Third Reich were systematically tortured. At 93 rue Lauriston, Paris XVI, the gestapo ran a torture chamber and brothel combined, ably assisted by the scum of the Paris underworld. At the Institute for the Study of Jewish and Ethnic Racial Questions, a Dr. George Montandon gave lectures on the phrenology of the Jews. "Look for the prominent lower lip, the curved nostril, partition between nostrils very low."

For the first time in my life I wanted to hide, to fall asleep and wake when it was all over. You will have noted, I suppose, that I had not been to see Lili. In fact I had no idea where she was. She had left my friends in the Dordogne. I wouldn't have been surprised to hear that she had gone back to the O-zone, to Paris. When Hervé came by one day to tell me that he had located her, at Megève, in the Alpes with Philippine, I set out at once, eager to see them.

Before the war Megève had been a fashionable ski resort. I was amazed to find that it was still the center of a sparkling social life. It was in one of the eight departments occupied by the Italians who resisted both the French and German measures against the Jews. As a result, a crowd of liberally minded rich still flocked there, including the Princesse de Polignac, the actresses Danielle Darrieux and Arletty, and a certain number of high-ranking German officers. There was skiing by day, parties by night. The war was forgotten on that magic mountain.

Lili, who adored the social whirl, had moved there as a change from her quiet retreat in the Dordogne. I found her in a pleasant ski hotel—a curious reunion. We met as friendly strangers. She told me she had worked hard for my release but once it was accomplished felt free to lead her own life again. I felt much the same, but there was Philippine, now a precocious, charming nine year old, with very nice manners. I adored her.

As a father I may be a bit of an amateur, but my daughter has always been the apple of my eye. She still is. In those days it was a completely new sensation, walking about with my own child, seeing things with her eyes, introducing her proudly— "my daughter."

In the evening she reminded me of the story I used to tell her when she was barely five. I had almost forgotten it, but she remembered.

"You made it up for me when I was sick, papa." It was the time she had been taken ill at Mouton. No one knew what was wrong with her and the doctors weren't proving helpful. I wrapped her in a blanket, took her in my arms and drove to

Paris with her. My doctor told me she had polio, and might never walk again. She did. He cured her. I had stayed with her night and day till she was better, and told her my fairy story.

"What did we call it?"

" 'Silver Wing,' papa. Would you care to tell me some more?"

I sat with her at bedtime as I had done years before, only now, thank God, her legs were steady and pretty, her face shining with good health and I knew she was happy to have me back.

One day, out walking, a gendarme accosted me, muttering something out of the corner of his mouth. He thought I ought to know, he said, that the prefect was having me watched.

"Really? Whatever for?"

I didn't care for the look of the man and he wasn't very forthcoming. I couldn't get another word out of him. Next day I decided to take the bull by the horns and go and see this prefect. He was very polite when I introduced myself, almost subservient. He had no idea what the gendarme was talking about. He certainly intended to close the nightclubs shortly and expel a lot of foreigners from the town. The place was infested with them.

"Infested with whom?"

"The aristocratic element, and with it the Israelite atmosphere. They're intermarried."

I looked him straight in the eye. An echo in my brain: "She wanted to marry a rich Jew." Someone had said it once when I was entering Ciro's with Lili. I had overheard it.

I decided to leave the place, not because of this wretched prefect but because I wanted to visit my dear friend Gaston Bonheur, who was staying in Antibes. Lili said she would come too, it was such fine weather, and we would all enjoy the sea. The sun is a mighty magician: walking by the seashore with Gaston and Philippine I could see the war dwindling as if in a perspective glass, my child's hand in mine was the only reality. Yet on the other side of that sparkling sea young Germans and British were savaging each other to death.

Gaston had been one of Jean Prouvost's editors, with Hervé. He was still writing, still managing to keep in touch with the world. In the evening we drew the curtains and listened to London on the wavelength which sent personal messages in code, mostly for the Underground—"The Red Fox will be at the junction at 5 A.M.," and so on. A friend of Gaston's came in two or three times to listen; his name was Vautrin, a colonel, I understood. He seemed to travel the length and breadth of France. How or why one didn't ask. He talked a lot about Colonel, later General, Pierre Koenig, and his Free French Army. Only a few weeks before, they had crossed North Africa from Dakar and stopped Rommel in his tracks.

One day we were playing a mild game of bowls—*pétanque* that is, the French variety. Gaston was there and Jacques Prévert, the poet, and his brother. We had been joking over the game when suddenly, for no reason, the reality of our situation hit me: should the Germans be defeated in North Africa, they would certainly occupy the whole of France. It would be the end of all of us. Gaston said no, Russia would win the war and put paid to the Nazis. I thought he was very optimistic, at that moment they were fighting with their backs to the wall. Leningrad had been holding out for six months, but they seemed to be at the last ditch. Voroshilov was dragging the wounded from their hospital beds to fight. I felt very pessimistic and Gaston won the game.

Lili and Philippine would have to go back to the de Fleurieu home in the Dordogne. It was the safest place I knew. And what should I do?

Vichy was planning a census of all the Jews in Unoccupied France, obviously a prelude to more persecution. I was forty, in the prime of life, and life was becoming impossible. I was not the military type; I couldn't see that I'd be much use, if I decided to throw in my lot with Vautrin and his people. I am no more a hero, or a coward, than the next man. A hero in any case is often a man who, finding himself in a tight spot, has heroism thrust upon him. On the other hand I had no taste for ignominy or martyrdom. The strongest force ranged against Hitler was England, but England seemed a mighty long way away. How could one get there now?

While I was pondering and planning, we heard dreadful news from Paris: a German naval cadet had been killed in the métro at Barbes Rochechouart, and Fernand de Brinon, Vichy's chief spokesman in Paris, had apologized to the Germans, telling them that he would punish the Parisians himself, six persons would be guillotined in a public square as a reprisal. The Germans told him not to bother. For every German killed, they would shoot fifty or possibly a hundred hostages.

Gaston was returning to his country home, Château de Floure, near Carcassonne. I would go to Marseilles and investigate the possibility of getting to England via Spain from there. At Marseilles I left a note for the Spanish consul. He replied, making a rendezvous at a private house. When I was ushered into a salon, I was very surprised to see Paul Morand, the fashionable novelist, and his wife, Hélène, sitting there. Madame Morand had been formerly the rich Rumanian Princess Soutzo; the consul was a rather elegant creature; and Morand, by then, a diplomat for Vichy. It was difficult in that company to speak frankly. When they caught a hint of my intention, Madame Hélène launched into a tirade. Was I mad? What was wrong with me? The Germans were perfect people with perfect manners. The decadence into which Europe had declined was entirely due to the corrupt Jews and Freemasons. The Nazis were the only ones who had the solution.

"You know my name?"

"But of course, Philippe, you are different. They won't touch you."

Paul Morand never said a word. He sat gazing into space, a man looking for a mirage, while his awful wife ranted on.

The consul was smiling as I left. There was no hope from that quarter. I'd have to think again.

I went to the de Fleurieu home in the Dordogne to tell Lili what I had in mind. She was shocked and disapproving. Jane and Pierre thought I had no choice. They were working with the Resistance and had their ear to the ground. There was a long argument with Lili, which got nowhere.

"And how will you get there?"

"How will *we* get there?"

"Please don't talk nonsense, Philippe. How could I leave Philippine?"

"She can stay with your brother Gérard, he has children. She is always happy there. In any case I don't think it will be for long. You've heard that the Americans have landed in North Africa?"

"I do not want to go. I am a Frenchwoman. Why should I leave my country? Apart from anything else, I don't believe you have the slightest chance of crossing the frontier. Supposing you were involved in a fight? You are not a strong man."

"Well, I certainly can't stay here. You are my wife, Lili, Philippine's mother, I cannot abandon you."

"You are being dramatic. Here I can live my normal life. What would I do in England? I don't understand a word of English. And you, do you think you would count for anything in that country?"

The fact of the matter was that my wife had no fear of the Germans; she was influenced by some of our former friends who had thrown in their lot with Vichy. "Why should the Germans harm me? I am from an old French Catholic family. The Germans respect that." She told me that if I went she would resume her family name and title, Comtesse de Chambure, and that she was quite able to take care of herself.

She had obviously made up her mind and I could hardly take her by force. "Above all, don't worry about us," she told me. "I shall go back to Paris: all my friends are there. I know I'll be safe in my own home and I certainly wouldn't feel safe anywhere else."

As I was preparing to leave, an exhausted couple arrived at the house, friends from Bordeaux of the de Fleurieu family. They had crossed the demarcation line on foot, barely escaping with their lives. They brought shocking news. Nearly one hundred hostages had been shot at Bordeaux and Chateaubriant, the Germans having decided that the fierce repressive measures of the Vichyites Fernand de Brinon and Pierre Pucheu were not enough. To hear of friends and acquaintances now collaborating made one despair. Fernand de Brinon had been a guest in my house. How had he solved the embarrassment of a Jewish wife? I learned later that the Germans had told him she must be hidden away. She was at his country house in the Basses-Pyrénées.

I asked if they knew what was happening at Mouton. Yes, it was now H.Q., South-West German Air Defense.

Nothing seemed to have any effect on Lili. She appeared to have her future all mapped out. I cycled up the road to say good-bye to Édouard Marjary, took a photo of Philippine holding her teddy bear, embraced Jane and Pierre and left. Lili came out to wish me Godspeed.

I made my way first to Gaston Bonheur's home, Château de Floure, not without misgivings. As we had predicted, the Nazis had occupied the whole of France; they chose November 11, Remembrance Day. Gaston would be taking a risk, harboring me, but I had no intention of staying long. I planned to cross the Pyrenees on foot. It was the only escape route left; all the other frontiers were now firmly closed to us. I needed a guide and I knew Gaston had contacts in the Resistance at Perpignan. We ate a quiet meal, Gaston brought out a bottle of his good wine and we didn't talk about the war. I left early next morning. He had asked me if I was prepared to risk the train journey. I was: time was short. He drove me to the station.

When the train drew in my heart sank—it was crammed with German soldiers. I couldn't retreat. Quickly I bought all the collabo journals, jumped in and stood in the corridor holding the disgusting *Gringoire* in front of my face. No one ever read the rag with such concentration.

Next stop, Perpignan. Two minutes' wait. This is it, Georges Philippe, alias Pierre Renard, watch your step. Get through

that crowd fast. The place is lousy with Germans. I tried to look
happy and relaxed, but I couldn't make it; my mouth was so
dry I couldn't swallow, let alone smile. I caught sight of myself
in a shop window, the one bare head among a crowd of helmets. They looked ridiculous.

Gaston's number one contact was the town clerk. I made
straight for the town hall, decided it was the wrong time of day,
too early, walked round the block two or three times, regained
my old confident stride, marched in through the front door,
located his office and caught a glimpse of him as the door
swung open to release an office boy juggling with a pile of files
that reached to his chin. Then I rushed downstairs and waited
in the street. I walked this way and that, trying to look as if I
had somewhere to go, while keeping an eye on the town hall
exits. Missed him. the concierge was locking up, going to his
lunch. I repeated the performance in the afternoon, with even
less success. My quarry wasn't in his office. He didn't appear at
all. I felt sick at heart as I watched the concierge lock up for
the night.

Better try the second contact right away. It was the old man
who kept the newsstand at the bus terminal. He was a pale,
stern old chap. I bought newspapers, went for a walk, came
back and bought more, without getting a word out of him. I
bought a pack of lead pencils, a tin money box and an India
rubber shaped like Felix the Cat, still not a word. Had I got the
wrong man? I was about to give up when he looked me straight
in the eye. "No sense in hanging about here," he said. "Get
yourself up to Font-Romeu, pronto."

"I'm not on a skiing holiday."

"On holiday, did you say? Oh yes, very nice place, do you a
world of good. Want some new clobber while you're there? See
my friend Josef the tailor." He scribbled a plan of the way to
Josef's shop on a scrap of paper and winked solemnly as he
gave it to me.

The evening was drawing in and I'd nowhere to sleep. I
decided to make for Font-Romeu straight away, if possible.

Maybe I'd feel safer there. I was in luck for a change, there was a train.

It was dark when I arrived, and deserted. Nevertheless I set out to check up on Monsieur Josef. The tailor's shop existed, but it was boarded up. I tried the neighbors. After a long time, an old lady answered the door, looked at me suspiciously, but gave me some idea of where the tailor was to be found. Up by the Bella Vista Hotel, she said, waving her hand vaguely toward the hills.

I found the hotel, a seedy-looking boarding house in the suburbs, and sure enough, two doors away, Monsieur Josef's new shop, which was even poorer than the one he'd left.

It was too late to call. I tried for a room at the Bella Vista. The foyer smelled of stale cabbage and rising damp and there were plenty of empty rooms.

Next morning I called on Monsieur Josef. He got the message straight away. "Oh dear no, nothing doing here. The last lot who tried it were brought back under arrest. You get back to Perpignan sharp, on your toes."

I thanked him and asked him to do a little job for me. He was a Jew and obviously sympathetic. When I left the shop, my precious store of banknotes had been carefully stitched into the collar of my jacket.

Back in Perpignan I had only one chance: the town clerk. This time I waited by the side door at the lunch hour.

I was lucky. He came out that way and he was alone. I went up to him, and casually asked the way to the nearest pharmacy. He looked just another fussy little bureaucrat close to, but he walked with me a few steps and I gave him Gaston's name, then told him what I wanted.

The only people who could help me were the Communists, he said. He gave me an address and exact directions, excused himself and quickly jumped on a bus. After going wrong in the back streets, I eventually found the place. It was a shoemaker's shop, small and dark; there were vases of gaudy paper flowers among the rows of broken-down shoes. The shoemaker was a subtle questioner, giving me an oblique glance as he worked over his last, throwing in a philosophical remark as the bell on the shop door rang and a customer entered. When he finally closed the shop he told me to follow him.

He took me to Juanita's house. Juanita was a Spanish republican who had organized the escape of a small army of her people and brought them to France. Now she was helping French refugees to return to the country from which she was exiled. She took me in. It was a very small house and she had a husband and two children, so my bed was in the loft. By chance one day I discovered that this young mother, so gentle and kind, was busily engaged in smuggling arms to the Resistance. She fascinated me, but that was as far as it went. She was in love with her husband and her Communism. The latter might have been overcome, but it is quite useless to try to seduce a woman who is happy with her husband.

It took fifteen days for her to make the necessary contacts, including fixing me some false papers. Prisons had taught me patience. In the evenings I lay on my bed listening to the street sounds. One day a traveling fair moved in and at dusk I could hear the hurdy-gurdy of a carousel, the shrieks of the girls as they dived with the big dipper and the roar of a motorbike, which never seemed to go anywhere; it just whirred round and round like a fly in an upturned glass.

"What is it?" I asked Juanita.

"That's the Wall of Death," she said.

I'd never seen one. I was so curious that, on the Saturday night, it was the night before I was due to leave, she risked taking me out, walking between her husband and the children, to let me see the strange death wall, a huge cylinder with a motorcyclist riding its inner surface.

A few nights before, a tall distinguished-looking character had appeared at the house. He carried himself with an air. His coat was long, of gentlemanly cut with a black velvet collar. I kept wondering who he reminded me of. Then it came to me. He was the spitting image of Louis Jouvet. He was speaking

Catalan and Juanita was translating for me. There was a long discussion about routes. Juanita asked which guide I would have.

"Sebastian, one hundred percent trustworthy," he said.

He assured me that he would himself be watching over me, from start to finish, though I wouldn't see him. The price was agreed and he left.

I asked Juanita who and what he was. "The king of the smugglers," she told me. "He controls fifteen miles of the border. His word is law."

The method of payment was ingenious. I was to deposit the money with the shoemaker, who was tried and true. Then a banknote was to be cut in half. I was to take one half with me. When my half was returned to the shoemaker, "Louis Jouvet" got the money and he paid the others.

Of course there was nothing to stop Sebastian slitting my throat and pinching my half. I didn't think he would, though, somehow. He and his boss were in a profitable line of business: their fifteen miles of border territory must have been a gold mine. The price asked was fifty thousand francs. I was lucky enough to have it.

I suppose Sebastian and the shoemaker got their cuts. After the war I heard how Juanita got hers. She was denounced, and died in a Nazi camp.

18

I must—I will—I can—I ought—I do.

RICHARD BRINSLEY SHERIDAN

IT was a dull afternoon when I set out on my journey into the unknown. There were banks of clouds on the distant mountains, snow clouds probably, and I was wearing my everyday clothes and shoes so as not to arouse suspicion. I had brought a cap and hidden my half banknote in the peak. My guide, Sebastian, was a sturdy Catalan, weather-beaten and taciturn; neither of us had more than two or three words of the other's language. We took the bus to Arles-sur-Tech, a village beyond the edge of town. If all went on schedule we should there pick up the connecting country bus without too much delay. Destination Saint-Laurent-de-Cerdan at the foot of the mountains. From then on it would be Shanks's pony.

It was at Arles-sur-Tech that I made my first and only blunder. I was standing at the stop in a cold sweat waiting for the little bus to leave. It was sitting there as empty and still as a church on Monday. All of a sudden the driver appeared and unlocked the door. He had been in a small lean-to of a place which I had hardly noticed. I did now. Two gendarmes came stepping out of it. I panicked, bolted blindly, then changed direction and hid on the other side of the bus.

Sebastian, inside, waved his arms angrily. I ran round to the door and he heaved me aboard. The driver pulled the starter, the little bus coughed and left. The gendarmes began to run. The bus continued on its way. Sebastian was plainly furious. "Si vous pas faire comme moi dire vous frappe." His French was obscure, but the accompanying pantomine—brilliantly clear . . . We sat in silence the rest of the way.

I would have liked to make a joke of it all, but I hadn't the words, and Sebastian looked too serious. At Saint-Laurent-de-Cerdan, another shock—two dozen Germans had descended on the village. For the moment they were rollicking in the one and only inn.

Sebastian, shepherd and smuggler, knew all the byways and sideways. He took me over some rocks, down into the inn yard and put me in a cupboard of a place below some stone steps. Safer, I gathered, as he locked the door.

Hours passed. The pattern of daylight in the small grille, high in the wall, was gone. It was night. At every moment I expected the sudden flash of a torch, the command in German. . . .

At last, a soft whistle, the door was unlocked. It was Sebastian.

In no time we were over the wall and away. There was no moon and a steady climb ahead of us. Sebastian had to keep waiting for me. It was rough going. At last I got my second wind. We were obviously keeping to the heights, avoiding the paths. I was terribly out of condition; I even cursed the small rucksack I was carrying and felt like dumping it, but it contained a change of socks and underpants and my mini electric razor.

As we were breasting the first high ridge, Sebastian began whistling "La Cucaracha." It was a prearranged signal. Danger ahead. I threw myself down and crouched under a rock. Then I heard it, the sound of men thrusting their way through the scrub. They were cursing the dark night, in German. The whistling stopped. I heard my guide exchanging a few words with one of them. What was he saying? I didn't understand German. Perhaps the whole setup had been a trap and he was going to hand me over.

No, they went their way and he came back for me. We plodded on, without speaking, my heart still beating fast. The long ascent began, scrambling, climbing, sometimes flattened against a wall of earth, sometimes pinned against a rock face, happy to find a handful of tough grass or an obtruding root which might furnish a handhold, as one heaved oneself up. Sebastian was always fifty yards ahead. I was glad when I tumbled, it gave me a couple of seconds' respite while I dragged myself to my feet again.

It was perhaps two in the morning when the moon was suddenly revealed, riding the dark clouds. As the pale light spread over us, I thought I saw a stone dwelling, or was it just a rock fantasy? I pointed: "Look, is that a shelter?" He nodded.

"Louis Jouvet" had told me there'd be a scheduled stop somewhere en route. Could this be it?

Rest?

Sebastian was obviously keen to push on and went into his "frappe" routine. I made him understand that I was at the point of exhaustion and very hungry. Reluctantly he changed his course and we headed for the farm—for such it proved to be: one meager stone building and an outhouse. As we approached I noticed a lighted window. They're up. There may be a bed.

No, no, too dirty, he said, doing a vivid mime of catching fleas and killing them. He indicated that I was to stay where I was, and made off to rap at the farm door. A burly shape appeared, holding a lantern. There was a bit of back slapping and ribbing as the man glanced in my direction. They went in and closed the door. I made for the window. I could see a man writing in a ledger by the light of a spirit lamp. I moved closer. There were three other men seated at the table. Sebastian moved into the picture, bent over the ledger, a mug in his hand. It was a while before he came out.

"Okay," he said, "a little . . ." and he put his head on his hand as we walked along.

"Where are we gonig?"

"Barn. Much cleaner." He held his nose and pointed at the farm.

"Friends."

"Smugglers."

"Doing their homework?"

"Accounts," he said.

I opened the food pack Juanita had given me and offered him some. He shook his head and strolled back to join his friends.

"Deo gratias," said I, when I finished my banquet of sausage, onion and bread and stretched along among the sweet-smelling hay. As I sank into nirvana I heard a soft munching and snorting and, through half-opened eyes, saw the cows' soft bellies and their vague, gentle eyes as they came toward me. Outside it was snowing. I remembered we were somewhere near Christmas. Away in a manger, no crib for a bed, the little Yiddisher baby, J.C., lay among the cattle feed. I smelled the sweet, warm breath of the big beasts as they lumbered around me, and I slept.

All too soon we were on our way again, and my feet were bleeding and swollen, much worse after the rest. Shoes? Worse than useless. On and up. All I remember is the encounter with thick ice when we reached the first peak; Sebastian floated in front of me, like a will-o'-the-wisp, then he'd disappear and I'd go on, blindly, occasionally feeling a shove up as he helped me over a wall of ice. Day and night dissolved into one. Would we never begin the descent? We did, sometime during the second night, but to descend was worse, and at times precipitous. I couldn't get the action right and I was exhausted. At one point I lost control of my legs and slid down five hundred meters of steep scree on my backside. I came to a painful halt. That was it, I couldn't get up. Sebastian tried to tug me to my feet, and managed it, but after two or three steps I was down again. He squatted beside me, waiting. It semeed to be getting lighter. He was pointing. Far below us, the light clouds parted for a moment, I thought I saw a thin gray ribbon of road.

"You are in Spain," he said. I couldn't speak. I made the supreme effort expected of me and he did his best to support me as we stumbled down a rocky slope, pebbles flying, birds uttering a warning cry as they rose from their nests.

I remember coming to an isolated farm. There was someone else helping me along. I remember being led to an enormous bed which filled the room and that's all. Sweet oblivion.

A minute later someone was nudging my leg. My eyes wouldn't open, the nudging went on. Where was I? I looked. Four men were sleeping beside me in the enormous bed and my guide was prodding me with a broom handle. "Up! Up!" he was saying. "You have had four hours." All I wanted was to stay there forever. "Up, up, and see your father hung," said he. I clambered over the sleeping bodies as they muttered and swore at me. "Bus," said my guide, "à Figueras."

The road was not far away, but I was nothing but a sack and Sebastian was determined to make that bus. He called to the owner of our mountain rest and between them they got me over the last lap. And, oh, the relief of standing on a smooth, rockless road. We were in a narrow gorge, small streams gushing from its sides, and a stone bridge pointing to the most beautiful sight in the wide world—a Spanish bus.

The driver eyed me stolidly. He knew where I had come from, so did the black-robed peasant women who were clambering aboard. They didn't stare, they didn't even look at me. I suppose they were used to exhausted Frenchmen falling from the hills. In fact thirty thousand Jewish refugees crossed those mountains to Spain; many more tried and failed.

As we sat on the bus I gave Sebastian my half of the banknote. He paid the bus fares. As we rode the hairpin bends toward the valley I wondered what the hell I would do next. I

1 *right* Maman, me,
James and Nadine

2 *below left*
A promising lad

3 *below right* Baron
Henri de Rothschild—
Papa

4   Nadine, me and James

5   The seriousness of youth

6   St Moritz. Let's go!

7   Annam, 1931. Blood sport

8   Speed crazy

9   Rothschild, air ace

10   At Le Mans

11   The *Eros,* Papa's pleasure boat

12   My summer haunt at Arcachon

13 A good catch

14 Lili

15 A devoted father

16 Philippine and her teddy

17 Filming *Le Lac aux dames*: Simone Simon, me and director
Marc Allegret in the leather jacket

18 With Jules Kruger, the cameraman   19 Colette came to the première

20 In Hollywood—Joseph Schenk, Harold B. Franklin,
    Governor C.C. Young, me and Louis B. Mayer

21 Papa in Hollywood with Shirley Temple and Anna May Wong

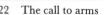

22 The call to arms

23 With the Free French, London 1943

24 Mouton in the nineteenth century

25 *above* Old-time *vignerons*

26 *below* The Association of Five — plus one. *From the left* André Gibert (Haut Brion), Philippe de Rothschild (Mouton), le Comte René de Beaumont (Latour), Pierre Moreau (Margaux), Baron Robert de Rothschild (Lafite) and le Comte Bernard de Lur Saluces (Yquem)

27 *above* With Philippine

28 *below* Amongst the vines

29 My *Commission technique* — Édouard Marjary and I are at the desk

30 Édouard Marjary with his mustimetre, checking fermentation

31 Raoul Blondin, *maître de chai*

32-5 Four artists who illustrated labels — *above left* Cocteau, *above right* Dali, *below left* Warhol, *below right* Picasso

36 Merilda of Mouton

37 *below left* Summer
wedding—Michel,
head gardener at
Mouton, marries his
Maria

38 *below right* The
Queen Mother and I

39   *above* Pauline in the *grand salon* at Mouton

40   *below* For the fashionable photographer

41 With Philippine in the garden of 'petit Mouton'

didn't have long to wonder. At the first village we came to, Besalu, the Guardia Civil were at the bus stop.

All out! I looked round for Sebastian. He had disappeared into thin air.

A small crowd gathered as I stepped down, helped by one of the old women.

The Guardia Civil arrested me. A young boy stood staring, he couldn't take his eyes off me.

"Comment t'appelles-tu?" I asked him. "Cómo te llamas?"

"Jesus," he replied.

That was a good sign, I thought—Jesus and Christmastide.

I was taken to the police station, bare and cold, one light bulb dangling from the ceiling. All that seemed to interest them was the amount of cash I might be smuggling. I produced a few pesetas from my pocket, and some notes amounting to twenty-five dollars. What about my hidden store? Obviously I was about to be searched.

"Could I shave?" I asked the captain of the Guardia Civil, who spoke a little French. "I feel dirty."

"With pleasure," he said, went to his cupboard, and produced a cutthroat razor, a mirror and a little wooden bowl of soap.

"I have my own, thank you," said I, fishing out my little electric job and looking for the socket. They were amazed and intrigued.

The second-in command began to frisk me. I had bargained on the sound of the razor drowning the crinkling of the dollars if he touched my collar. It did. They noted the twenty-five dollars, the pesetas and the electric razor.

With charming politeness, they took me to their one hotel and locked me in a bedroom. I slept. At midnight the church bells were ringing and someone was banging on the door. I tried to get to my feet. Impossible. The door was unlocked—a beautiful woman wearing a red dress and an embroidered fichu stood there. She was holding a bowl of steaming chocolate and a plate of little almond cakes. "Feliz Navidad," she said. Happy Christmas. I realized then that the bells had been ringing for midnight mass and that was why she was wearing her very becoming national dress.

Off she went and I slept again, a day and a night, on and off. Meals were brought on trays and left on the table. I would hear the door being locked afterwards.

I was up, washed and dressed, when the captain of the Guardia Civil came by on St. Stephen's Day. "I have to deliver you to the authorities in Figueras," he told me. "Let's go," I said, and off we went to catch the bus. At Figueras, said my friendly captain, I would first have to face the charge of importing currency illegally. That wouldn't be serious but afterwards he would have to turn me over to the police. I asked him what might happen.

"Difficult to say."

"So long as they don't send me back."

"I don't think it will come to that, but there is a camp. . . ."

My heart sank.

The Imposing Official who dealt with *delictos monetarios* was reading a racing paper when we entered. The captain produced the twenty-five dollars I had declared and the I.O. threw me a stern glance over his pince-nez. Then, with a flourish, he read out the currency regulations.

"So, I'm afraid your dollars must be confiscated, señor."

"All of them?"

"All of them."

He was already folding the twenty-five into a drawer and bringing out a sheaf of forms.

The captain looked at me sadly. The I.O. was doing a lot of rubber stamping. He thrust a paper at me: "Received from Pierre Renard, etc. . . . ," my false name, chosen to keep the initials the same.

"You will hand this form to the immigration authorities."

With the form there was a small dirty banknote, five pesetas.

"Receipt please."

"What for?"

"Five pesetas, expenses. Returned to you by courtesy of the Spanish government."

I glanced up at the forbidding face of Generalissimo Franco.

"Gracias, mon general," I said.

As I took the money my collar blushed. We were dismissed. "Next, please."

"Let's have a drink before you turn me in," I said to the captain as soon as we were out on the street. He agreed, but glanced around uneasily. Obviously he didn't want to be seen drinking, especially with a prisoner. "Not in that bar," he said, and began walking down the street.

I was hungry and I'd taken a liking to my amiable escort. I wanted to give us both a treat. I spotted a discreet-looking restaurant. "What about this one?"

He hesitated for a second, but then pushed open the door, made straight for the bar and ordered two beers. I slipped into the dining room, grabbed a waiter and asked what was on the menu.

"Today it's tortillas, señor."

"Two double portions."

"You will take wine?"

"A bottle of your best. Have you any of that delicious almond cake?"

"Turrón cake, señor? Our speciality."

When I got back to the bar my captain was paying for the beers. "I have a table," I said. He looked very uncomfortable. "I'm supposed to be delivering you to the police and, apart from that . . ."

"Don't worry about the money," I said, "the proprietor is my long-lost uncle. Let's eat, drink and be merry, mon capitaine, you know where I'll be tomorrow."

"In clink," he said, "and I'll be lucky if I'm not there with you." He took off his shiny *bicorneg* and smoothed his hair as he followed me to the table. He looked different without his headgear—young Pedro Cuevas, father of three, the friendly cop.

We settled down to the best meal either of us had seen for

many a long day, finishing up with ersatz coffee and fiery Spanish brandy. The bill arrived.

"Don't try to do a bunk," he said, "or I'll have you."

"You lend me the money then. I'll send it back to you."

"What?"

"Then lend me your pocket knife instead."

He would not give it to me. So I took off my coat and asked him to slit open the collar. He flipped when he saw the dollars.

"You see? I fooled you, didn't I? Have some more brandy."

"How could I have missed all that?"

I acted out the razor trick for him.

"Very devious," he said, "I congratulate you, but you'd better not try any tricks here, Figueras division is very tough."

We finished the brandy as the sun was setting. I asked him what time the night shift came on at the police station. He began looking for his hat.

He was right about the Figueras cops. They gave us a hard look as we . . . well, I won't say rolled into the police station, but we were a little unsteady.

Pedro made his report, grasped my hand when no one was looking and made rapidly for the door.

"See you after the war," I called after him.

"Sergeant!"

"Sir!"

"Put this man in the chokey."

Well, I'll spare you my prison journal at this point; all I can say is that Casablanca was a three-star hotel compared to this. In the one cell there were twenty of us, all sexes and persuasions. There were faces that would have graced one of Goya's gibbets; there were pale martyred faces with closed eyes, one grinning dwarf and a triumvirate of foul-mouthed thieves. I kept my money next to my belly.

We slept on the floor and we stank. Our nourishment a tin bowl of tomato soup and hard tack, issued once daily.

I demanded to be taken before the prison governor. The

guard turned a deaf ear. I shouted, protested. I wasn't the only one protesting. After three days I was taken out for questioning.

"We know you've been telling a pack of lies and your papers are false. . . . How did you get into Spain? Who brought you? Names."

I invented names.

"Which route?"

I told them I could not remember.

"Perhaps you can remember your own name."

I decided to tell them.

"You are a Jew?"

"I am."

"Where were you making for?"

I told them I had friends in Madrid and named a distant relative who lived there, though I thought there was very little chance of her being in residence.

"Take him away and check his story."

And I was taken back to hell's waiting room. The next day they marched me out again.

"We are releasing you, provisionally. You will stay at this address and report here twice a day. In due course a member of JOINT will be coming to collect you."

JOINT was the international organization for helping Jewish refugees. Until then I had never heard of them. Thank God, they seemed to have heard of me.

I went to the address they'd given me; it was in the main square of the dreary little town, a small hotel inappropriately named Hôtel de Paris. I settled in to wait for my deliverers.

Here follows one of the dullest paragraphs in my whole story. There is absolutely nothing to tell. I just waited. There were no books, no radios, I couldn't read the papers or talk to people and it was all made so much worse by the suspense. I didn't even want to go for a long walk for fear of missing the unknown friends who were coming to take me away. To freedom? To Madrid, anyway.

The worst lay behind me—I hoped. What lay ahead? The chance of getting to England.

One day I was called down to the small foyer, with its yellow flowering wallpaper and perpetual smell of warm olive oil. Someone was asking for me. A dapper little man stood there, dressed in black. He was very polite.

"JOINT?" I asked.

He didn't reply. "Moi, ami famille," he said, or something to that effect.

We had difficulty in understanding each other. He seemed most anxious for me to go somewhere with him, and having nothing whatsoever to do, I went.

We came to a small, dapper factory, painted white, and he bowed me in. There was a wonderful smell. Then I saw trays of small chocolates drifting by, crowned with sugared violets or rose petals. My mouth was watering. I couldn't remember when I last tasted a chocolate cream. He gave me one.

"My factory," he said. "Please!"

At last I was being rewarded for all my trials and tribulations, with a chocolate. Scrumptious! He was dropping several of these luscious *bonnes bouches* into a paper trumpet.

"To what do I owe such pleasure?" I asked him, using my Spanish phrase book.

The explanation was laborious. It was a while before I got it right. His mother had been a consumptive child, cured, he said, at —. I recognized the name, Berck-sur-Mer, my grandmother's clinic. He had never forgotten it, nor the name of my family.

A marvelous moment, but the dialogue was necessarily limited. I sauntered back to my room and slowly ate my chocolates. When deliverance arrived at last, I left the dreary little town with an even larger paper trumpet, full of chocolate creams.

On the way to Madrid from Figueras, the official from JOINT who was escorting me went out of his way to inspect a camp of eight hundred women.

"From France?"

"From everywhere."

Eight hundred women and none for me. That, I'm afraid, was the only thought I had. They turned out to be refugees of every nationality who had found a shelter in Spain.

The Franco regime was a blight over Spain, there is no doubt about that, but had their government shared the rabid racism of Germany or Vichy France, or had they closed their frontiers like Switzerland, many thousands more would have died. Ninety-five innocent men had recently been shot as hostages at Mont Valerian, Paris, fifty-three of them Jews. The mass deportations began in 1942. Before the war was over one hundred twenty-five thousand Jews were sent from France to the Nazi camps, one-third of them French citizens, two thousand under six years of age. Three percent survived.

In Madrid I decided to take the smallest room in the biggest hotel. As I passed through the foyer I could hardly believe my eyes. There were Germans chatting with English, Russians with Poles, Italians, Austrians, Spaniards, all drinking and gossiping in the friendliest manner in the world, yet I was the only one who aroused suspicious glances. The reception clerk's eyebrows hit his hairline when he saw me. I caught a glimpse of myself in the mirror behind him. It gave me quite a shock too. Wind-beaten, scruffy, my jacket stained and ragged, the battered rucksack still slung over my shoulder, I looked the perfect bum. As I wrote my name in the register someone tapped me on the shoulder. I turned. It was Paul Morand, suave and immaculate. He certainly hadn't arrived in Spain on foot by way of the Pyrenees.

"Philippe! How amazing! What are you doing here?"

"I have nothing to say to you," I told him, and turned away. All the same, if this distinguished gentleman hadn't claimed me at that moment I don't think they would have given me a bed in their Grand Hotel.

I cleaned up a bit and went down to dine, checking my fellow guests as I passed them. Any or every one of them might be a spy. Morand, I was told, was there on a diplomatic mission for Vichy. Later he became Pétain's ambassador in Rumania, took refuge from the Russian advance in Switzerland and sent de Gaulle a message of congratulation when Paris was liberated. De Gaulle would have none of him, so he went to ground in Berne, but in the end, all was forgiven and forgotten; he was elected to the Académie Française, our famous Hall of the Dead.

I wanted to be away from Madrid at the earliest possible moment. I felt ill at ease and unsafe. I went to my room and tried to phone my father in Portugal. Once there I would be more than halfway to England. I longed to breathe clean air.

The next morning the phone rang in my room. Now who's found me? Should I answer?

"Maggie de Zuylen here."

The lady was related to a distant Rothschild by marriage. She was the one I had named in Figueras.

"Monsieur Pucheu is dying to talk with you. I promised to contact you for him."

"Pierre Pucheu? The last I heard of him he was Pétain's minister of the interior. Surely you know that it was he who set up the anti-Jewish police force in 1941? He outdid the Germans with his summary executions."

"I only know that he is a desperate man."

"What on earth does he want with me?"

"Only a few minutes of your time. I beg you to see him."

"Well, certainly not in public. . . ."

She knew I was weakening and went on with her pleading. I gave in.

"Tell him I'll be walking by the Prado under the trees at ten o'clock this evening."

Why did I agree to see this creature, who had almost the worst reputation of any traitor in France? I don't know. I certainly could not have imagined the man he turned out to be. When a miserable, tight-lipped being approached me, I turned away.

"Pucheu," he muttered.

"Let's walk," I said. He talked, I listened.

He was not so guilty as they made out. There were others more to blame. All he had tried to do was save France from the worst horrors of the Occupation. A Frenchman executing orders was preferable to a German. Pierre Laval was the villain of the piece. Monsieur Laval's concessions to the Nazis had gone too far, said Monsieur Pucheu, so he had fled to Madrid, where he lived in hiding.

"How many Frenchmen did you send to their deaths?"

He turned to look at me.

"The Germans threatened to kill five times as many. They do not make idle threats. In the main I only went for the far left, the secret societies. Communists . . ."

"And Jews."

"At Nantes I saved the war veterans who were to be shot as hostages. I replaced them with Communists."

"What do you want with me?"

"I want to fight for France, go to North Africa, join General Koenig and the Free French."

"But when they find out who you are they will shoot you. You won't even be a blot in the history books. If you really want to wipe away your past, change your name, join the Foreign Legion."

"I will not disguise myself. I am what I am. If I did wrong I will face the music."

The man beside me was no back-street collaborator, doing it for a handful of ration tickets. He had been a Vichy minister, with power of life and death over us, ruthless in his dealings with anyone opposed to Pétain—the "bomb throwers in the pay of the British and the Jewish Bolshevik plutocrats," known to us as the Resistance.

I felt sick in his presence. What was I doing with this man? I had left France to fight for France, and here I was hanging around in this cesspool of a city. Not that I had anything much to be proud of. We had all been collaborators to some extent, defeated, occupied, what else could we be?

He was waiting for me to speak. What could I say? I told him that it was not for me to judge him. I had never had to take life, nor had I been forced to make odious decisions.

I looked at him, a washed-out rag, no longer a man.

"I chose the lesser of two evils," he said. "Thank you for seeing me, Monsieur de Rothschild. I have made up my mind. I shall go openly to Algiers."

He went, and, as I had predicted, they shot him.

After the Pucheu encounter I was prepared to leave Madrid on foot, if there was no other way. There was some hope that JOINT might help me to England, but that would mean waiting around indefinitely. I sat by the phone for hours till I got through to Portugal. My father came to the phone. "Come," he said, "try from here." I took the first train available.

We embraced. He looked old and spent, but he wasn't grieving about his losses. He had his faithful Marthe Régnier with him and they were living simply, from day to day, as well as one can at such a time. They were in a small villa outside Lisbon, where, they told me, de Gaulle had a consul. At the first opportunity I went to see him. He was not optimistic.

"Getting you to England may take some time. In fact you'll be lucky if you get there at all. It all depends on the British consul."

I tried to see the British consul, but he was not available. I had to face another wait. My father told me that my brother, James, had been hoping to get to England but he had as yet no news of him. Nadine was still in Grasse.

I made the best of quiet days with my father and Marthe, and I had my usual luck. I met a strapping Austrian girl on the beach. She had been a bareback rider in a circus. Among other things, she delighted me with stories of her roving life, traveling with the big top to all the capitals of Europe. The war had put a stop to the circus. The animals had to be sold or slaughtered. Her beautiful horses had finished up "steak cannibale" long since.

19

Quoique leurs chapeaux soient bien laids
Goddam! Moi, j' aime les Anglais.

JEAN BÉRANGER

AT four o'clock one morning the phone rang. "Get to the airport immediately and report to the British officer in charge. There is a military plane leaving at 9 A.M. and they say they can squeeze you on board, if you're not too fat." Luckily, I'd lost about six kilos on my long hike; all the same they had to get me in with a shoehorn. The plane was packed with British officers, all squatting on the bare struts. I couldn't understand a word they said. What did it matter? I was on my way to the Land of the Free. After a bumpy ride and a terrifying dive into the clouds to escape a Messerschmitt I stepped out into a misty place called Swindon and was promptly arrested.

"As a French officer, I refuse to be locked up," I told them. They scratched their heads. "I'll go into the cell, but only if you leave the door unlocked."

They left the door open after I'd promised not to run away. Where would I run to, I asked them. They gave me a mug of tea, with sugar.

And then what? The British coppers seemed pretty relaxed

after the other guardians of the peace I'd been meeting lately,
but when I told them I'd come to join the Free French and
would like to get on with it, they looked dubious.

"You'll 'ave to be over 'auled first, " they told me.

What did that mean? Medically?

"No, no, no, they'll 'ave to look into your credentials, won't
they? We can't 'ave any Tom, Dick or 'Arry turning up claiming
'e's fightin' for freedom can we? You'll 'ave to be turned over,
foroughly."

It really annoyed me to think how long it had taken me to
learn to pronounce "th" and "h," only to find this character
dropping his aspirates all over the place and saying "fings" for
"things"; I ask you.

Happily, the sergeant who escorted me over the next stage
of the journey was a Highlander. En route I was given more
tea and a doorstep of bread smeared with rubbery cheese. At
the end of the day we drew up in the laurel-lined driveway of
a large and forbidding Victorian house.

In the bare dining room, where I took supper with twenty
other inmates, I learned that I was at The Patriotic School,
somewhere in the suburbs of London, and we were all there to
be vetted before being let loose on the island race.

The British being a very fair and democratic sort of people,
I had to wait my turn like everybody else; there was no jumping
the queue, pulling rank and all that. In any case, I'd not much
rank to pull—officer of the French air force? Where were they
now? And was I so sure that I wanted any more to do with the
air force after that flight from Lisbon?

The other residents in that Tower of Babel were refugees
from every occupied country; most of them spoke very little
English. The officers from British Intelligence who interro-
gated us and checked on us were very thorough. This time the
waiting was rather like purgatory, and what's more I had a
peephole to paradise. Every morning and evening I walked to
a little hillock at the farthest edge of the grounds, and watched
a small green train go rattling by. The railway line disappeared

into a tunnel which seemed to run under the house. I would wave happily to the people crammed against the windows. I didn't think they could see me, but one evening a girl in a red tam o'shanter waved back.

As soon as I'd been accepted and given my British identity card I would board the little train and go straight to London-town.

My overhaul took a little less time than the others who'd gone before. Well, after all, I did have a lot of English relatives. Most of them were away, in the forces or on war work, but the bank was still functioning and Anthony, an elderly cousin who was running it, spoke for me.

The moment my clearance was through and I was awarded my British identity card I was off. The little green train deposited me at Charing Cross. It all looked very cheerful—the red buses, the flower seller outside the station, the graceful Eleanor Cross.

I was walking on air but I'd no idea where I was going. I showed the name and address of my billet to a policeman, with my new identity card. He began to direct me. An oldish man, in a uniform strange to me, stopped beside us. "I'll take him," he said. He was an air-raid warden, one of the many volunteers who were on duty each night during the raids. He asked about France as if it were his second home.

He found my billet for me, a small hotel in a side street near St. James's Palace. The room was cold, the blue flames of the gas fire went out with a pop every few minutes, only to reappear when you'd thrust large pennies into a slot. I had to go wandering in the darkened street to find them, encouraged by the concierge, who couldn't understand a word I said. What a miserable way to spend your first evening in London. You think so? Never. I looked in the mirror, I grinned at the man I saw.

"You're free!" I shouted. "Free!"

It was one of the happiest evenings of my life.

Next morning I had an appointment at de Gaulle's H.Q. in

Carlton Gardens. I was received with open arms; there were friends all around me. At last you could talk openly without looking over your shoulder. I realized then with a shock how much one had been conditioned by occupation.

I was surprised to hear that my brother, James, was already in England and had joined de Gaulle's rather diminutive Armée de l'Air.

What was my job to be? They needed someone at once in the decoding department. I would sooner have worked on the BBC program, "Les Français parlent aux Français," but perhaps it was just as well; it might have endangered Lili and Philippine if my voice had been recognized. The decoding was easy, monotonous even, though sometimes the information was very disturbing: the day I learned that Pauillac had been bombed and a British aircraft brought down by flak from the German battery at Mouton, or when I noticed Colonel Vautrin's name on a list of missing, shot down over Libya. I managed to get the news to his girl friend in Paris, via the secret service BCRA, Bureau Cent al de Renseignements et d'Action.

Like my admired ancestor Nathan before me—Amschel's son, who landed in England in 1798 with a few words of English in his copybook and all his worldly wealth stitched into his jacket—I decided to avail myself of the Rothschild network. My army pay was peanuts and Carlton Gardens were about to pack me off to the wilds of Sussex, so I went to see Cousin Tony at the Rothschild bank, New Court, St. Swithin's Lane, in the City of London, established 1810.

I borrowed twenty-five pounds and was offered three or four pounds a week for the duration, to be repaid when the war was over. That was fine, I'd few expenses, I needed the twenty-five pounds to buy some needlework for Mouton which I'd seen in a Pimlico shop. It would fold into my kit.

Why was I leaving London? I'd got bored with decoding, it was anybody's job. Hadn't they something more useful, more suitable to my many talents? Liaison, they said, you have good English. I may have some knowledge of English, but of the army and its language I know sweet Fanny Adams, I told them. (Actually I didn't pick up that expression till some months later on a commando course.) Don't worry about that—we'll send you on a few training courses down in the wilds.

They could have been trying to get rid of me. The atmosphere round Carlton Gardens was getting a little too dictatorial for my taste and I've never been slow to put in a few criticisms and suggestions.

The wilds turned out to be pretty Tenterden, with its shades of Ellen Terry, plus the remains of a Roman barge from the days when the sea was lapping round the field where we were camped, myself and the British infantry.

The next course they found for me was at Fort William, in the Highlands of Scotland, with the commandos. Shit a brick! It was murder. The air was blue, the language was bluer and my small parts were mauve. Up hill, down dale, up to your neck in icy water.

"To kill the f—, get him in a half Nelson, thus, and break his f— neck."

It took me quite a while to decode our P.T. instructor.

"All right, chaps, breakfast at four and the road's ice bound."

We'd no fuel for a fire, so one or two of us would watch the railway line for passing coal trucks, then climb down and pick up any droppings.

I was glad when that little lot came to an end.

"Lieutenant Rothschild? You're for Ulster with the Yanks."

"Ulster? Where's that?"

"Northern Ireland."

Ireland? Great! For me, Ireland was Yeats, Lady Gregory, the Abbey, the Gate, the Book of Kells and sweet Irish blarney.

"Hey, who's this guy?"

"Free French."

"De Gaulle and all that crap?"

"He's attached to the unit for three weeks."

"Oh yeah?"

The Americans didn't recognize de Gaulle, who had been

loud in his denunciations of Roosevelt for failing to come to the aid of France in 1940. Roosevelt in return regarded de Gaulle as a threat to the war effort. "All he wants is political power."

There was no love lost between our leaders, and the Ulster Yanks insisted on treating me as de Gaulle's personal representative. They weren't going to have some Frog muscling in on their territory. "He's welcome to stick around, but strictly extramural, okay?" And I was supposed to be patching things up, explaining French political systems, manners, customs and all that to our friends the Americans. It was, after all, important that when the time came there should be some understanding between French civilians and their liberators. I gave two or three lectures—how to explain a necessary search to some reluctant French peasant, the rôle we might play as Free French when the time came, but I could have saved my breath to cool my porridge. Perhaps they'd had some experience of the Vichyites in North Africa; for whatever reason I was clearly not *persona grata*. There was nothing I could do about it. I simply took what the English call "French leave" as often as possible, and that was very pleasant since Ireland was then, and believe it or not, still is, the Land of Faerie.

One fine day, I know you won't believe me, but one fine day I saw four fairies, sitting on a fallen tree by a lake sharing a pair of binoculars. I asked them what they were looking at. My accent must have betrayed me, for they replied, in fairy French, that they were bird watching, and was there anything wrong in that? They were ruffled. I apologized hand on heart. Then they wanted to know what business I had there. I sat down beside them and told them how lonesome I was in their lovely country. I was playing for sympathy of course. "Pauvre garçon," said one, she was the eldest, and they all invited me to tea. As we walked through a wood, sufficiently enchanting, they showed me four trees, each with a name carved on it—Rose, Daisy, Violet, Iris. "That's us," said the youngest.

We came to a Georgian castle. "Our home," they said, "and

you were trespassing on our estate. Don't worry, we're used to it, everybody does it these days." As we moved through the hall, I stepped over a mound of letters, overflowing from a cloakroom.

"Sorry, we can't throw them away because we don't read them," said the prettiest.

"Rose, I'm sure our guest isn't in the least interested in house keeping," said Iris, the eldest. "Why don't we show him our Buffon?" Violet and Rose gave a silvery laugh.

We came to an inner room, shelves from floor to ceiling bulging with books, books too big for the shelves stacked on the threadbare carpet and two lecterns covered with velvet cloths embroidered with laid work, threaded with silver gilt.

Violet blew on one to scatter the dust and whipped the cloth away to reveal a rare edition of Buffon, the great eighteenth-century French naturalist. It was illustrated by Picasso.

We took tea in the music room, strong tea poured from a pot of bright yellow Delft, served with soda scones and whiskey. Then at Daisy's insistence, Violet stood and sang "The Last Rose of Summer" for me, and the Rose herself accompanied her on the clarsach.

Before I left I asked why they had been so cross with me when we met.

"The uniform," they said.

"Every year at this time the wild geese visit us," said Iris. "This year we haven't seen one. Those army persons have scared them away."

At the first opportunity I meant to visit Dublin and take a look at the famous Irish theater. The only problem was—the republic was neutral; I would be in forbidden territory when I crossed the border. I decided to take a chance. Well, the Irish didn't seem to bother. They waved me merrily on my way, though one pretty girl on the train advised me to change my uniform for mufti. I'd already thought of that and emerged from the toilet in a new Irish suit and canary yellow sweater.

I saw Mac Liammóir's Hamlet, went backstage, talked theater

and strolled round beautiful Dublin, blazing with lights. Then I went to the Shelbourne and ordered myself a steak. It came with a fried egg on it. An egg! In London it had been: "Egg, sir? Don't you know there's a war on? Eggs are powdered, but you may have them scrambled, sautéd or curried. No? What about today's plat du jour, corned beef à la mode? Spam? Shall I see if there is a little whale meat left? Thank you, may I have your coupons, sir?"

I stayed over in Dublin to see *Juno and the Paycock,* visit the university library and the Martello Tower immortalized by James Joyce, and of course was shown the Post Office, where Irish patriots held out against the British during that tragic Easter week. . . . What an unromantic place to die.

Dublin is a difficult town to leave, but I thought I'd better get back before I had to face the firing squad.

"I see that French guy has turned up again. Where in hell does he get to?"

They couldn't have cared less, but I got a rocket from London. In fact, they recalled me.

"What do you think you were doing in Dublin?"

The Americans had sent a stinking report about me. "Constantly absent without leave."

I told the truth and got a black mark. From now on, they told me, you'll be staying in London. I was delighted.

Despite rationing, bombs and blackout, I still thought London paradise. It was an international city and there was a camaraderie on the streets such as I've never known anywhere since. Passers-by cracked jokes in impenetrable cockney or tried a few words of French. One night I bumped into an old cockney in the blackout.

"Pardon me."

"That's all right, young'un. You polish off this geyser 'itler and we'll 'ave light enough—prettiest sight in the world, the old Pall Mall at night."

But the prettiest sight for me was the girls. None of us had ever seen a girl in uniform before. They looked so smart, so sexy. My neck ached, turning my head from side to side to look at them. I fancied them all.

One dark night, strolling along Piccadilly, looking for somewhere to eat, a streetwalker accosted me, in perfect French.

"You've strayed a bit, haven't you?" I said. "Where are you from?"

"Brest," she said. "We're the tarts of Brest, aren't we, girls?"

"Yes, and proud of it," came the response from along the street. There was a whole chorus line of them.

"Our pimps used to bring us over for the season and then call back to take us home for Christmas; but once the war started, we saw them no more—they're either dead or in the black market."

"Aren't you homesick?"

"You get used to it. We were coming over here for years, long before the war."

"Don't ask her how many."

"Hundreds of years. The tarts of Brest are historical."

That was true, the seasonal whores had been as much part of the London scene as the Breton onion sellers.

I found a good meal that night, by chance. I thought I'd come to the end of nowhere; there was only Hyde Park, black as pitch, farther on. There would be no clubs or eating places there. I noticed a crack of light showing from an inner room as someone pushed open a large imposing door. I heard the sound of a French accordion tune and decided to investigate. I recognized the place at once, there was no mistaking that rococo ceiling, the imposing entablature above the mantel. It was a Rothschild house. I'd actually stayed there once as a child. It had been built by Lionel, son of Nathan, grandson of Amschel, the father of us all. Now it was an army club, crowded with French servicemen and their girls, and I had a sumptuous meal for five shillings.

There was still a social life in London and a deal of kindness toward lonely French officers. I began to get invitations to parties.

"Our boy has got his wings; we're having a little celebration. Do come."

"The girls and boys are all home on leave together for once. It'll be such a reunion, you must be with us."

Bombs might be falling, the fire engines tearing through the streets, but the party would go on. If the bangs got too close we would adjourn to the basement or the nearest underground station.

Each evening a procession of Londoners made their way to the tube, carrying their bedding and refreshments. In the dawn light, when the full extent of the damage was seen and the fires were still burning, it was amazing how many people turned out to help, and how many different kinds of people. London seemed classless and the cockneys incorrigible.

> Hitler has only got one ball
> Goering's are very very small
> Himmler is somewhat sim'lar
> But Dr. Goballs has no balls at all.

They sang it in every pub to the tune of "Colonel Bogey." Each army unit marched to its own bawdy songs. No wonder the French think the British are barmy. . . . The worse it got the more they mocked the war.

> Even a private's privates, boys, enjoy no privacy
> You sacrifice all that to save democracy.

We were more serious.

Did you ever hear the French partisan song? After the war people said it was more popular in London pubs than in the Maquis, the usual rivalry between the ones who got away and the ones who stayed put.

*   *   *

Ami, entends-tu le vol noir des corbeaux dans la plaine?
Ami, entends-tu le bruit sourd d'un pays qu'on
enchaîne? . . .

I heard it first in a chintzy little apartment near the Lancaster
Gate underground station. A few of us had been invited for
cocktails and we gathered round the piano singing. As we were
about to leave, the young composer Jeff Kessel struck up a tune
on the piano. None of us knew it. Somone joined in with the
words. It was Maurice Druon, writer, friend of mine before the
war and after. He and Jeff had just written the song that evening.

Our hostess was a typical English lady married to a typical
English lord, but she loved France and all things French. I had
met her at a party given by her aunt Emerald Cunard, famous
hostess and bitch queen of the *bon mot* in London's 1920s, born
Maud Burke in 'Frisco 1872, and still plying her Irish wit and
hospitality in wartime London. I noticed a quiet, softly dressed
woman, rather overwhelmed by Emerald's glittering court, and
asked her about herself. Her husband was a drunk; too old for
military service, he had retreated to the Highlands to stay soz-
zled for the duration. She was doing some sort of war work,
mostly making up food parcels, from what I could gather. It all
seemed rather sad.

"And you haven't a lover?" I asked.

"I had. He was a Frenchman."

Perhaps it was thanks to him that she showed such kindness
to me, and all my friends. She kept open house for us, scouring
the shops in her lunch break to find tidbits for her soldiers'
soirées. All her sweet rations went on me, I'm sorry to say.
Dear, kind Riette, her pretty flat was a haven. It wasn't long
before I found myself spending all my spare evenings there,
and what's more contriving to be alone with her. She would
listen to my stories, sitting on her footstool, hands clasped
round her knees, her blue eyes fixed on me. Of course I

couldn't resist her. I found she was lovelier than I'd imagined, all milk and roses.

Just another wartime affair? Yes, if you like, and of course I can't say that there weren't a lot of others. We were like lobsters in a boiling cauldron, sometimes fastening desperately onto the one next to us as we bobbed up and down. Even at the best of times one has to allow for the accidental—which may simply be incidental if only as a marginal note, but nevertheless valuable. There is also the impossible. One night in a small restaurant I caught sight of a back view which looked familiar: lean, brown shoulders, a low-cut summer dress, a cloud of auburn hair. So like . . . could it be? She turned. It was. Anne Marie, the tigress. She looked marvelous. She knew me at once and pounced on me as she always had done, like a friendly Labrador.

"Are you alone?" I asked at once.

"No, I'm with my husband. He's just gone to the men's room."

"The same husband?"

"Quite different. You might even know his brother, Oswald Mosley."

She was naming the leader of the English Fascist party, the Blackshirts, the leading anti-Semite of England. Did she know?

I didn't have time to ask her. As always, without warning, she just cleared off. She must have known.

III
It's the Wrong Time and the Wrong Place

20

It's the wrong time and the wrong place,
Though your face is charming, it's the wrong face,
It's not her face but such a charming face
That it's all right with me.

COLE PORTER

AFTER my recall from Ireland, army life seemed more boring than ever. There were translation jobs, lectures, exams even, but everybody knew we were simply cooling our heels, hanging about, waiting for the great day, the opening up of the second front, which would put paid to Hitler —or us.

The general feeling was that it would be France, though whether by the south, north, the Atlantic wall or all three, nobody had much of an opinion. Someone opened a book and the betting was lively.

One day I was told to join some of de Gaulle's aides at the Hyde Park Hotel. I left my name at the desk and turned to take a stroll round the foyer. Someone touched my arm; I nearly jumped out of my skin. A stout little man, ugly and rather scruffy, was staring at me. I'd never seen him before in my life.

"I know who you are but you don't know me."

"Who are you?"

"Cyril Connolly."

I was delighted. I knew him from his marvelous book, *The Unquiet Grave*. How did he know me?

"Heard your name at the desk, had to speak. I've so much to thank you for."

"Really, what?"

"Mouton '21, '24, '29, '37."

I could have hugged him, not for knowing the best, but for the word "Mouton"—it was a very long time since I'd heard it.

"Saved my sanity for what it's worth. How else would one have got through those boring air raids? I have a few bottles left: care to share one or two? The accompanying meal will be quite devastatingly bad, but the company should be good."

I told him I'd given up wine for the duration.

"How noble. Like the patriotic plumber of Dolphin's Barn who swore to let his hair grow till Ireland was free?"

"Partly noble," I said, "partly practical, bad wine doesn't agree with me."

I accepted his invitation, but kept my vow about the wine. Calling on Cyril became one of my few real pleasures. He was an amusing man, such good company that when you were with him the war and all that dropped into perspective.

I couldn't take him to Riette's; he had a caustic tongue, and she could easily have been hurt by one of his sallies. Part of Riette's charm lay in her naïveté; you'd never believe she was in her fifties, a lot older than me. Nice for a change; recently all my women had been young. She mothered me and at that time it was just what I needed—a soft bosom, tranquility, peace.

Outside, the raids were getting worse. It didn't worry me. I am a fatalist. If the bomb has your number on it, that's it—but I didn't fancy being cut by those long slivers of glass which you saw on the pavements every morning. Sometimes the police wouldn't let you out on the streets while the bombers were overhead, so you'd have to dive into the nearest funk hole and wait for the all clear.

After spending two nights under Riette's bed I was bored with sheltering, and took to spending all my time at the French club. One morning, after a hell of a night, who should I run into in the canteen but Yves Rocard, my professor when I was at the Sorbonne. I asked him if he knew whether Planet Philippa was still safely in place, up there beyond the trouble and strife. He was deafer than ever, with no idea what I was talking about.

"Very well, thank you," he replied. "Had a little trouble last night though."

"How was that?"

"Went to bed, slept well, woke up this morning, house gone."

One Monday morning I was given my marching orders: Camberley. I knew what that meant; we were lining up. It wouldn't be long now. In the barracks on the Kings Road I was issued a tin hat and a sleeping bag.

I took Riette to Hampton Court and as we stood looking at the Great Vine I said good-bye. When we got to the herb garden she began to discuss our future.

It took me a long time, several repetitions in fact, to explain that my future was a little uncertain, that I was not by any means a good, steady feller and that, come to think about it, after the war I would have my wife back and she would have her husband.

She didn't seem too pleased about this and declared that I was happy to leave her. In a way she was right. At the time I had only one thought in my head: soon I would be back in my own country. I longed for that moment as for nothing else.

All the same I tried to cheer her up. I told her she should keep the ram's head Nancy Mitford had bought for me in Brighton, and when the war was over bring it to Mouton and meet my wife and daughter.

At Camberley I found I'd been posted among the British, which meant that wherever Tommy went, I'd go too. All right by Major Rothschild. Me. I should have been a colonel, it might have saved me a lot of trouble later with some of these generals, and other idiots. At the time I hadn't fancied the identity change, I was enjoying the company I was in. There were plenty of Rothschilds lording it around, without me.

The English branch were all carrying the flag aloft, my

brother, James, was doing his bit for France in de Gaulle's air force, and some months after I arrived, Cousin Guy was washed up; he had been snatched from the wild Atlantic and went to stay with my nice cousin to recover—Miriam, the etymologist. I must admit I kept away from the family, they had enough on their plate without their mad cousin Philippe, as they called me.

Well, if I was mad I was in good company. The British Canadians, camped next to us, were the wildest lot I'd come across, and on the other side were the Yanks. It remained to be seen who would be first for the trip round the lighthouse.

We listened to the news on the BBC Home Service with close attention, and weighed every word. Just before lights out, I'd switch on the last bulletin of the day. First there'd be the boom of Moscow's guns saluting another Russian victory. Where were we?

> Severe blows were struck at the Germans today when more than two thousand Allied aircraft went out on varied and widespread missions. More than seven hundred and fifty American Liberators and Flying Fortresses bombed targets in northern France, and at the same time, Mustangs and Lightning fighter-bombers, accompanied by Thunderbolts, attacked the same area. Four enemy aircraft were destroyed in the air, others at ground level. Nine of our heavy bombers were lost. . . .

How many French lives?

Obviously it was all a preparation for our landing in northern France. When we were going in? We felt sure that the generals and politicians would be havering and hesitating, disagreeing among themselves as usual.

I was playing cards with a Belgian friend, Henri Spaak, one night when the order came through. June 6. D-Day! And the Yanks were going first. One or two of the chaps raised a satirical cheer, some were so tired of waiting that they would have preferred to be going over with the first wave. In fact, as the great day dawned, I wondered if anybody would be leaving at all. The weather had been vile for days: the worst storms seen in the channel for twenty years, we were told. It was rumored that the whole operation had been postponed, but that was impossible. We waited. The sky was black, overcast. We thought we could hear our bombers. Then there was a break in the clouds and we saw them. They were returning from their D-Day mission.

Curtain up. Even if you weren't the praying kind, you held your breath. The greatest armada ever assembled was on its way to France. Later we heard that the seas had been mountainous, nearly everybody had been seasick: very much later we learned what that day had cost, nine thousand wounded, three thousand dead.

Our turn came on D+15, June 21. We landed before dawn at some tiny place in the Bay of the Seine; we never saw it, but pushed on toward Bayeux. There was no encounter with the Boche; on D+3 their army had retreated to Caen, the key to northern France, and dug in there.

At Bayeux an H.Q. had been established. My companions went foraging, for news as much as anything. I went and took a look at the tapestry which I'd never seen—worth a detour, even during an invasion.

When I got back I was plied with news and gossip. Courseulles was the pretty name of the place where we had landed, and we would be going to Le Havre. The top brass considered D-Day a success. Surprise had worked, and many of the beaches had been captured as planned. The Yanks had suffered badly on the beach just to the west of us, tank landing craft had gone astray in the sea mist, and the soldiers already ashore had no backup. There had been heavy slaughter.

Bayeux was the beginning and end of my sightseeing. From that time on, we just plowed on; the roads were rivers of mud, such people as we saw—sullen or expressionless. Nobody was sure that the Germans wouldn't be back, they were defending

Caen with everything they'd got. We, in turn, were dropping thousands of tons of high explosives on that unfortunate city and, inevitably, on some of our own ground forces besieging it.

Our advance was very slow. The railroads were unusable, pulverized by bombs. We moved from village to village; occasionally, a little crowd would cheer us on our way, others took pot shots at us. We might call it liberation, but for many of my fellow countrymen it was just another invasion, the same old looting, raping, summary reprisals.

I was in charge of civil affairs, organizing supplies of food and water, electricity, all essential sources.

At Douvre-la-Délivrande the Boche found us and the bombs started falling. I rather enjoyed it, but one had to try and carry on working. It was there that a boy came running through the streets to tell me that his mother was having her head shaved by the neighbors. I told the nearest gendarme to go and arrest her. She would be safer in the police station.

While we were held up there, a matter of a few days, more and more such stories came to me. I intervened whenever I could and did my best to protect these hunted creatures; whatever they were, or had been, they were entitled to fair trial.

I was having my troubles with the army types too. It was my job to reduce the chaos when the liberators moved on; and it was difficult to persuade some of these gentlemen that civilians existed, and that it might be as well to have them on our side. All they thought about was troop transport, all I wanted was food, drink and medical supplies. There were a few clashes. Nevertheless it was at Douvre that somebody noticed my brilliant organizational ability and saintly patience. I was told that I would be put in charge at Le Havre, if we ever got there.

It was, in fact, September when we found ourselves picking our way through smoking ruins, looking for the port where I used to embark on those luxury liners for America. Throughout August I had been installed at Bolbec, not far away, and there it was that the women came running to me, begging me to save their menfolk from the Resistance. I had to put a stop to it, I hated being mobbed; even so one of them got past the sentry, announcing that she was la Baronne de Kainlis, a friend of my family. I took a look—elegant, impossibly so in those surroundings, and keeping a tight hold on herself, but I was sure it would be the same old story. It was.

The Resistance were camped all round her father's country house not far away, they wanted a word with him. He had barricaded himself in. When she told me his name I was not surprised. President of the Jockey Club before the war and during the occupation, the Marquis de Triquerville had had no need to change his tune when the Nazis arrived—his club had always barred Jews. Except the Rothschilds, of course. They were rich enough to be exempt. Cousin Édouard of Lafite, the racing baron, was a member right up till the day he found himself fleeing to Normandy to hide his art treasures on his stud farm. The Nazis also had good taste.

I had no recollection of ever having met this lady, but she assured me that her father had often been entertained at Ferrières. That explained it, she was confusing me with Édouard's son, Guy. It often happens, we all look rather alike. I told her my name. She looked shocked.

Wasn't Lili my wife? Did I not know that she had been arrested?

"What? By the Resistance?"

"By the Germans."

I didn't believe her. Why would the Germans arrest Lili? Just before I left England, I had heard that she was in Paris safe and well; but the woman had made me uneasy. I would do what I could and then be rid of her.

The story about the father was true enough. When I arrived at his house, accompanied by two members of the local gendarmerie, the place was guarded by three or four men wearing FFI armbands. The FFI, Forces Française de l'Intérieur, was the new name for the Resistance. I told them I was acting under direct orders from General de Gaulle. They'd never heard of him. I tried the firm authoritative act I'd picked up in the

British army, and was surprised to find that it worked. The gendarmes went in, arrested Triquerville and hurried him into the police van. We never saw his face, and the Resistance men made no move. I've no idea what happened to him, but whatever it was, it was better than being a bloody mess on his own doorstep.

The daughter's words kept coming back to me, but her story was so unlikely. Paris would be full of such rumors, the town was in a state of chaos, I knew that. On August 19 whole districts had been taken over by the Resistance, and the Germans had fled or capitulated; in other sectors sporadic street fighting was still going on. Lili would surely have the sense to keep her head down.

In any case, there was nothing I could do about it then. The long siege of Le Havre was over. We were going in.

I had never seen total devastation before, nor smelled that sickening, all-pervading stench of burning. It wasn't only the town which had gone, but the cliff above it, the railway line under the cliff, the sewers, the cemetery—there was no electricity, gas, water, food; the cheese factory was just being looted. And of this Golgotha I was mayor. The rightful holder of the title had disappeared.

The main thing was to act quickly. I moved into what was left of the town hall, mobilizing a few activists among the locals en route—clerks, honest gendarmes, anyone who could be handy. Outside Paris, the gendarmes had mainly remained loyal to the true France. It was only in the capital that many of them went round arresting Jews and dissidents, keeping in with the occupiers.

In no time I had the makings of a local authority, and they knew where to find anything there was to find, including all the carefully hidden German supplies which had been left behind.

The gendarmes went off to stop the looting, with a couple of soldiers to help, and I made a list of priorities. One old man, a prewar councillor, felt very touchy about the dead buried in the railway tunnel when the cliff collapsed under the bombing, so I left him to organize the gruesome job of digging them out.

At the end of September the town was in some kind of working order, and the army was due to move on. Soon I too would be able to get away, but first I had to do something to try and lift people's spirits. The locals were facing the second phase of their rehabilitation, it would be drearier and lonelier without us, and the army had heard about Hitler's deadly new weapon, the V-2, which had just been launched against London. What we needed was a victory parade. I got together a band, told everyone to smarten up a bit, and we marched through the town, colors flying, and laid a wreath on the 1914–18 war memorial. I think we all felt better afterwards. Next day I left for Paris.

It was a fine, sunny morning, and the road was quiet. As I reached the suburbs and caught my first glimpse of the tall gray buildings, bright sunblinds at the windows, I had to choke back the tears. On such a morning it seemed that the war had never been—not a building was scratched, there were no ruins, no destruction. The Germans had respected our fair city, and Paris was still Paris, but the roads were terribly empty; there wasn't a car to be seen. Then, nearing the center, bicycles began to appear, and round the Arc de Triomphe and all along the Champs Élysées they were whizzing by, the girls light skirts billowing out behind them. There they were, on either side of me, all the pretty girls of Paris.

I had never seen the house where Lili and Philippine were living—17 rue Barbet de Jouy. When I got there it was shuttered, and the lodge where one would expect to find the concierge was empty. I crossed the courtyard and rang the bell. Marcel Tortet, my butler, came to the door; he must have known that I'd turn up sometime, even the German-controlled radio had mentioned the fact that my brother and I had landed in France, yet he went white, he looked shocked. Anna, his wife, stood on the stairs behind him.

"What has happened here? Where is madame? And Philippine?"

I had known Marcel all my life. He had served me, and my
father before me. He turned his head away.

"What's wrong?"

Neither of them could speak.

"Well?"

"Entrez, Monsieur Philippe. There is no one here."

He closed the door, bolted it carefully and just looked at me.
Anna spoke first.

"It was three weeks after the Normandy landings, about 8:30
in the morning, I remember the time because Philippine had
just left for school with her governess, Mademoiselle Duplé.
The doorbell rang. I went. Two men in gray suits were standing there. 'The Comtesse de Chambure?' The man was soft-
spoken but I knew he was German. 'She is resting,' I said.
Madame had been out late the night before. It was the night
Monsieur Mille had been waiting to see her."

"You mean Monsieur Mervé Mille, from Lyon?"

"Yes, monsieur, and when she did not return, he gave us a
message for her: 'Tell the countess that she must leave this
house at once, this very night. She is on the next list.' "

"List?"

"For deportation they had lists, monsieur. They knew everything about everybody. Marcel waited up for her. . . ."

"I urged her to go, monsieur. Even at that late hour it would
have been possible," added Marcel.

" 'Do you know the time, Marcel?' she said. 'I am rather tired,
I am going to bed. Don't worry, nothing like that will happen
to me.' "

"And the two men?"

"When they made no move to go I picked up the house
phone to call Marcel. They snatched it from me and made for
the stairs. Marcel came. He tried to stop them. They pushed
him aside. They were at Madame's door—'Open up! Gestapo!'
It was the first time we had heard the word. 'What are you

doing here?' we heard her say. 'What does this mean?' They ordered her to get dressed and they took her away in a van. Marcel followed on his bicycle."

"I pedaled as fast as I could and managed to keep them in sight. I knew where they were going."

"The gestapo H.Q.?"

"Yes, place Beauvau, monsieur, near the Champs Élysées. I waited an hour, two. Then I managed to bribe one of the guards with cigarettes. He told me she would probably be sent home after questioning. I hurried back."

"When Marcel arrived," said Anna, "Philippine was home from school. She was in her room. It was a Thursday, there was no school in the afternoon. She usually took her guitar lesson, then went out with her mother. Shortly before one o'clock we heard the prison van pulling into the yard. I went to the door.

"And I ran for the child, snatched her up, signaled her to be quiet, and carried her down to the basement. I hid her behind the boiler. We knew the Nazis took children."

"I was shaking, monsieur. There she was, poor lady, between those two men. She told me to prepare her some lunch and asked the Germans if they would take anything. They said no and hurried her up to her room. Marcel followed on tiptoe to see what they were doing. He said they were turning the place over and told me to take her lunch in to her. As I entered with the tray I heard them asking if she had a daughter.

" 'Oh yes,' she said, 'tell Mademoiselle Duplé to bring Philippine here, Anna.' I didn't know what to say. 'She is not here, madame.' 'Where is she?' 'At her guitar lesson,' I said. It was all I could think of. Mademoiselle Duplé was struck dumb when I told her what she was supposed to do. She asked us if she should take the child and run for it. The bell rang from madame's room.

" 'Where is my daughter? She must have returned by now. Tell Mademoiselle Duplé to bring her here at once.'

"What could we do? We gave the child her white gloves and her gray coat to make it look as if she had just come in from school. Mademoiselle Duplé took her hand and they went to her mother's room; she told her to do her best.

"We waited. Marcel tried to hear what was going on. He said they were speaking German. We heard them moving in the room. So we went and stood in the hall. It wasn't long before madame came out followed by two Germans. She stopped and turned, 'Bye-bye, Philippine,' she said, 'see you later.'

" 'Where are they taking her?' I asked Mademoiselle Duplé. She didn't know. Marcel followed them again. Philippine went back to her room. I don't think she knew what was really happening. How could she? A child of ten, she thought her mother would soon be back. Mademoiselle Duplé told us what had gone on: 'They asked her where her father was. She did very well. "We don't know," she said, "he disappeared one day and we don't know where he went." Then, they showed her some dinner party lists from before the war. They had turned madame's little desk upside down. They asked Philippine if she knew any of the names. Of course she did, they were all friends and relations. My heart was in my mouth, but she just shook her head. 'You are sure?' said one. 'Yes, I am sure, I was too little.'

"Madame tried to dismiss the Germans. 'You've seen everything, gentlemen,' she said, 'and I have a hairdressing appointment.' 'I am afraid not, madame,' said the French-speaking one. 'You are coming with us.' 'Why? What for? Let me lead my life.' They didn't answer. They began arguing in German. Mademoiselle Duplé understood German. 'Are we taking the girl?' said one. 'Why not?' said the other. 'Well, she is no more than a child.' 'So what?' 'It's only that I have a daughter that age in Germany.' "

"They didn't take Philippine?"

"No, monsieur. She is safe. She is at madame's father's house at Escrignelles. Monsieur Hubert de Chambure came for her. He smuggled her out of Paris in an ambulance, her legs bandaged as if she'd had an accident."

Marcel had again followed the gestapo van, this time to the prison in the rue du Cherche-Midi. From there, she was taken

to Fresnes, the female prison, which seldom released any prisoners. An actress friend, Elvire Popesco, managed to see her.
"Get me out of here," said Lili, "they're going to deport me."
Friends and relatives did all they could. Fernand de Brinon was
asked to intervene. He was still Vichy's main contact with the
Nazis, their representative in Paris, and Lili had considered
herself under his personal protection. He was said to have done
his best with the Germans, but failed. He wouldn't have had
much time; the Allies were already in France. When the last
train carrying deportees to the death camps left, Lili was on it.
It was frequently bombed en route, and many escaped. She
didn't.

Escrignelles, where Philippine was living, is a little village near
Gien. When I got to the house there was only a housekeeper
there. I learned that Lili's father had recently died.

"Where is Philippine? Is she well?"

"She's fine, she's at school now."

I ran there as fast as my legs would carry me. The children
were out in the playground. I stood by the railings—a strange-
looking man in khaki battle dress, a beret over one ear. I spotted her. She glanced at me and went on playing. I smiled. She
looked at me again, then rushed towards me. "Papa!" My little
girl was in my arms. "You know they arrested mama? Have you
news of her?"

All I could say was, "Not yet, but I soon will have."

It seemed best to leave Philippine where she was. Where else
could I put her? The war was by no means over; the Allied
advance had been halted. The Germans were fighting fanati-
cally all along their west wall and they still held the ports of
Dunkerque, Lorient, St. Nazaire and the mouth of the Gironde, just above Bordeaux.

I still had two days' leave, after which I would have to report
back to Paris. I badly wanted to see Mouton again. I explained
the position to Philippine and she understood—"Only don't
stay away so long this time, papa."

To reach Mouton I would have to go via Bordeaux. I skirted

the town, calling on one of the Cruse family, the wine merchant Christian. "You'll never get to Mouton," he told me, "I'm not even sure the Germans aren't holding it, the FFI were still attacking yesterday." Well, if the fight was on I'd join 'em. It was my home they were scrapping over. All I had to do was get there. By now I was convinced that my little army jeep would get me through anything.

What I saw of Bordeaux looked untouched; a bit drearier, perhaps. Was it only two years since I went away?

At Pauillac they told me the Germans had retreated from Mouton. Five hundred FFI had driven them out and the fight was going on somewhere along the road to Lesparre. Mouton was a sorry sight—telegraph poles down, wires cut, breast-works, guns, concrete pillboxes everywhere. I stood outside the gate, gazing at the wreck. I hadn't the heart to go in. A few blokes gave me an easy salute—vignerons from the look of them, with FFI in red on their armbands. I knew them, but I'd forgotten their names. I didn't want to stay and talk.

"Where is it happening?"

"They're in the outskirts of Lesparre."

Lesparre is a little market town twelve miles from us. It was in the auction rooms there that my great-great-grandfather had bought Mouton. I raced along the road, hardly noticing the burned trucks and the bodies. I'm afraid I'd become hardened to such sights: it happens all too quickly.

I heard rifle fire. Someone shouted to me to take cover, the tangy Médoc accent again—quickly I backed off the road. It was a squad of FFI, all local men, some very young. They seemed in fine fettle, confident, professional.

"They're caput. It won't be long now."

"They may try to hang on to their Atlantic wall."

"Not if we chase them to the mouth of the river and drive them into the sea."

The Atlantic wall was the series of huge concrete bunkers built by slave labor, French slave labor, to resist any invasion from the Atlantic. They are still there today, indestructible.

One of the men told me there was another Resistance army at Royan on the other side of the river. "A friend of yours commands it," he said.

"Who?"

"Monsieur de Fleurieu from the Dordogne."

Pierre, in the land of the living! I would have to see him. I doubled back to Bordeaux, crossed the river where the one bridge was still intact, and made for Royan. It wasn't difficult to find Pierre; everybody knew where he was. He was the local hero, my fine, brave old de Fleurieu, and he looked the part when I came upon him, towering above his old guard, chest covered with medals, brandishing his one arm at me. His right arm had been blown off in the First World War. He had managed to bring together all the scattered Resistance units in the Dordogne and make an army of them. As the first representative of the Free French anyone had set eyes on, I was invited to make a tour of inspection.

You should have seen those chaps, thin blue peasant suits, improvised armbands, berets and any old weapon they'd managed to lay hands on. The only good stuff had been pinched from the Germans, but Pierre was tremendously proud of his ragged army.

I was due to report back to H.Q. in Paris in a matter of hours. I embraced Pierre and climbed into my jeep.

Having nearly broken my neck to get back on time, I found myself hanging around for days awaiting further orders. I mooched about with nowhere much to go. I didn't want to occupy Lili's house in the rue Barbet de Jouy. There was still no news of her, but there was always my prewar bachelor home in the avenue d'Iéna. I wouldn't mind having that back.

There was obviously someone living there, and the lock had been changed. I rang. When the door was opened, who should be standing there, wearing my dressing gown, but Henri Lillaz, a cabinet minister before the war, and a renowned collaborator. He also owned a shop called Le Bazar de l'Hotel de Ville. I introduced myself.

"Good morning," I said. "And now will you kindly get out of my house?"

"This property was confiscated. . . ." he began.

"Out," I said, producing a revolver. "And don't forget the key."

Henri Lillaz was the resourceful type—he asked for a few days, grace, which I granted him. But no sooner was my back turned than he brought a van and took away every stick of furniture I possessed, stripped the place down to the floorboards—he even took my nightshirts.

Such games were all the rage just then: collabos playing hide-and-seek, skipping, fiddling, forging, but an awful lot of them seemed to be making a beeline for me. Once I was back in avenue d'Iéna there was almost a queue. They all seemed to think I was a soft touch. One day this gift-wrapped thing arrived; it was Germaine, one of my prewar flames, still pretty. She and her husband had been as thick as thieves with the Germans and were now lying low. There were tears and trembling smiles. Could dear Philippe help, for old time's sake?

"Well," I said, "if I do, it won't be much."

I gave her a letter of introduction to the acting minister of justice and he simply went and fell in love with her, so that was that.

When my new posting finally came through it was, as I expected, Germany and, once again, liaison with the British. Not surprising, as very few French officers spoke English.

As the German army was pushed back, the places we had called concentration camps were opened up. When the first reports came through, they were not believed. People have long memories for some things. During the First World War there had been atrocity stories of bodies boiled down for glycerine, babies tossed onto bayonets, which were afterwards discredited as mere hate propaganda. But this time there were eye-witness accounts from soldiers and war correspondents who entered the camps and saw what they contained. Delegations of politicians, lawyers, doctors, were sent to verify these reports. I was appointed to such a mission, by the French government. It is possible that they had heard Lili's story. I don't know, or maybe I have forgotten. I know I didn't ask for the job. I didn't want it. The possibility of finding Lili was too remote to be contemplated. She was one of millions.

Belsen came first: the furnaces used for burning corpses were still smoking. To enter the camp area we had to wear gas masks, protective clothing and gloves. Once inside, all we could do was wander among the half dead, murmuring useless words, trying to avoid the eyes of men and women who were not much more than skeletons in rags.

I was shown the files in the administration section, the bills and receipts, neatly typed and rubber stamped, "We beg to acknowledge delivery of your improved gas chambers. We have found them most efficient."

I discovered that Dr. Zadoc-Kahn and his wife had died here, gentle old friends. The Nazis kept careful records. They had been stripped, shaved and had their spectacles taken away from them. I saw collections of spectacles, false teeth and human hair in the hut labeled "Stores."

Hamburg-Neuengamme had been a camp for children; it was now empty. When the guards heard that the British were approaching, they took the children who were still alive and hanged them. They wished to hide what they had been doing, but the bodies were found, and post-mortem examinations showed that the children had been used for experiments, injected with various bacilli and kept under observation. I saw the medical reports, signed by a Dr. Trebinski and SS Kurt Heissmeyer.

Going through the list of dead children I found the name of my cousin Armand's son, Georges André Kohn, age twelve. Later I heard what had happened to the rest of his family. My aunt Marie Jeanne Kohn, age seventy-two, her son Armand, his wife and their four children were deported in a cattle truck. Tante Marie Jeanne had turned up at the station with her clothes and toiletries neatly packed by her maid, and the Croix de Guerre and the ribbon of the Legion d'Honneur pinned to her breast, next to the yellow star. She explained to the SS man in charge that she was quite unable to climb into the truck as there was no step, and in any case she was used to traveling first class.

It was at the time of the Allied advance, and no one thought the train would ever get to Germany; nevertheless half the deportees decided to make their escape. Cousin Armand forbade his children to go with them.

"No harm will come to us. Let us stay together."

Philippe, age nineteen, and his eighteen-year-old sister Rose Marie defied their father, jumped for it and survived. The rest went on to meet their terrible end. Only Armand came home, brought back half dead. My aunt Marie Jeanne walked to the gas chamber at Auschwitz.

In the POW camp at Lübeck, standing among a crowd of French officers, handsome, tall, smiling at me, who should I see but André Wisner, my André, my oldest friend. It was the one bright moment in that ghastly landscape.

One day I heard that Lili had been taken to Königsberg. Was there any way of getting there? Useless, said the British, all the inmates had been evacuated to Ravensbrück, and that was now in the Russian zone. There was no chance of getting through.

Back in Paris I was given a sound ticking off for not sending better reports on what I had seen.

A Commission for the Relief of French Deportees had been set up, its headquarters in that same Hotel Lutetia which had housed the gestapo during the Occupation. I went there for the second or third time to ask if any news of my wife had been received. A group of French women had just arrived, not long out of Ravensbrück. They looked as if they had risen from the grave. Among them one recognized me. I looked again. It was Tania, Comtesse de Fleurieu, Pierre's cousin, a brave woman in the Resistance. She had been very lovely but now all her teeth were smashed. They had beaten her across the mouth. She knew about Lili, she had been there, in the same hut.

Beaten, degraded and too broken to move, Lili had been dragged from her plank bed by the hair of her head and thrown into the oven alive.

She died because she had borne my name, there was no doubt about that, but how did they know? She had called herself de Chambure. Had she been indiscreet? She must have been. Was she denounced? It's possible. I wanted to let it rest. I did not make any more inquiries, and to this day I have never received official notification of her death.

Our married life had long since broken up, that you will have noted. When? Difficult to say—one stops then starts again for all sorts of reasons. I had proved too much for her from the outset. She was jealous, I was promiscuous. She blamed me for the way our son was born, but I knew that it was rather the fierceness of her feeling against me which was the cause. His death was the end of us. Yet she was loyal, a dutiful wife and mother. She had done all she could to help when I was in prison, and I was considerate where she was concerned. All the time I was in England I had tried to watch over her, to guide her. She had many messages and letters from me by the underground post, though some, I must say, were disapproving. I did not much care for Lili's behavior during the German Occupation. Why had they taken her? Lili dead obsessed me more than she'd ever done alive. Poor pretty woman, until they came for her that morning her life had been so easy, all silk and roses.

I have heard that someone told her she would have done better to have remained as she was, the name Rothschild would only bring her harm.

"Whatever it may bring, it has brought me more joy than sorrow," she replied. I hope she did say that.

21

For Mercy has a human heart,
Pity a human face,
And Love, the human form divine,
And Peace, the human dress.

WILLIAM BLAKE

MAY 8, 1945—peace? The French were tearing each other's hearts out. There were accusations, counteraccusations, bitter recriminations: the most respectable reputations, the nicest names, were being dragged through the mud, and the jails were getting so full that the old inhabitants, veteran streetwalkers, pimps and petty thieves, were having to move over to make room for all the distinguished ladies and gentlemen accused of collaboration. The Resistance had already polished off quite a few without waiting for trial by jury. The trainloads of men and women arriving at the Gare de l'Est, wearing the striped uniform of the camps, drew tears and a burning desire for revenge. The trials were speeded up, so were the executions.

Pierre Laval took poison in the prison at Fresnes, where Lili was last heard of. They managed to revive him sufficiently to take him out and shoot him. Many were let off, many had run off, others were kept locked up: Pétain, for instance, for life. Later, as the storm died down, de Gaulle started handing out pardons. That was when people like Paul Morand came drifting back, without having changed their opinions one iota.

I was fascinated by the accusers and the accused. I went out of my way to attend the trial of Admiral Esteva in Paris, a typical navy man, erect, spare, sharp eyed.

"You called on German parachutists and Italian forces to assist the French fleet under your command, and held Bizerte against the British and Americans from November 24, 1942, to May 1943?"

He shrugged his shoulders slightly and gave the usual answer. He was obeying the orders of Marshal Pétain.

I couldn't sustain the loathing I had felt for the criminals. Angry feelings soon died in me. It's not that I'm a pacifist, far from it, but of what use is revenge? Shooting a man against a prison wall will not bring his victims back to life. But, of course, I was one of the lucky ones—I had escaped. Those of us who had been exiles were almost the only ones above suspicion, apart from the dead.

After the politicians, the army and the navy, came showbiz. One after another the idols were pelted with muck. Yes, they had sung and danced for the enemy, performed in Germany, performed in bed. The men were cross because C— had always been a woman's woman till she met her German officer—it was a slight on French virility—and if poor M—— L—— had not been in an automobile accident while out driving with her German, nobody would have been the wiser. If I were to name all those stars of yesterday, or show you their now aged faces, I doubt whether you would turn a hair. Then it was different; spitting on gods recently brought down has always been a popular show, but people soon forget.

Louis Jouvet—the real one, not my smuggler—put up a large map in the foyer of his theater when he returned to Paris with his company after the liberation. He wanted everyone to know exactly where he had been during the Occupation.

I was surprised to hear that Jean Prouvost, who had been our most famous newspaper proprietor, was on the run, under threat of arrest. The fact that he had sustained the only non-collabo newspaper *Sept Jours* throughout the war was forgotten. It was enough that he had worked for Vichy in 1940, for one month. I got a message to him by Hervé Mille or Gaston Bonheur, I've forgotten which, offering to let him lie low at Mouton till the hunt was called off, which he did.

The one man who should have been shot was Pétain, the hero of Verdun. The people of France had trusted him, venerated him, and he had betrayed them. From time to time, his followers have tried to exonerate him, even wanting to dig him up and rebury him at Verdun. I was approached for my support quite recently; I would have none of it.

When I went back to Bordeaux after my visit to the camps, I was shocked to find one of my oldest friends imprisoned as a collaborator. It was Louis Eschenauer, doyen of wine merchants, Uncle Louis to all the wine growers in the Médoc.

What had happened? I knew he came from a German family, though born and brought up in France. He had always had links with German wine merchants; Kurt Böhmers, Nazi-appointed wine führer for the Bordeaux region, had learned all he knew about our wines from Louis long before the war.

When he was sent to Bordeaux during the Occupation, Böhmers at once set out to find his old master. Louis agreed to advise the German, and at his trial pleaded that by doing so he had helped to preserve the standard of our wines. Also that it was his friendship with the Nazis which had saved the Bordeaux bridge: he had interceded with them when he heard that they meant to blow it up. It was the usual type of plea and was not accepted.

The memory of the Bordeaux hostages and the yellow star were still fresh in people's minds and, it was maintained, Louis had not only worked with the Germans but enjoyed a social life with them, attending race meetings and such. One or two of the wine merchants disagreed. They felt that he was an honorable man who had been caught in a trap. I knew the minister of justice and offered to intervene. I did so and was refused.

He is safer in prison, I was told. Six months later, he was released.

"I want to shake hands with Philippe de Rothschild, if it's the last thing I do," he said. He was in fact a dying man. I invited him to a meal at Mouton. When he saw me he broke down. I did not want to hear his story but he had to tell it. Three days later he died.

At Mouton a delegation came to me, intending to denounce two men to the authorities. Why? They had been too friendly with *them*. I took the two aside. One was the bookkeeper, an old man, the other had worked in the cellars. I didn't know him.

"You'd better go or there'll be trouble. Maybe when things cool down you can come back."

The old man returned a year later and worked with me until he retired.

There'd been enough of hatred. I wanted to see Frenchman reconciled with Frenchman. As if that could ever be. Sometimes it seems that France has never recovered from those bitter years: Frenchmen rending Frenchmen has become a national sport. I felt I had no right to judge my fellowmen because I did not know whether I would have had the courage to stand up to torture and death. Most of us find it easier to drift with the tide. I had been angry with Duff Cooper in England during the war when he threw the word in my teeth. "Another French collaborator," he'd say, repeating some unpleasant tidbit. Would England have done any better if she'd been occupied?

Duff Cooper certainly changed his tune when he came to Paris as ambassador in 1944. The embassy was said to be a hive of collabos. The difficulty lies in identifying them, was Duff's excuse, but his judgment may easily have been swayed by his affair with La Vilmorin, my one-time flame Louise, who was by no means free from taint, having spent a good deal of her war careening round Germany with a Hungarian husband.

The only peace I could find was at Mouton, walking among the vines, but what was I going to do with the hundreds of

"collaborators" camping in the park there, our German prisoners? They were billeted in their own huts, guarded by the
FFI. It struck me that they might as well make themselves useful, instead of sitting around, smoking. They could clear up
some of the bloody mess they had made, for a start. What was
I supposed to do with that damn great tower with the gun
emplacement on it? I got permission to put these chaps to
work, and they went to it willingly enough, bored with their
enforced idleness, and none too eager to go home.

The park at d'Armailhacq was now completely overgrown.
The old Comte de Ferrand had died soon after the Occupation, and the roof had been blown off the half château during
the bombing of Pauillac. The Germans had patched it up with
any old stuff. I hadn't been able to do anything about d'Armailhacq before the war; now I had an army at my disposal. I
set them to work clearing the park, demolishing broken-down
sheds and fences and making a road to the southern boundary,
on the Pontet Canet side.

My old team began to reassemble. Édouard Marjary arrived
with his 'sonsy' wife, Hélène, on his arm. We embraced, delighted to find ourselves alive and kicking. Smiling Eusèbe returned, Raoul Blondin was back from Germany, reunited with
his sweetheart, his dark beauty, Henriette; she had been a girl
working in the chai when he left. I inspected the vines with
Marjary. They had been well cared for. Albert Blondin took
me aside.

"Come with me, monsieur."

We walked the length of the chai, then through the door at
the far end. Why was he taking me to the old storage dump?
He wasn't. It was no longer there. Instead there was a wall
covered with algae.

"You had no sooner left than I sent for Blanchard, the stone
mason. All your best wines are behind that wall, monsieur. We
didn't want Goering to get them."

"The first one we bring out will be for you, Albert."

"The wall was well done, wasn't it, monsieur? We had a job
with the moss, though."

The old house itself had been the officers' quarters. Strange people: they had kept a vase of flowers under my mother's portrait all the time they were there. But all my furniture had gone; they'd auctioned it. The FFI attacks hadn't damaged the fabric of the house, but afterwards, when they were in occupation, floorboards had been ripped up for fires, and the walls had been left spattered with mud and blood.

We could find plasterers and carpenters—that wasn't difficult, everybody was out of work—but I'd no ready money to buy materials and pay the men.

I decided that I would have to sell something, yet I could not bear the thought of parting with any of my treasures. There was that Sèvres dinner service, made by the workers in their homes during the revolution of 1789. It wasn't very pretty, the colors were dingy, but it was a collector's dream.

Nobody offered to buy.

Jane de Fleurieu helped me out.

"You can pay me back when you have it."

I thanked her. I knew I would be able to lay my hands on some money once I got down to the problem. All I could think of at the moment was pulling Mouton together. My lost furniture began, mysteriously, to reappear, and work started on the house, so I had no alternative but to clear out and busy myself somewhere else. It might be a good idea to salvage my mind, if anything remained of it. I had one or two half formulated ideas for films, so I located Gaston Bonheur—he was in Paris trying to settle to his old job, journalism, but none too happy about it —and suggested we might work together on a couple of film treatments I had in mind. He was quite keen, and for weeks we spent every spare minute composing a wildly romantic scenario. It was to be pure escapism: no whistling bombs, Resistance fighters or camps, just love-in-a-mist, but it wouldn't come right. The story was feeble; there was no humor in it. Then Marie Edmée turned up again and that was wonderful. We went dancing and swimming, played and made love. It was my postwar honeymoon, but in the early morning or the too-long afternoon, my postwar blues would be lying there with me and nothing could banish them. Life without a purpose tasted stale.

I tried my second idea on Gaston, but he was beginning to talk like a journalist.

"How many thousand words do you think, this time?"

I made a synopsis and this one didn't click either. Dammit, I'll come back to it another time. I turned over the idea of developing the lens factory, which had originally been one of my father's interests. I had kept up to date with the development of optics, but when I checked up I saw that, like the rest of our property, it was all tied up in governmental red tape, so that idea was stillborn too.

Pierre de Fleurieu had a scheme for selling good tea—I started work on a ballet.

My God, I was getting like my father, a dabbler. I fled back to Mouton. There was an enormous improvement. The workmen had finished and lovely Jane de Fleurieu had organized a squadron of cleaning ladies who'd scrubbed and scoured until the last trace of occupation had gone forever. How had they managed to get all the fabrics so clean without soap? There was none to be had anywhere. They had returned to their grandmothers' methods—used cinders.

As soon as two rooms were habitable I went to Escrignelles to fetch my daughter. I wanted her with me. She was sorry to leave her schoolfriends but delighted to see Mouton again and to be with me.

The park at d'Armailhacq was cleared and the road finished. It had taken four months, but it looked good—a wide graveled avenue, running from Mouton to Pontet-Canet. Even today when I look at it I say, "There it is, my road of revenge."

The wilderness which had threatened to overwhelm d'Armailhacq had been hacked away and in the spring wild cyclamen reappeared in the shadow of the old house. I had a magnificent stretch of land to call my own, so I began planting trees: magnolia, cedar, cypress and the lovely lagerstroemia, which only grows in the Bordeaux region. To mark the entrance to the park I brought out two tall eighteenth-century urns, found in England long ago, and threw the whole place open to the public. Everybody told me I was mad; it would all be vandalized. It wasn't. I saw one or two local schoolboys stoning ducks one day—I caught one and tanned his backside and that was the end of that. I don't like barriers, keepers, notices telling people to keep off the grass, and there are none. It's my park but I'm happy to share it.

Philippine settled in at Mouton and soon made new friends. I began to feel that I should do the same. It seemed to be the right place for us. But could I settle anywhere? We all know what they say about rolling stones, and what about the chap in the Bible who planted his vines, built his presses and his wine store, then cleared off to some far-away country for a very long time? Nothing came of that. He lost his vines, his wines and his beloved son and heir. What was he doing in that faraway country? Just playing, time wasting, amusing himself, probably. At least I'd written a few lines of poetry. No, if you plant a vineyard, you have to stay with it. It's worse than marriage, but it's the only way to get good wine . . . and good poetry.

"Wine, bewitching wine, which sets even a wise man to singing and to laughing gently, and rouses him up to dance and bring forth words which were better unspoken." Yes, Monsieur Homer, but where would all our occasions be without it, the first night of love and the last, the wedding, the christening, the funeral and coming back to Mouton after so long absence and abstinence. The first glass I drank put me on my back. Apart from all that, wine, like the devil, has all the best tunes.

> Fill every glass for wine inspires us
> And fires us with courage, love and joy.
> Is there aught else on earth desirous?
> JOHN GAY, *The Beggar's Opera*

My life! If I could make Mouton a place of love and joy, I might stay forever. The only trouble was, it didn't belong to me; Vichy had taken away my French nationality and usurped my inheritance. All I had in exchange were a couple of decorations, the Croix de Guerre and the Legion d'Honneur, which President Coty had handed me. They would not pay the wages.

The nationality problem was solved at the stroke of a pen: all French Jews had their Frenchness restored to them, passports stamped with the word Jew could be burnt, one need no longer be frightened to show one's private part—but I still needed cash. My father wanted to stay in Portugal, so I would have to begin sorting out his affairs, and sooner or later something would have to be done about that great pile of rubble which used to be our Société Vinicole de Pauillac. The whole area had been flattened when the British bombed the town.

While I was in the park one day, planting a blue cedar and brooding over these matters, what should I see walking up my wonderful new driveway but a ram's head. If it had been an ass's head I would not have been surprised. Shakespeare's enchantments could easily unroll in my park at Mouton.

The head, with its curling horns, came closer and under it who should I see but Riette, my London war bride, my lovely Lady Lamington. She couldn't have chosen a more inappropriate time to reappear in my life, but there she was, smiling shyly as she held the head on high, the monstrous head Nancy Mitford had bought for me in Brighton.

I'd no idea where I was going to put it, or the Lady.

22

His opinion was that there was a strange kind of magic bias which good or bad names, as he called them, irresistibly impressed upon our characters and conduct. . . . How many Caesars and Pompeys, he would say, by mere inspiration of the names, have been rendered worthy of them? And how many, he would add, are there who might have done exceeding well in the world, had not their characters and spirits been totally depressed and Nicodemus'd into nothing?

LAURENCE STERNE

THE house was still not entirely habitable, so Philippine had to be made comfortable in a box-room. Riette was given Philippine's room and we all sat down to tea—orange pekoe—in anticipation of a few quiet country days, *en famille.*

Apart from the ram's head, which we left in the rocking chair because there was nowhere ready to receive it, Riette had managed to bring all the needlework samplers I'd bought in Pimlico. I was delighted to have them. I'm always buying things for Mouton, all over the world, and I never know how I'm going to get them back. As it happens, I can't go out anywhere, at any time, without prowling round the first antique shop or flea market I see, and I nearly always buy something. It may be a tuppenny-ha'penny Victorian mug with an amusing pattern, or a classic Bacchus in soapstone. When it does arrive, it has to wait in my dump, *la réserve,* till I find exactly the right place for it.

Riette's first day passed pleasantly enough, with us selecting samplers for the stairway and showing her around, but my heart wasn't in it. Usually I'd be criticizing, rearranging, adjusting every object within sight to a centimeter. I did a little of all that, to be sure, but my worries kept coming up; it was worse than the hiccups. Even the fresh white walls reminded me of the money I owed Jane de Fleurieu.

Goddammit, I was a Rothschild after all, the name must be good for something. I should fix myself some credit, and plenty of it. After that the vines must pay for themselves, Mouton must pay. I needed one of my ideas, a good one.

I had half a one—a publicity stroke, my strong point. I only needed to find the other half. I shut myself up in the tip, laughingly called the office, which I shared with Monsieur Marjary. Riette was left to her own devices—you are—at Mouton, frequently. Philippine had disappeared altogether with Babette, her pet dog. She often did.

The two halves of my idea were coming together, like a happy sandwich. I went into the chai to check up on Jean Carlu's cubist design. I'd had a blown-up version painted on the far wall. Before the war, I'd been mad about it. Funny to think what a furor it had caused in those days, but then so had my rams—and that was the point. Whatever people thought of them they noticed the changes, and sales increased, and that was all any of us really worried about.

You've guessed that I was thinking of—a new label. Well, that wasn't the whole of it, as will be seen.

I told Riette what was in my mind at dinner.

"I can think of something you need much more than a new label," she said.

"Really?"

"A new look. If you don't think so, try sitting in this house all day, on your own. It is very gloomy."

"What do you suggest?"

"Chintz. Sunny chintz everywhere, primrose yellow for preference, with a touch of daffodil. We should be able to get those lovely Lady Hamilton prints again any day. Things are coming back. I actually saw some cramoisie scarves in Harrods the day before yesterday."

I put my nose deeper into Merilda's noodle cake.

At that moment my twelve-year-old came bursting in, late for dinner, disheveled. Without a smile for either of us she took her place at table. I told her to go out and come in again, bringing her smile with her.

Dear Riette, she wouldn't hurt a fly, but as soon as Philippine had left the room she couldn't resist mentioning her bad manners. I knew at once, as Philippine came back, that she'd heard. We didn't get another word out of her all evening, and when Riette and I settled to backgammon she disappeared.

I had tried a wartime vintage for the first time with dinner. It was good wine. I asked to see the bottle. Surprisingly, they had kept my rams on the label and the elegant lettering—Château Mouton Rothschild. What a Jewish name for those Aryan Allemands to find on their table; how could they bring themselves to drink the stuff? They had also kept the record of bottles for each vintage in the style I had instituted long ago—without my signature, naturally. Imagine printing my name on the wine they were pinching from me.

Victory year would have a completely different label; I made up my mind there and then about that.

Riette was yawning. As soon as we finished the game I would see if Philippine was still awake and maybe take a stroll among the vines before turning in.

A slightly tearful voice spoke to me from the darkness:

"How long is she staying, papa?"

"You mean Lady Lamington? Why?"

"I would rather like my room back."

"Of course, poor child. It was sweet of you to let her have it."

"I am not a child, you know, papa."

"No, indeed. In fact I was thinking of asking you to play hostess for me tomorrow. I've an important meeting with Monsieur Marjary and I have to go to Bordeaux."

"What do you want me to do?"

"Entertain Lady L. for me."

"But what can I do with her?"

"Take her to Vertheuil, Fort Médoc, l'église de Moulis; that would make a fascinating tour."

"Yes, papa, maybe I'll take her to the ocean."

"A hostess has to be able to entertain people, you know."

But she was asleep.

The walk among the vines was dismal. Thunder was threatening and all the chained dogs in the village were barking in chorus. I had been stupid about Philippine. Why hadn't it occurred to me before? It wasn't a child I had on my hands but a woman, someone new to take out at night, to show to the world.

"And this is my daughter, Philippine de Rothschild"; but it made me feel middle-aged. How long before I'd have to start thinking about her future, her career, her marriage maybe.

My new idea for the labels was good. Change them every year, give each vintage a personality of its own. Use illustrations of topical events perhaps. What happened in 1946? Nothing very amusing. Gandhi screwing the British, de Gaulle the French. Well, they might do for corkscrews but you couldn't put their holy faces on a wine label. Forget events. Better to find the right artist and leave the design to him. For Victory Year, Oberlé and the young artist I'd met in England, Jullian. Bébé Bérard would be marvelous, but he'd never bother himself with a design the size of five postage stamps. He had painted Lili's portrait in 1942 at Jean Hugo's house, near Nîmes. Jean Hugo, there was another idea, an artist himself and a discriminating wine bibber. I would offer wine in payment for the label. Wine for art. Art for wine, five cases of the year of the label and five of any year of his choice.

I was so excited about artists and new designs that I even told the bank manager all about it the next day. I got all the credit I asked for, and more. It must have been a wonderful idea; all that remained was to implement it.

That evening my two women came home dusty, bedraggled and rather silent. Weren't they on speaking terms? I cornered Philippine. "Is there anything wrong?"

"It's your fault, papa. You obviously want me to be a prissy little English miss."

"Why do you say that?"

"Why does Lady L. keep correcting my manners?"

"Well, perhaps they are a little neglected, Toto."

She turned away from me. I didn't quite know what to make of her mood. It wasn't always easy to understand her, this lonely child growing into young womanhood without a mother. How much did she know about what had happened to Lili? I didn't think the loss of her mother had affected her deeply. How could I be sure? It was long after, a very long time after that, I noticed her mother's picture beside her bed. It is still there.

"You're not thinking of marrying again, are you, papa?"

"No, why should you think that?"

"I just thought. Please don't ever do so on my account. One parent is quite enough for me. And if you want me to speak English and know how to handle *le style Anglais,* why not send me to school there? I'd much rather that than some amateur governess you found somewhere."

My daughter has always known her own mind and nearly always had her own way. I had also known that ever since Riette arrived there had been a certain design in her pretty head, and I felt sure that sharp little Philippine had sensed it too. God knows Mouton needed a mistress and doubtless Toto would be the better for a good mother, but the two of them hadn't exactly clicked. In the end, it was the thought of all that sunny chintz which finished it. Something told me Riette would never be right for Mouton. I have always been frank with my women. I resolved to make a clean breast of things, as soon as I could face it. The only problem was not to hurt her. With some women you don't mind, but she was really a sweetie.

She said nothing but she left early the next morning, went back to her little flat near Lancaster Gate. She didn't live very long. I never saw her again.

Philippine went to school in England the next year, and became completely bilingual, like the rest of the family.

The quest for labels became a full-time job. They make a neat collection now, thirty-six of them, mounted in a glass case in the Grand Chai, but they were rare specimens, difficult to pin down.

Among the early ones, Philippe Jullian produced the prettiest victory label. others sent us patriotic designs, all red, white and blue. We had to use the rather ugly V-sign popularized by Churchill, but Philippe made it look attractive and the wine was superb.

You could say that though the first were hard to get, the rest came easy, like pickles from a jar. Cocteau was prompt and happy with his design; some of the rest said yes but took seven years to produce anything. It was a relief to arrive at our centenary and use the portrait of my great-grandfather, Nathaniel, painted the year he bought Mouton.

Max Ernst produced a highly unsuitable design and when I turned it down he gave the job to his wife, Dorothea Tanning. Delvaux worked on a design for a while and sent it to me. It was beautiful but he changed his mind at the last moment and withdrew it, because he thought it was being used for advertising. Nothing I wrote could persuade him, so I went to Brussels to plead with him. No go. But I had a wonderful time talking, drinking, envying his virility, nearly ninety and a beautiful woman at his side.

The famous were all difficult and the obscure too eager. Bona was almost unknown, the artist wife of a friend, but her design was very pretty, and so was she. Though I assure you that was not why I chose her. Look at the list and you'll find that the other women were already famous.

Dali took the whole thing as a joke, but then everything about him was a joke too, especially the place where he lived—a rock face of shelving levels, hung with nets and shells, his bed balanced somewhere on the top.

It was very difficult to turn down designs, often magnificent but useless on a bottle. My fault. I should never have approached artists whose paintings would be more at home on the Empire State Building than on a label 10 centimeters × 3.5 centimeters.

In 1973, after handling the job myself for nearly thirty years, I asked my friend the Baroness Cary de Vendeuvre to take over. Her first assignment was a tough one—the Picasso label. He had said we might use it, but only after his death. I wanted it for '73, the year Mouton Rothschild was legally accepted as a *premier cru*. Picasso was dead by then, but his affairs were in such a tangle that I thought the design lost. Cary sorted it out. She knew the artist's daughter, Paloma, took tea with her in the Café de Flore and persuaded her to let us use the design.

Queen Elizabeth's acceptance of the 1977 dedication was a joy to me, and an honor for Mouton. The Queen Mother stayed with us that year during her official tour of the Médoc. All along the route from Bordeaux to Pauillac people came out to cheer her on her way. In her speech to the citizens of Pauillac assembled in the town hall, she felt she had to mention the British air raid which had caused severe loss of life in that small town. The mayor replied that it was the price which had to be paid for liberty.

France has always been very dear to her. In June 1940, our darkest hour, she broadcast a message from London:

> I want tonight to express to all the women of France, of
> that glorious heroic France fighting at this very moment,
> not only in defense of its frontiers but for the freedom of
> the whole world, the affection and admiration that their
> suffering and their courage evoke in our hearts. We salute
> the leaders and the soldiers of the French army, but also
> the women of France, anxiously watching the development
> of the gigantic struggle in which their sons, their husbands

or brothers are engaged. For myself I, who have always loved France, suffer at this hour with you.

I hope the love of England for France will endure forever. My love for this gracious lady will outlive me—the lady they call the Queen Mum.

23

L'autre la nommait sa branche de corail.

RABELAIS

My inheritance, how lordly wide and fair.

GOETHE

Lez moi vos coucherez tot nuz
Pour avoir plus pleasant delict.

ANCIENS FABLIAUX

I have put most of my cards on the table and if you haven't taped me by now you never will. What's on my label? Full bodied, rich red, sparkling, blended, dry? I'd like to be around to read the post-mortem edition. At least I've made no secret of my wickedness, nor has anybody much ever reproached me for it. I don't think I am wicked: in fact I'm a rather conventional person, and dislike brazen behavior, particularly in woman.

For a while in the postwar gloom my fires burned low, but then a breeze from the south kindled them—my lovely Marie Edmée, sweet on the tongue, light on the palm of your hand, the prettiest woman I've ever had. We would spend a few days together, then go our ways, but I always took care to keep her warm because the others were really nothing but hors d'oeuvres to raise my appetite for the main dish.

All the same, I take great pleasure in the unforeseen, a sudden prick of venery while sheltering under the same umbrella, an unexpected encounter in the lift, a hand under the table at a formal dinner, knee tremblers, one-night stands, passing gropes, all the embroideries on the breeches of the almighty *branche de corail*.

I make two exceptions. I never deflower and I do not persist if the lady doesn't want me—there are plenty more fish. And don't think I don't have pure friendships with all the sexes; after the fluttering dies down, the feeling for me often endures. (Sometimes annoyingly, as when after only one incident, she attaches herself to you for life.)

Once I'd settled down at Mouton I took to spending my summers with my princess: Marinetta. Well, before the war when I first knew her, she had been a princess, since then she'd stepped down to marry a count.

She took me round her native Italy and she took me in hand. We visited churches—St. Bernardino, St. Domenico, St. Marco, St. Petronio; and palaces—Bartolini, Piccolomini, Rucellai, Giraud-Tortonia. She preferred the churches, where she prayed devoutly for me.

In Rome, where in 1822 my grandmother's grandfather Kalman had prevailed on the Pope to abolish the ghetto, I wanted to look and see if anything remained of the old site.

"No, no," said Marinetta, "you must forget about being a Jew."

"Well, I can't forget being a Rothschild, nor that it was Kalman, with his Rothschild money, who restored the Vatican's failing fortunes, and was allowed to kiss the Pope's hand."

"His ring, Philippe, nobody ever kisses the Pope's hand."

"Well, as Kalman had rescued the kingdom of Naples, drained the Tuscan marshes and repaired half the Roman roads in Italy, I guess the Pope didn't mind what he kissed."

"Philippe, please! Mind what you are saying."

She found me rather upsetting, told me that I was like the rest of my people—stiff necked, cussed and proud. Why couldn't we eat pork chops and settle down?

"We are God's chosen people, Marinetta. We couldn't die out and let him down."

"All this pride gets you into a great deal of trouble."

"We're used to it. Long before Jesus of Nazareth Jews were having their tabernacles smashed, but we were a pastoral people, good at packing—even our tabernacles folded up. We should have been able to avoid trouble, except that whenever we were crossing those deserts or wine-red seas, there was always somebody crooning, which may possibly explain how pogroms began."

She sighed, folded her hands and listened.

"It was wandering all over those frontiers, Marinetta, which gave the smart ones ideas about international banking and *bureaux de change*. On the other hand, there were many good doctors among us, the community suffering, as it did, from the effects of their mothers' good Jewish cooking."

"I must say I've always admired the way the Jews take care of their relations."

"They had to. With their distinctive clothing and choiffure, they were an easy target for anyone who didn't like the look of them. They simply had to stick together for mutual protection, but when it came to camping under city walls, they were asking for trouble. I guess they only risked it in the hope of a little barter. Naturally, when plague or earthquake struck, or the neighbor's wife had an unexpected baby, it was blamed on those weird devils out there in the park, and they had to get going again.

"One dark night in thirteenth century Frankfurt, two thousand Jews didn't move fast enough. A city elder suggested that the survivors should be walled up in a small section of the city, with strong gates which could be locked at night, and on Mother Church's holy days. There they would be safe, family planning could be introduced by limiting their marriages to twelve a year—since there seemed to be some danger of their seed outnumbering the stars, as prophesied in their holy book —and of course they would be glad to pay protection money and be thankful for their new home, the ghetto. The word comes from Italy, dear Marinetta—('borgetto.') Nevertheless, we must never forget that Italy was kind to a persecuted people in the recent great pogrom, and a service rendered to a Jew is never lost."

"Thank you, Philippe."

"As Amschel Meyer said, the father of our house."

She had listened patiently enough, but I could see she wasn't very impressed.

"That is all very well, but it doesn't excuse your speaking so disrespectfully of the Pope, and you don't mention any naughty Jews."

"Come to bed and I'll show you one."

But in that respect I could do nothing with her. She just couldn't be too sexy, she was too shy and well mannered. We flirted and argued, she was erudite and witty, a perfect companion, except when she tried to improve my manners, my way of dressing and of course my dangerous background. She thought there was no hope for me without baptism.

In July 1947 the art tour had to be curtailed; my father died suddenly. He was seventy-five. I hadn't expected it, he didn't seem old to me. I found it very sad, the thought of him dying without seeing his own country again, without having his property restored to him, that is what was left of it.

His yacht was no more, it had been commandeered by the Nazis and sunk by the British. Four-fifths of his art treasures had been lost; he had sent them to England when the war broke out, but they had been destroyed in the bombing. Only one of his eighteen Chardins survived, the exquisite *Girl with the Shuttlecock*, and I have it. Last year she toured the world.

Disentangling my father's affairs was a nightmare. There were donations and gifts in his will, properties we couldn't trace; there was poor little Marthe Régnier. Meanwhile everything was in the hands of the state. Nothing would be released until the deeds, titles and securities secreted all over the place by friends, or Jardot's faithful team, had been located and verified.

A year after his death, it was all settled, and Mouton was ours to be divided equally between Nadine, James and myself.

Three bosses? My team was horrified.

"Don't worry," said Monsieur Marjary. "Our Philippe always gets his own way, and now he's a baron he'll be throwing his weight about more than ever."

That was true; I was thoroughly enjoying my new role. At first I'd turn my head looking for a baron, but I soon got used to it. Not that it's to be taken too seriously—a Habsburg barony, 1822, in republican France? Originally it was awarded to every member of my family in perpetuity by Emperor Ferdinand, so that he could keep some of the Rothschild weath in his anti-Semitic empire. I find it useful, though. In this world, titles will always count.

The other new baron and baroness, James and Nadine, were comfortably settled in their own lives; both served good wine at their table but that was as far as their interest went. Mouton had long been Philippe's baby. It might stop him running after women and driving fast cars all over the place. They enjoyed their share of the wine, but neither of them ever thought of visiting the place, or asking to see a balance sheet. I decided to buy them out.

There was no problem; nobody wanted any disagreement at such a time. Nadine's banker son, Jacques Thierry, took care of the details. We all decided that we'd done rather well out of the deal. Nadine and James thought hard cash was more to the point than an estate in deficit; I had my beloved Mouton, and my team there breathed a sigh of relief. There wasn't much that didn't come to my ears. They had me well weighed up: "He never seems to be listening to us, but he does." "He shouts and bawls and throws his boots at the ceiling, but his heart's in the right place." "Very hard to please, but he makes you laugh."

Well, at least after twenty-five years we knew each other and I believed that, underneath it all, they were proud to work for

Mouton, and for themselves. I had devised a system whereby each vigneron worked his own plot of land and was paid according to its yield. As a result we have never had a strike; but then, of course, we have never had a trade union either, except among the office workers.

The postwar years were tough. In the countryside there was an equality—of poverty. Many of the small châteaus stood empty, their owners departed or dead, and dying vineyards were a common sight. What could be done to introduce a little good cheer? A touch of glamour might help. I thought of reviving the club I'd started before the war, my Commanderie du Bontemps: if it were tuned up, given some *cachet*, we could invite distinguished visitors to the Médoc and receive them in style. Each member would have to be an authority on Bordeaux wines. To do the thing properly there should be a robe of office for official occasions, and why not a title for every member— "commander"?

Monsieur Marjary revised the rules, we formed a committee and I designed the costume: a flowing medieval robe, wine colored, with a toque to represent the *bontemps* itself, the *bontemps* being the wooden bowl into which we tip the white of egg which clarifies the wine. Funny thing to put on your head? It looked splendid. For the white of egg I had a froth of beige silk, for the bowl of a circlet of dark velvet.

If you want to see our commanders in full regalia, come to the mass of St. Vincent at Pauillac on September 27; it's then that we go to church in solemn procession to pray for a good harvest. Did you know that Vincent only became the patron saint of wine because of his first syllable? How do I know? The archbishop of Bordeaux, Monsignor Richaud, told me so.

As the 1940s drew to their unlamented close, there was more sadness and upheaval in the family—this time at Lafite. Like my father, Robert, the good-looking baron, died in exile. He left when the Nazis came, and never returned.

On June 30, 1949, Édouard, the elder cousin, died. He was eighty-one. He had always been kind to me and I felt his loss keenly. His son, Guy, replaced him as head of the bank. One of Robert's two sons, Alain, became a leader of the Jewish community in France, and Élie, the younger one, took over the running of Lafite on behalf of his brother and his cousins Guy and Dollie.

Élie at once took an interest in the commanderie and all the affairs of the Médoc, and I was delighted. Later I wished he had stayed at home.

A bitter feud developed between our two houses, which had strong roots: family jealousy and rivalry between the House of Lafite, descended from Banker James, born Jacob in the Frankfurt ghetto, and youngest of the five original brothers, and the House of Mouton from Nathaniel, son of Nathan, son of Amschel, the brilliant, irascible genius who ran the show from London.

Nathan's son simply could not understand the family obsession with money making. "I find it sheer madness, jumping into the bath up to your neck in the hope of gaining a few more sous. My dear uncles are ridiculous with their love of business for its own sake."

So he and Charlotte, his wife, turned to other amusements: traveling, collecting books and paintings, among them the Chardins, an unusual taste then—a "modern" painter, the bankers of the family preferred old masters. Charlotte was herself an artist, and I have a collection of her water colors at Mouton. They are lovely.

My father's history and character I have already tried to unfold for you. So we have, on one side of the family, books, theater, poetry—on the other, banking, politics, hunting, shooting and fishing.

Cousin Élie of Lafite shoots, hunts and is president of a chain of hotels. He was on the Maginot Line in 1940, taken prisoner, tried to escape, caught and sent to Colditz. He married a childhood sweetheart, by proxy, while still in prison and, after nearly five years of captivity, came home fighting fit.

On my right, Dashing Élie, age thirty; on my left, Battling

Philippe, age forty-five, both quick on their feet and both Rothschilds: that is to say, quite unable to take orders from anyone, each utterly convinced that he is Number One.

To cap it all, you could spit on Lafite from the tower at Mouton.

Trouble ahead.

24

Let us ponder this basic fact about the human:
Ahead of every man, not behind him, is a
woman.

JAMES THURBER

ONE fine day in 1950 I found I had accepted an invitation from Hervé Mille to what promised to be an amusing luncheon party, but of course you never know. So, to be sure of not missing anything, I accept all invitations and take the rough with the smooth.

A tall, striking-looking woman arrived rather late, and I didn't catch her name. I found myself placed next to her at table. Her French was impeccable, but her amazing chic was not French. I tried English; her English was perfect, but the studied charm of her accent was not English. I usually plunge in with "Who are you? Where do you come from?" But she was telling a story and everybody was listening. She was an amusing person; the whole room was smiling. I noticed the place card near her hand and quickly slipped it under my napkin: Pauline Potter. Everybody else seemed to know her. Where had I been? The situation would have to be remedied, at once, before we finished the asparagus. I'd tried one or two jokes; they didn't go down too badly. Over the cheese, she asked my name. I did my baron act, it sometimes works. It didn't. I corrected myself: Philippe de Rothschild, I said.

"Oh, the poet!" she replied. I don't know how she knew. I have never made a song and dance about my poems. I asked if she would lunch with me. She accepted. Long afterwards she told me that I fell asleep over the coffee. I don't believe I did —I was too fascinated by Miss Potter, already in her forties who, once she was away from the glittering set which gathered round her, had the naïveté of a nun. She wouldn't talk about herself but I knew that this bird of paradise had not spent much time preening herself in the sun. I didn't need to be told that she had not had a very happy life. They told me she was one of the highest-paid women in America. I asked what she did—not that I was particularly interested; she had walked into my life and I wanted to keep her there. I did not care what she had done before.

A dress designer? She was certainly a lot more than that. I invited her to Mouton. She came, bringing her friends, David Bruce, American ambassador in Paris at the time, and his wife, Evangeline. She fell in love with the place. I fell in love with her. (Well, I think that had happened a little earlier, almost the moment I saw her—"Who ever loved that loved not at first sight?" and all that.)

I told her she could come back to Mouton whenever she wished, and stay as long as she liked. Next time she stayed.

One could never be quite sure when she would emerge from her room, but one teatime when there'd been no sign of life all day, I went to look for her. She was in her bath reading, a magnum of champagne beside her, unopened.

"Didn't they bring you a glass?"

"I didn't ask for one. I only wanted to look at it."

And she sank back into the perfumed water, turning the page of her book.

"What are you reading?"

"St. Augustine's *City of God*, a very good read."

I found the lady's taste in books unaccountable. All fashionable books were quickly devoured—romances, philosophies, autobiographies; no sociology, no politics. Ancient esoterics from every known culture, except Greek and Hindu, filled the lower shelves in her room. She collected coffee-table art books, kept every catalogue of every private view she attended, her impressions carefully penciled in against marginal sketches for reminders. She had every known history of costume, jewelry and furniture, and critial works from Vitruvius to Mumford. No music, dancing or theater. She hated music. I found that a little sad. Later, when she told me her story, I knew why.

Her father, Francis, had been a ne'er-do-well with social pretensions, almost a caricature of the gentleman con man from the deep South; her mother, Gwendolen, a sweet, eighteen-year-old flibbertigibbet from Baltimore, her genteel relations rich enough to persuade Mr. Potter he was on to a good thing.

After a smart wedding in London he took his bride to Paris, leaving a trail of unpaid bills behind him. In Paris, more unpaid bills. When Pauline was a year old, Mr. Potter vanished. He reappeared twelve years later, looking for his daughter. By then Gwendolen had become a hopeless drunkard, trekking from one cheap hotel to another, relying on casual lovers and occasional money orders from home for her sustenance.

The prodigal husband found his wife and daughter in a mean hotel room. They were half starved—Pauline suffering from rheumatic fever—on the table a huge bouquet of lilies and white lilac.

Mr. Potter had a rich woman in tow who sweetly offered to take Pauline away. Mrs. Potter cried, Pauline clung to her feckless mother. Mrs. Potter declared that it was only right that the father should get to know his daughter and to love her, that he had been deprived of her sweet company too long. So Pauline went off to a good meal, and Mrs. Potter went back to her endless traipsing round the fourth-class hotels of Paris.

Back in Baltimore, Pauline was adopted by a series of elderly aunts and great-aunts, who seemed to die off or move just as she was getting to know them. Two years of this and she ran off, looking for her father. When she found him, he was busy with a new family. He threw some dollars at her and told her that was it, she would get no more from him. So it was back to Baltimore. She heard that her mother had been found dead in some sordid hotel in Brussels, age thirty-six.

Pauline gilded her hair, wore garish dresses which she designed herself and looked for a way out—a career, marriage, any escape route would do. She fixed her sights on a local celebrity, a tasteful designer, heavy drinker, restorer of old paintings, well connected and one hundred percent homosexual.

Pauline designed the entire wedding, the church filled with white lilies, lit by giant candles, her frock—gold satin, to go with her bright gold hair. When she appeared, very late, everybody gasped. She carried an ivory-covered prayer book and a lily, but it was her train that caused the sensation. . . . It was very, very long. Although Pauline was always late for everything, on this occasion she had been stalling, waiting for her father to come and give her away. He didn't show up.

The morning after her wedding night, the maids at the hotel found her clothes ripped to pieces, the newlyweds—nowhere to be seen.

As for her father, she saw him again once by chance, just before the Second World War. She was walking along Fifth Avenue.

"Excuse me, but aren't you Francis Potter?"

"Yes?"

"I'm your daughter."

He was flustered, muttered a few flattering words, made a lunch date and again failed to turn up.

That was that. She did not forgive him. After she'd told me her story she never mentioned his name again. She refused to attend his funeral.

That father of hers had been a compulsive piano player; apart from conning people, it was his only activity. Perhaps that was why she hated music.

Not long before our first Christmas together at Mouton, Pauline disappeared. I was told she had gone to Bordeaux, and when night came and there was no word I set off to find her. I drove round the town; it was nearly two in the morning, but one shop on the main street was ablaze with lights. There she was, wandering around a toy shop, while an assistant slept in a hammock.

A rap on the window—"What are you doing?"

She unbolted the door. "It's very difficult choosing the right present for each child."

"I didn't know you had children."

"It's for the children of Mouton, silly one."

"There must be rather a lot of them."

"There are one hundred and two." She had them listed, name, age, sex.

"It will soon be Christmas, and that has to be done rather well. I would like to decorate the banqueting hall myself, if nobody minds. What would you think of white lilac and lilies of the valley?"

"At Christmas?"

"That's just it, winter will seem like spring."

Christmas and New Year, which I've never liked, became something fresh and different with Pauline—new games, dressing-up parties, excursions to the sea. New Year's Eve was her birthday, which made her very cross. "If only it had been the next day," she said, "I could have been a year younger, at least on my passport." Always, after that first year, the team at Mouton brought her armfuls of white lilac on that day; and at midnight, with all the windows open, we embraced, toasted each other and thanked the gods for the blessed gift of wine. Pauline would organize a procession with candles and music, then the party would begin all over again.

All her ideas were original; one wanted to have her opinion on everything. I would walk her round Mouton, rain or shine. At the time there wasn't much to be proud of, but she found beauty where no one else would, in the steeped roofs of old farmhouses, for example, which reached almost to the ground (we imitated them later when we started rebuilding), the branched wooden pillars supporting the galleries in country churches and the fine proportions of some of the old chais, built by nobody knew who. She didn't like my eighteenth-century urns. Too showy for Mouton, she said. I was curious to know what she'd make of the house, by then filled with Victoriana, mostly discovered in England, and a lot of my favorite knickknacks and whatnots from before the war. "Very Philippe," she said. I wondered what that meant.

She had one or two ideas for improving the house, so clever that when they were tried out you couldn't even see them; they just made the space you moved in more enjoyable.

Nothing escaped her eye: a stitch needed in the corner of a cushion cover, the tiniest speck of dust on my collection of glass wig blocks. You'd never put a wig on them, they're too pretty —light, jazzily decorated globes, very fragile. Pauline was an impeccable housekeeper, and a fascinating companion. I began to think that on no account must this pearl of a woman be allowed to escape.

The only other jewel in my collection was Marie Edmée. It had proved impossible to give up seeing her, even for Pauline:

> How happy could I be with either
> Were t'other dear charmer away.

I managed to keep both my charmers happy until one day, a day of days, I found myself lunching with Marinetta, Marie Edmée and Pauline—with Hervé Mille looking at me satanically across the floral arrangement.

"All your nurses?" he said.

Pauline told me later that she could only admire my taste, and I had been in the pit with Don Juan, flames all around us, throughout the meal. Soon after, staying with an old flame near Beaulieu, I heard that Marie Edmée was near at hand at Lord

Beaverbrook's place and took it into my head to visit them. Things had to be straightened out.

I adored her, my sweet Edmée, but it couldn't go on. I'm sure you don't believe me, but it was tearing me in two. I explained and we said good-bye. She didn't seem unduly surprised or upset. She may have been glad to get rid of me, you never know. We embraced, but we didn't go to bed. I was crying. I felt my heart was broken, and I cried all the way back to Mouton. Pauline seemed to understand. She knew about a lot of my affairs, treated some of them as a joke, though not, I think, this one.

Marie Edmée went to live with Lord Beaverbrook, and shortly after, when that broke up, she became ill. It was cancer. She had to go back to her parents, she was penniless. They were very cold with her—because of me, they said. I heard that she had collapsed and died at the foot of their bed at three o'clock one morning. I still have her photo near me: she was so pretty, almost unreal.

25

Because the birthday of my life
Is come, my love is come to me.

CHRISTINA ROSSETTI

IT is April 13 and I am fifty: half a century! It's always a
frightening date. I'd long since given up celebrating my
birthdays, except secretly of course, but this one was
going to be an exception, and I could hardly wait to share it
with Pauline. She never woke up in the morning, so I had to be
patient. As soon as I dared, I tiptoed into her room. The light
was burning; she was reading.

"You are awake."

"I haven't been to sleep yet. Yes, I do know what day it is but,
as you don't like presents or birthdays, I simply offer you my
good wishes."

"Well, I have a present for you today."

"Is it nice?"

"I have it here."

"Where?"

"In my head."

"That's a problem!"

"No, it's a good idea. It came to me in the night."

"And it's still good this morning? What can it be? A poem?"

"A museum."

"Here in Mouton? Then it will have to be a wine museum."

"It is. 'The vine and wine in art.' Say you like it and it's yours."

"Thank you. I don't just like it. I think it's the most precious present I have ever received."

We talked about it all day. We threw out folklore, farm implements, processes. There would be paintings, statues, tapestries, amphorae, drinking horns, vials and nipperkins, chalices and galipots, anything lovely or amusing that wine has inspired since someone first trod on a bunch of grapes. We would have to comb the world, quite an undertaking, but it was going to be tremendous fun.

First we brought out all the old Rothschild heirlooms which had been stored away and forgotten and selected anything interesting. There were seventeen pieces of silver gilt from my father which Pauline quite liked. Then her eye lighted on the old storage for disused casks, beyond the chai, Aladdin Blondin's secret cave. It was roomy, of good proportions, the very place for our museum.

We worked night and day, practically living in the old chai. It didn't matter to Pauline, who had still to discover the difference between night and day. Cardboard mockups were made of every object and the shelves and showcases which would hold them. They were then placed approximately, and carefully adjusted. Even the pattern of the floor tiles was tried out first in colored paper. Pauline would stand at the door, and I would move the colored squares.

"That one a fraction farther to the right. That's it."

The lighting was my territory, with Pauline as critic. We were aiming at perfection.

Lucky man, I say to myself, as I think of those years with Pauline. We were doing very well, the vineyards were flourishing at last, and all my innovations had been a success.

I believed I was working for the whole of the Médoc, not just for myself. We were opening a window on the world and the prospect was good. Until . . .

One morning, not long after my birthday, Édouard Marjary came running into my room. It was early, I still had my nose in a mug of tea.

"I'm sorry to intrude on you at this hour, but I have the most extraordinary piece of news for you."

"Yes, well?"

"It is so extraordinary that you won't believe it."

"What is it?"

"I can hardly believe it myself."

"Monsieur Marjary, do spit it out."

"Your Association of Five. It isn't any more."

"What?"

"They've turned themselves into Four."

"What are you trying to say, Monsieur Marjary?"

"They've had a meeting and decided to call themselves the Association of Four. You are out. They say you have no right to call yourself a premier cru."

I grabbed the phone prepared for murder, but nobody was available. At last I got a response from Margaux, where Pierre Ginestet and his son Bernard had succeeded my old friend Pierre Moreau.

"What's this I heard? What's going on?"

"Meaning?"

"Is it true you've been meeting without me?"

"Yes."

"Why wasn't I sent the usual notification?"

"Your cousin Élie doesn't want you in."

I went into a tailspin, threw away the morning paper—France's war in Indo-China was going badly; mine had just been declared. I knew what had brought things to a head—Mouton's success. My wines were fetching top prices everywhere, sometimes more than the other premier crus, and Mouton Cadet was the most popular Bordeaux wine in the trade. This was particularly resented.

Worse was to come. When the Sunday *Sud Ouest,* the Bordeaux paper, arrived, imagine my reaction on opening it to see a large advert:

Les Quatra Grands. Noblesse Oblige.

So they were telling the world that they were of the nobility, and I was not. They obviously meant to do me all the harm they could. I wasn't just angry for myself; they were harming my associates, my colleagues and friends, my team, everybody who had worked so hard and loyally for Mouton.

That loyalty, and my long fight for the honor of Mouton, were inspired—partly at least—by a tradition. If you don't like tradition, you'd better skip the next couple of pages. I only like it myself if it suits my book. This one is not very old, it dates from 1851, when the Great Exhibition, the wonder of the age, opened at the Crystal Palace in London, displaying all the luxuries in the world, including the wines of Bordeaux. The Rothschilds of France and England were there in force; admiring the architecture and tasting the finest of French wines.

The Bordeaux stole the show with their odor of violets, strawberries, roses, and there and then my great-grandfather Nathaniel decided to buy himself a vineyard in the Gironde. It was two years later, in May 1853, that he bought the obscure property of Brane Mouton: sixty-five acres, plus stables and outhouses.

The Great Exhibition had been such a success that New York decided to mount an even bigger one two years later and Napoleon III, not to be outdone, planned to trump the two of them in 1855, and build one in Paris. He put his cousin Prince Jerôme in charge of the whole affair. Jerôme made a thoroughly dull, conscientious job of it. When it came to the Bordeaux wines he wanted them displayed in ranks, and the Bordeaux Chamber of Commerce was ordered to undertake the job of grading them.

Did any classification exist? Nobody seemed to know. Some sort of notation had been made by English and Irish merchants in 1740, but that wouldn't do—a jury was picked from among the local wine establishment and the classifying was left to them.

Sixty red Bordeaux were selected, and thirty white sauternes.

The reds were then divided into five classes, first to fifth, and the awful term premier cru was invented for the first class. It's even worse translated as "first growth."

Mouton Rothschild was put at the head of the deuxième crus, while Lafite, owned then by Sir Samuel Scott, was named a premier—the other Rothschilds only bought Lafite thirteen years later. Latour, Margaux and Haut Brion were also placed in the front rank.

The smart Parisians drinking Nathaniel's good wine were hardly aware of Jerôme's paperwork, but the provincial jury were proud of themselves and used their classification on all occasions. It became a bible, more and more respected as its leaves yellowed with age.

Nathaniel, a foreigner and newcomer, meant nothing to them; less than nothing—his vineyard couldn't even boast a house—nothing but stables and outhouses which had once belonged to Lafite.

The steward at Mouton was hurt and angry. He was proud of his wine, and could accept the verdict. He got together with the local schoolmaster, and they thought up a motto:

> *Premier ne puis, second ne diagne, Mouton suis.*
> [First I may not be, second I disdain, I am Mouton.]

And the 1855 classification was challenged at the very next expo,

> Like all human institutions, this one is subject to the laws of time and must, in due course, be rejuvenated and kept abreast of progress. The vineyards themselves, on changing ownership, may often be modified. A certain wine site, neglected by a careless owner or by one who has run into debt, may fall into the hands of a rich, active and intelligent man, and because of this give a better product. The opposite can also happen.
>
> Charles Cocks, in his classification
> of Bordeaux wines, 1867

Others opposed the judgment on Mouton. Danflou, Lorbac, Dr. Aussel, historians and experts, pronounced it a wine of the highest order. Since their time, Mouton Rothschild has been accepted as one of the greats all over the world, and in the Médoc. What about my Association of Five? Granted Lafite had always refused to sign anything, their word was enough. "He who breaks an oral agreement which is not legally binding is morally wrong," said the Hebrew sage Baba Mezi'a, and that was just what the House of Lafite was doing, one hundred years after Napoleon's forgotten show. But since Élie and whoever else he'd managed to win over, were simply using the old *classement* to boot me out, there was only one way to put a stop to their capers. Ditch the 1855 altogether, and replace it with a new, up-to-date table, with Mouton in its rightful place. That would fix them. I knew that old documents with seals on them were highly prized in France, until they finished up in the flea market. I couldn't have imagined that it would take me twenty years to get this one torn up.

I was told that the only legally constituted body which had the right to appeal to a higher legally constituted body was the SCC, the Syndicat des Crus Classés, an ancient order of wine growers which was responsible for the observance of wine laws in the district. If I could interest a majority of the members in a revision of the 1855, it would at least start the ball rolling. It was a long time since this organization had shown any sign of life—they never seemed to meet. It looked as if I would have to winkle them out, one by one. The first problem was to locate them since they were scattered all over the Médoc, some pushing up the daisies, other gone away, leaving empty châteaux and rows of withered vines. It was not unlike Gogol's *Dead Souls*, and I too was looking for votes. In one dilapidated, out-of-the-way place I found the owner standing among his vines, sighing over the price of weed killer. I told my story and he listened politely, but for him the problem was purely academic. He knew the famous date, of course.

"Oh yes. But you know, my boy, the 1855 was the reward of

quality at a given time. Nobody has the right to withdraw that honor."

Nobody ever asked me in. It was not unfriendliness: their homes were very poor in those days, and they were very proud.

I'd trace another one to a dusty club in Bordeaux.

"Of course, but you know what they're saying, don't you? 'He thinks his name on the bottle counts more than the 1855.'"

I'd roar along the road, back to the calm of Mouton, and we'd spend all evening examining some Elizabethan parcel gilt which Pauline had unearthed in an old packing case.

I enjoyed her company so much. She was amusing, eccentric, subtleminded and a glorious piece of woman, long legged, deep breasted. For me the physical passion lasted six years, longer than with any other woman. For her? Well, truthfully, she wasn't a sexy woman, but she loved good talk, like a lot of bright women, enjoyed the company of clever homosexuals and cared for me tenderly. When she knew that I had been ill all my life with stomach pains, at least ever since Miss May's gruel and powders, she carted me off to Boston and left me in a hospital there for a month. But every day she flew from New York to see me. She was still working for six months of the year for Hattie Carnegie, the designer, at the time.

I was put on a diet of tea and rice; no wine for ten years, but it cured me.

During that ten years I also had the museum on my hands. When the syndicated wine growers got too boring for me, and the design racket got Pauline down, we would fly off on a hunt for treasure. There wasn't an antique dealer in Milan, London, Amsterdam, Dublin or Copenhagen who didn't see us coming before we turned the corner of the street and begin to dust his treasures. But we weren't so dumb—we both had eyes.

One morning, after working all night in the museum, we stepped out into the fresh air at that moment when moon and sunrise share the scene. The world was rose colored. Everything was transformed: the deserted stables which ran the length of the courtyard, my white doves strutting in and out of the empty windows, us. The glamour only lasted a few seconds.

"There! Look!" said Pauline, in her shooting-star voice.

"Look at what?"

"Our cloud-capped towers, our gorgeous palaces."

"Where?"

"Don't you see? The stables. I never noticed how good those proportions were till now."

"But it's a total wreck, a ruin."

"It is deteriorating slightly."

I had tried to ignore those stables for a long time, they depressed me so. I couldn't pull them down, and I didn't know what else to do with them.

"If the dawn can transform the place, we can."

"The dawn doesn't cost money."

"Imagine a graceful château, with rooms for entertaining, a huge library, a studio, a proper office. We're so cramped as things are, and what will happen when Philippine leaves boarding school? There will hardly be room for her, let alone her friends. We'll have to move into a tent. You know, it would make a perfect château."

"What would?"

"The stables."

She convinced me, but our transformation scene took a long time. The design of Château Mouton, as you see it today, took shape piece by piece, each of us adding our own notions to the overall design, though neither of us ever knew whose idea came first and neither of us ever acted without the other.

We knew we wanted to take full advantage of the length of the building, with a corridor full of light for promenading and enjoying the view when the weather was inclement. On the first floor there were the remains of fireplaces and dividing walls where there had once been coachmen's dwellings. The building had to be virtually gutted and new rooms constructed, though Odette, Merilda's daughter, still says, 'I was born in the baron's bedroom." The main stairway was built first in wood so that we could test the proportions and change them before having it constructed in stone.

In April 1954 Pauline proposed to me. I was fifty-two, she was forty-six, we'd both had our fling, but I don't think either of us contemplated fidelity.

"I've seen the way you behave with women, in that respect you are totally unreliable, but we could have an interesting life together."

She gave up her work with Hattie Carnegie.

In Paris she'd been sharing a flat with a brilliant gasbag, Marthe Bibesco, but that didn't suit when I wanted a session. Pauline thought it wasn't *comme il faut*. I made room for her at my bachelor flat, avenue d'Iéna, very male 1930—she didn't like it at all. I asked Pierre de Fleurieu, who had gone into real estate, to help me. He found a ground floor empty on rue Méchain, between a morgue, a nunnery and the Santé prison.

"She'll never accept that," I said.

She adored it, or so she said, but after two or three visits and a good deal of scribbling on her small memo pads, she had plans for the thousand jobs which would have to be done before she could even look at it again.

Pauline wanted solitude, needed it, yet above all she seemed to like the idea of marriage. I couldn't understand why until she gave me a list of the men in her life:

NUMBER ONE: you already know about.

NUMBER TWO: ex-grand duke, white Russian, she was simply added to his list of scalps.

NUMBER THREE: Irish diplomat who thought she might be an impediment to his career.

The rest were passing clouds: two tough American diplomats, both comfortably married; a nonstarter with a film director, who adored her but left it at that; and lots of worshipers, among them André de Vilmorin, brother of Louise, and very many women. But Pauline was fastidious and now, poor girl, she had me—at least I gave her a ring. We were married at Auffargis, where my parents and my baby son are buried. In the town hall there was made our contract. I liked her hat. Her friends Evangeline and David Bruce had insisted on laying on a wedding breakfast for us at their pretty house in Versailles. It seemed a bit silly at our age but there we were, carving an enormous wedding cake, giggling like two teenagers. On the way back to Mouton . . .

"I've been thinking," she said.

"About me."

"About the cottages over at d'Armailhacq. If we're going to make ourselves a lovely new home, we should smarten up those cottages at the same time."

"What for?"

"They're not very nice inside."

Naturally, the cottages were restored. I couldn't refuse her anything. She designed a children's playground at the back of them and we made some progress with the stables. On the west side, looking out over the vines, and running the length of the building, we would have our grande pièce and, backing onto it, an enormous library. Pauline liked to be surrounded by books. The grande pièce, formerly the barn, already had seven half-moon openings, which would make beautiful windows. She couldn't find the right tiles for the floor and searched high and low. Eventually she saw what she wanted in a fourteenth-century Florentine painting of an imaginary village, tiles of orange-rose and eggshell blue. She had them made in Italy.

In contrast to the Victorian villa, where we had lived, which we now called Petit Mouton, we decided to be very moden, with an occasional surprise from the past. So, beyond Brancusi's *Oiseau* and Lippold's delicately vibrating space jewelry, we placed a regal, high-backed settee covered in figured velvet, a seventeenth-century piece; beside an orrery, a Paul Klee. A sixteenth-century wooden horse from Milan, life size, dominates the far end of the room. I can't think how we ever got him there.

Pauline had always loved the subtle colors of Mouton's well-washed pebbles and changing skies, and wanted to reflect them in the house. She mixed the paints herself: faintest pinks, apricots and blue-grays. You would recognize her taste anywhere, but not her surprises.

The first inspiration was not lost in the detail. We wanted a place where our guests could enjoy Mouton to the full. The grande pièce looks out over a sea of vines and wide vistas of sky, with only an occasional island of trees in the distance, often appearing to float above drifting mist. At night, I floodlight the vines.

In 1956 we decided we were ready for a housewarming, and invited our friends to see what we had done, among them Jean-Louis Barrault and Madeleine Renaud. Jean-Louis fell in love with the Milanese horse at first sight, and began prancing along the room to embrace it.

Nothing went unnoticed in the rival camp. Publicity-monger. Exhibitionist. "Lafite c'est Rothschild et Co., Mouton c'est Rothschild ego."

It all came back to me and it made me angry. I knew it was silly, simply playing into their hands, but really:

> Monsieur Le Baron (among his vines at Mouton, on a rainy
>   day): Do you realize that's gold falling on our vines?
> His Steward: Really! Then why isn't monsieur's umbrella
>   upside-down?
>
>   Bernard Ginestet, at table

My fair lady, sitting up a ladder, trying to choose between two swathes of sea green brocade, simply couldn't understand what all the fuss was about—why was I so cross? One mustn't be impatient. It will all come right.

She didn't know the Médoc. While I stormed and raged, Pauline would sit there, cool as a cucumber. She didn't know what it was to be angry, but she knew how to calm her battered knight.

I would set out with my Sancho Panza, Monsieur Marjary, at my side. He'd sit back, shake his head and wriggle his mustache when I tackled one of my windmills. He was always convinced that there must be an easier way round the problem, and I knew there wasn't. I had to win over an army of old fuddy-duddies.

Mouton was busy enough during all this time. We were clearing land, planting new vineyards, filling in an enormous quarry right in the middle of the Carruades vineyards, and I had been carefully watching the d'Armailhacq harvests. By 1956, the wine was good enough to join the family. I rechristened it Mouton Baron Philippe.

Pauline and I now took our evening promenade in a pony and trap, trotting round the lanes and woods which bordered our Abbaye de Thélème, our "love and do what you will" land. We thought up some startling ideas to mark its boundaries. Some worked, a lot didn't.

We could never find what we wanted even when, after a good deal of argument, we knew what it was. Mostly we came upon things by accident. Looking for a gatepost, we would like the look of a moss-grown Dionysus at the back of the junkyard, then when we got him home, we'd go off him.

"We could plant him among the laurels, a few leaves round his neck might improve him."

Eusèbe would whip up a team of four or five of the strongest vignerons, rig a pully and hoist Dionysus into place. Pauline would wander off looking for wild flowers, while I fiddled the silly grinning god this way and that, till he looked presentable.

Wandering one day in the woods of Gretz, near the old Rothschild palace Ferrières, we came upon an eighteenth-century obelisk, looking forlorn and neglected, as things we have an eye on often do. It was not forgotten at all. It belonged to the Péreire family, bankers, traditional Sephardic enemies of the Ashkenazi Rothschilds, and we were trespassing on their estate.

What's more, the Péreires intended it for their Place Péreire in Paris, so that was that. Luckily for us, that obelisk was so heavy that the Ministry of Works wouldn't allow it in the Place Péreire for fear it might disturb the roof of the métro. It now watches over the southern boundary of the park, with a golden polyhedron poised on top of it. The frustrated Péreires were glad to have us carry it away.

The park was beginning to look something like a park. Between Mouton and d'Armailhacq we drained a swamp and made a mini-Holland, four small canals, a flotilla of white ducks imported by Pauline and a wooden bridge. And what with arum lilies along the ditches, mimosa in the yard and the smell of cooking coming from the gatehouse kitchen, it was beginning to be my idea of heaven. What's more I'd finished my rounds, I'd seen every member of the Syndicat des Crus Classés. I could only wait and see if as a body they would take any action.

They did. A printed slip in an unsealed envelope arrived on a Monday, second post, inviting me to an extraordinary general meeting of the SCC. At this stage I'd better give you some idea of the pecking order.

1. *Le Syndicat des Crus Classés*. Sixty-one wine growers of the Médoc, answerable to:

2. *L'Institut National des Appellations d'Origine (INAO)*. Eighty wine growers from all over France, appointed by the government. They meet four times a year, thrice in Paris, once in any of the great wine-growing areas.

   FUNCTION:
   1. The prevention of fraud in labeling.
   2. The supervision of growers and merchants.
   3. The strict enforcement of the wine laws.

3. *The Minister of Agriculture*. Measures proposed by INAO are submitted to him and through him may become law.

We arrive at the town hall, Pauillac, for the meeting. It's a lovely day, autumn 1959. The old boys are assembling. They haven't seen each other for years judging by all the back-slapping and embracing going on.

A sudden silence as I walk in with Pauline on my arm, this striking, unconventional woman, serenely undeterred by the rude stares, the gleaming eyeglasses.

"Good God," under my breath, "they are all here."

"I should hope so, considering the time it's taken you to round them up."

"Order, order."

The chairman looks round sternly, rustling his notes. There is a good deal of beard scratching and staring at the ceiling. The chairman gives his introductory cough and goes into a long preamble in dry-as-dust French, mentioning several members who've passed on and giving each a short obituary. Then he brings out the minutes of the last meeting and asks if anyone has a moot point. Nobody has. Several of the older ones are already asleep. The preliminary business is concluded. It has taken twenty-five minutes. The room is stuffy and the lady is trying not to yawn.

"Wake up, he is coming to us."

". . . I take it this proposal has already been explained, severally or distributively, to each and every member here present?"

It had indeed. There was a rumble of assent.

"I will put the proposition to the meeting in the form of a resolution: We the . . ."

A holdup on protocol. Five minutes.

"It is proposed that INAO be requested to update the classification of 1855. All those in favor?"

Half the hands in the room are raised.

"Those against?"

The other half raise their hands. We've lost.

The chairman counts them, twice, the second time calling on an assistant. Carried by two votes. Even Pauline gives a long sigh of relief.

". . . Hence it would seem right and proper, *propter hoc,* for Monsieur de Rothschild, Mouton, to present his recommendation to INAO in his own person at the next meeting of the aforesaid body. All those in favor . . ."

We had got away with it, but only by the skin of our teeth.

There would be five months to wait before the next meeting of the mighty INAO, long winter months which we could spend happily working on our Mouton projects. Pauline would love it; winter was her season, walking bare-headed in the rain, trudging through snowdrifts, tracing the spoor of wild fowl through the woods of Béhérré, and then in the evening, after dinner, lingering at table talking, while a log fire burned itself out on the hearth, and the night was far gone.

Often the talk would be of poetry and poets, and usually finished with my bringing out one of my favorites, Paul Valéry, Rimbaud, Apollinaire, Aragon, or even something of my own. She was an attentive listener, never making a direct criticism, but rather . . . "Perhaps that line needs a little more thought."

In 1959, with all our works merrily in progress but none of them anywhere finished, she suddenly announced that the Elizabethan poets had never been properly translated into French and asked me if I didn't think it was a problem I should tackle.

I was excited, appalled, flattered, but above all I didn't think.

"Yes," I said, "if you'll help me."

We dipped into the *Oxford Book of Seventeenth-Century Verse* that very night. At that time it was all we had. It was enough, a dazzling display of prosody, names to make your ears ring as well as the ubiquitous Anon.; but then what else would you expect of a time when there was a cittern in every barber's shop, and maidservants were only engaged if they could sing in harmony?

Previously I had translated plays from the English, including poetical plays by Christopher Fry. They were difficult enough —but to attempt the complicated measures of Elizabethan lyrics, the marvelously subtle beat of the simplest song, written with a musical setting in mind, and to translate the carefully balanced prosody, undreamed of in any other age, in which the chief charm of many of the lyrics lies . . . oh Pauline!

BECAUSE THE BIRTHDAY OF MY LIFE IS COME 263

> I wonder, by my troth, what thou and I
> Did till we loved.
> Were we not wean'd till then,
> But sucked on country pleasures, childishly?

I translated with her help over 120 English poems, some of them only fragments. It took me over ten years. I strayed beyond the pastures of the Elizabethans, from Wyatt's introduction of the sonnet form at Henry VIII's court, to the anapests and octosyllables of Dryden and Co., the decline of English lyric poetry, the Age of Prose and Reason.

Each night I would read Pauline the lines I had struggled with all day. Hervé Mille told everyone that I was playing Scheherazade to Pauline's Haroun al Raschid. Our doings were always the talk of the town.

It was springtime in the Champs Élysées, when I arrived on time for my INAO appointment and was kept waiting forty-five minutes in an anteroom.

I was prepared for INAO in all its high solemnity, but when I was ushered into the inner chamber all I saw were nine old fogies from the Bordeaux region, sitting in a row. The one in the middle started questioning me without so much as a by your leave. In any case it didn't matter, because he didn't expect any answers. At least he didn't wait for them, but waved his hand toward a shadowy eminence and closed his eyes tight while the SCC resolution was read out. I was then invited to enlarge on it, and waded in with an analysis of the problems of the Médoc wine trade, peppered with facts and figures, and finishing with a flourish. There was a long silence.

"Thank you."

And that was it. *Ite missa est.*

I made a quick exit, threw my notes into the wastepaper basket, and asked the doorman the name of the chairman.

"Monsieur Pierre Pestel, monsieur."

*   *   *

It was a November morning in 1960 when the newsroom of *Sud Ouest* got through to me. It was Jacques Prévost, a friendly columnist, very excited. He read out a new classification which INAO had been preparing in secret.

"Mouton Rothschild to be promoted premier cru. Fifteen wines which earned honorable mention in 1855 to be completely dropped."

"How did you get your hands on it?"

"That I cannot say."

"It's not for publication."

"Oh yes it is."

He published and had the wine world about his ears. Lafite (Élie that is), and Margaux (Bernard Ginestet), grinding their teeth, the fifteen rushing around looking for lawyers, and INAO livid with rage over the theft of their document. I added fuel to the flames by writing to Monsieur Pestel and denouncing the new classification, on behalf of the fifteen. Well, what else could I do? One needs allies. On the other hand I was getting a little tired of this provincial storm-in-a-teacup so I went to town and buttonholed Edgar Faure, ex-prime minister, himself a wine grower and interested in the trade. He opened the door to the minister of agriculture, a Monsieur Pisani, who told me that the affairs of INAO were shortly to be discussed at ministerial level, and invited me to attend and voice my criticisms there.

Some account of the meeting at the Ministery of Agriculture. The minister himself, not present. A Monsieur Lamour in the chair. As soon as I enter the room, I notice Monsieur Pestel of INAO seated at the chairman's right hand. Introductions, formalities. I am asked to speak.

"Gentlemen, among the many precious things France offers to the world, our fine wines must take pride of place. At its best, wine making is an art, but it can be and should be at the same time profitable. Unfortunately, the organization that controls our wine laws is singularly cut off from the realities of today and the possibility of increasing our wine trade internationally. Frankly, our approach and our style are equally out of date. So are many of our wine laws, to such an extent that, in many cases, they are simply ignored or evaded.

"The committees appointed by INAO in 1936 certainly do not fill the bill. They are not sufficiently representative, composed as they are of wine growers, with neither brokers nor merchants being included. I suggest that a complete reappraisal of the situation is called for, proper regional bodies should be constituted. . . ."

Monsieur Pestel jumped to his feet.

"Nothing this man says corresponds to reality. He is simply out to destroy INAO, thinking thereby to ga.   ablicity for his Mouton Rothschild no doubt. I take his attack on INAO to be aimed at me, personally. I am well aware of his machinations, his meetings with ministers, he is well known for his ability to pull strings. . . ."

Monsieur Lamour tried to quiet Monsieur Pestel. In vain. I simply agreed with him, which made him angrier than ever.

"Gentlemen, please. I think it would be more constructive if Monsieur de Mouton, sorry, Rothschild, were to submit his criticism in the form of a written report. I propose we move on to the next business."

26

Entr'acte—My Daughter's Wedding

A man may deceive his mistress as much as he likes, but a daughter is a different matter.

ANTON CHEKHOV

PHILIPPINE had chosen the theater as her profession and I had encouraged her. At nineteen she enrolled at the Conservatoire, and at the end of her second year met the young man she was to marry.

It was the day of the annual competition, a great occasion, but as Philippine had failed her end-of-term test, she was not eligible. They had given her the seemingly thankless job of holding the book and cuing the others, who were either very dull, or had stage fright. Whichever it was, Philippine was getting all their laughs for them.

In the audience were two successful young actors: Jean-Paul Belmondo, who had left the Conservatoire the year before, and Jacques Sereys, already at the Comédie Française. They were highly amused by Philippine and started a round of applause whenever she came on. She did look rather comic, wearing thick glasses, a peasant scarf over her head. After the show the two young men fell into the brasserie on the corner. Jacques was asking about the girl reading the cues.

"She's over there," said Jean-Paul.

Jacques was stunned. She was wearing the same awful scarf and glasses in real life, and on top of that she was looking depressed.

Jean-Paul called her over and she brightened up a little in the presence of the two dashing young men. She told them she was about to chuck the Conservatoire, the theater, everything, but they laughed at her and told her how good she was.

She won the critics' prize at the drama school and a Prix du Conservatoire shortly after, which encouraged her, and when she left, a place in the Comédie Française. Jacques became her director. They seemed to get on very well, since they were always quarreling.

But before, they had a lot of fun together, playing Courteline, doing a circus act for the Actors' Annual Charity Matinée. It had involved months of practice, twirling on a rope high above the safety net, hanging by their teeth.

"It made my legs hurt so much I had to go away and cry," she said.

One evening after Jacques's production of a children's matinée had gone very well, he invited his cast to a little restaurant to dinner. Philippine said she would like to split the bill, but Jacques wouldn't hear of it. "Let me bring some wine then," she said. "No, no. Why?" said Jacques, unaware of her connection.

"Just tell me what you want," she said. "I know about wine."

"All right then, champagne, lots, but only the best, mind."

She arrived at the party with a case of champagne.

"But I was joking," said Jacques. "I've already ordered the wine."

It was a merry night.

When the theater closed for the summer, Philippine was going to Venice, where I'd taken a house for her and her friends. By this time she'd changed her specs for contact lenses, and looked as fresh as paint in her bright new clothes. She never bothered about *haute couture,* though Pauline tried several times to influence her. Philippine preferred to shop for zazzy clothes in the new shops for students.

Jacques, who was a solitary, suddenly said, "I've always wanted to see Venice."

"Then come with us," said she. And off they went.

On the train back to Paris, while they were lounging in the corridor together, Philippine told Jacques she didn't think anyone would ever want to marry her.

"I'd marry you," said Jacques.

"Quoi?" said she. Next day she rang him up.

"Did you mean that, about marriage?"

"Yes," he said.

They announced their intentions back in Paris just before the dress rehearsal of Marivaux's *Le Legs*. Director Sereys marries his soubrette.

"How does it feel to be marrying into the Rothschilds, Jacques?"

"I know all about banks, I used to be a messenger in the Crédit Lyonnaise at Marseilles."

Philippine left the Comédie Française because of the soubrette tag. "Why should I forever be playing the maids' parts? After all I am a Rothschild."

And here they were, riding in a limousine lined with orchids, Philippine in white satin crowned with a mink pillbox studded with diamonds, the town band heading the procession, followed by the M.C. carrying an ivory staff. The fleet of cars behind him carried the whole tribe of Rothschilds, nearly eighty of them. They'd arrived from the round earth's imagined corners.

I had chartered a train for the guests, and provided the ladies with the most famous hairdresser in Paris. Alexandre and his team had been prinking and preening the hairdos all along the route, while champagne and caviar were served *ad lib*.

When the train stopped at Poiters: "A holdup," cried one old dame. "How clever of them."

Apart from a few nails planted on the road outside the church all went well, and the guests were received at our new Château Mouton, where Pauline had just put the finishing touches to the library.

The wedding breakfast was in the banquet hall. Cold chicken and lobster, and the smilers hid their knives as we toasted Philippine and Jacques in Mouton Rothschild 1933, the year of Philippine's birth.

In the evening we all strolled through the vineyards to Lafite, where Cousin Élie and his wife, Liliane, offered a candle-lit supper in the chai. Liliane is known as the peacemaker in the family.

Before we left, Élie had a word with Jacques. "You don't know what they're like, the Rothschilds. They're touchy. Their self-esteem complicates their relationships with each other to a point you wouldn't imagine."

The cuckoos were send their mocking note across the vineyards in March that year.

>   Be it ever so humble
>   There's no place like home.
>   FOLK SONG

Well, my lady was in her castle, and we her slaves awaited her orders. We were a motley crew. There was Mesmin, her cook from Paris, a genius. Marie Gieselinck, a Flemish girl who had come to Pauillac with her father, a gardener. She learned the names of all the wild flowers and decorated every table and tray with them. We christened her Marie la Fleur. And Odette, Merilda's daughter, now a highly efficient housekeeper. Henriette, Raoul Blondin's dark beauty, could sew and pack and run an army if need be. Then came a chorus of village girls, all of them courting or married to vignerons working on the estate. They had the pride and courtesy of our country people, and the good French, but not one of them had any experience of spreading sheets of lightest lawn, encountering a bollocknaked genius in the passage before breakfast, pressing the confections of Monsieur Laurent and Co. or serving *îles flottantes* at a crowded table without letting one or two slide down the gesticulating arm of an honored guest: but—they were unflappable—"Twenty Chinese generals to dinner, Mesmin."

"Yes, madame."

And adaptable. They knew at once how to address a prince or a president, a queen, or quean, a count, or what you will, a baron, or baronne, an honorable, or an anarchist, or even an ordinary citizen. They got into a bit of a muddle with the bedrooms once or twice, because Pauline had renamed them. On one occasion L'Oiseau Lyre almost got into the bed in La Chambre Singe. I called them my Ballet Rose, they'd catch a petal if it fell out of place.

On Fridays a flight of guests would descend on us. Sometimes these weekends stretched into weeks, not often; most of our friends were working artists, writers, painters or journalists. A program developed—first a look at my new works, then perhaps a visit to the museum, a promenade in the park or among the vines. There would be trips to the sea, and swimming, playing, flirting, talking far into the night, alfresco when the weather was fair, cozily inside in winter.

And the sweet Gironde might have flowed softly till my song was done, if it had known its business. But no. Romans we'd had, savage Britons, Normans in their serpent-prowed longboats, and now BP-Shell, an oil refinery on the skyline. It was already approved and on the drawing board. It was too much, especially as one of my relatives was on the board.

What planners! The river should have been developed as a playground for townspeople, with yachting, swimming, fishing, fishfarming, what you will, but not an oil refinery to stink out the most precious vineyards in the world.

I fought that invader, single-handedly. In the end I forced them to put most of their damned refinery underground, but the rest is still an eyesore.

I must admit I had plenty of diversions in those years. I was either fighting or flirting, fantailing round the planet or filling the museum with wonderful things, and in 1962 it was ready. All the time we'd been working on it, nobody outside Mouton had any idea what was going on. We had asked everybody to keep it secret. What a team, spurred on by Eusèbe, who is not only a great carpenter, but a very amusing clown and particularly good at imitating me. The work was incomparably well done. These local craftsmen had come to admire our style, and enjoy our method of work. Eusèbe still makes life-size models of any design innovation, which was Pauline's way.

Monsieur André Conte, our architect, oversaw every change at Mouton. He joined us in 1953 and is with me today, on the current restructuring.

When we opened the doors of the museum, the word spread like wildfire . . . a wine museum! The world and his wife came to gape. No one had seen anything like it before, not in France anyway.

"It's not a museum, it's an experience."

That was true. And apart from the rare and lovely objects you will see there, it has a quality almost unknown in a museum —a sense of humor.

The next year, an unexpected piece of luck, Latour, one of the Five, was sold to an English firm, headed by Lord Cowdray. I had reason to believe that I might now expect some friendship from that quarter, or at least no antagonism. My joust with INAO had roused the wrath of half the countryside.

Monsieur Ginestet was still busy. "Floundering on 'gainst wind and tide, Philippe de Rothschild tries his charm or vents his spleen, turn and turn about."

"You are attacking a fortress," said Edgar Faure. "You need Joshua's trumpets."

"That is possible," I said. "Meanwhile I'll batter them with words."

I wrote articles, gave lectures, cornered ministers. In all, during my long battle, I had audiences with five successive ministers of agriculture, Monsieurs Pisani, Duhamel, Faure, Cointat and finally Monsieur Chirac.

But it was the coming of the Anglo-Saxons which finally

saved me. Lord Cowdray, and Douglas Dillon, who now owned
Haut Brion. He was American, perhaps I should say Irish; in
fact I never met him, but my spies told me that there was a
rumpus going on over there.

"Everybody wants his place in history. You underestimate
people's vanity," said Pauline. "You have wounded their self-
esteem."

Poor girl, she must have grown tired of hearing about my
never-ending quest. We'd change the subject, and dwelling on
the nuances of

> They flee from me that sometime did me seek,
>   With naked foot stalking within my chamber:
> Once have I seen them gentle, tame, and meek,
>   That now are wild and do not once remember
> That sometime they have put themselves in danger
> To take bread at my hand: and now they range,
>   Busily seeking in continual change

was a wonderful antidote to the *longueurs* of committee meetings, subcommittee meetings and ministerial antechambers.

Meanwhile my report to the Ministery of Agriculture was
slowly, oh so slowly, going the rounds. Then in 1969 France
had a new president, Monsieur Pompidou, once a Rothschild
banker, and Edgar Faure was appointed minister of agriculture.

I was at home, we were correcting the proofs of the English
poems, when a bolt from the blue descended. Monsieur Faure
had signed a decree authorizing the reform of INAO. Shortly
after there was a totally new committee with a new president,
Pierre Perromat, introducing a new member . . . me. Nobody
wanted to touch the classification.

"It's a hornet's nest, let's give the job to the Bordeaux chamber of commerce. After all, they started all the trouble," said
Perromat.

"They did?"

"Who thought up the—classement in the first place?"

So the chamber of commerce, Bordeaux, received a missive, bearing a government stamp.

> Good God, the time, thought, money, energy wasted on that fight for prestige, for something totally artificial.
>
> Bernard Ginestet

"We are instructed to prepare a new classification, gentlemen. How are we to go about it? We can't get out of it."

The elders scratched their whiskers.

"There's only one thing we can do—give it to the lawyers."

Perre Siré, doyen of the Bordeaux barristers, was brought in, and went home to consider the matter in depth.

While he was doing so, in 1970, I bought the vineyard of Clerc Milon, which lies on a gentle slope beyond Pauillac, bordered on one side by Lafite.

The village and chai have a charm I cannot define, the air is always calm, and even on a dull day the light is softly translucent. I always go there with pleasure. I am not the only one. The team of three who work there, a young maître de chai and two others, take great pride in Clerc Milon; witness the impeccable condition of the small chai and the outbuildings, the touches of artistry they have added to the place. The Mouton style has greatly influenced the people who work here, and even the people who live round about.

27

The secret of being a bore is to tell everything.

VOLTAIRE

I assure you I have already cut four-fifths of my classement story. The following is kept for any students of French law who may have strayed this far.

Maître Siré presenting his conclusions to the chamber of commerce.

Gentlemen, having exercised my mind on the problem of the classement, it appears to me that the primary consideration is to define the rights of each party. In the first place, whence cometh the term cru classé? In which legal statute does it first appear? I would refer you to Dalloz, the Civil Code, Tome 217, section XY, concerning property, case of Achille de la Vigerie versus the state. It would seem, according to the law of this country, that the term cru classé establishes, in any given classification, the senior rank of a certain wine-producing domain, domain being taken to mean the private property of one person or family. The key word here, gentlemen, is "private."

Since, therefore, the term cru classé refers to a private

property and springs from its soil and its wines, the patri-
mony or acquisition of a private owner, it should follow as
the night the day, that the term cru classé is likewise an
endowment, asset or peculium, de jure et de facto, of the
said owners, possessor or proprietor. In a democratic society, gentlemen, an owner of property cannot be dictated
to, neither can his products be classified without his consent.

Chairman: Which boil down to this, Monsieur Siré. We
cannot change one single rating without the approval of
the owner of the vineyard.

Monsieur Siré: Quite.

Impasse.

Monsieur Siré: What about a competition, gentlemen? You
could ask the owners to enter their wines, as for a horse
show; that might appeal to them; the rules to be worked
out with circumstantiality; but all sixty-one vineyards will
have to compete; that is bound to be the government
ruling.

There was general agreement and the meeting was breaking
up, though we seemed to have gotten nowhere.

"You can't judge sixty-one horses at the same time," I said,
"much less sixty-one wines. You'll have to make your revision
class by class."

"Beginning with the premier crus, I suppose?" said Monsieur
Siré.

There was a deep sigh and everybody went their way. They
decided to try the competition idea and on September 2, 1972,
it was announced. Nobody entered.

The next day a letter arrived from Lafite: "We are not enter-
ing because we have no intention of risking our 1855 rating."
The letter was forwarded to the minister. The minister replied:
"Of course you won't lose it, one can't change history."

Then one cold evening at Mouton, two days before Christmas, while Jacques Prévost and I were enjoying a convivial cup, a surprise visitor was announced, and Bernard Ginestet entered the room, smiling.

"I have a proposition to make. . . ."

Prévost moved to go.

"Stay where you are, Jacques, I need a witness."

"Take Mouton Cadet off the market and we'll drop our opposition."

He went out quicker than he came in.

So for all those years I had only been attacking windmills after all, and the windmill keeper was a little green-eyed god who lived over the hill.

Suddenly Latour and Haut Brion pulled down the curtain on the whole unfunny comedy.

"The harm done to Mouton Rothschild must be put right," they said, and they demanded a private meeting with my cousin Élie and Bernard Ginestet. It must have been quite a session. Two days later a letter arrived from Lafite. It was courteous enough and well it might be, it had only taken twenty years to write it. They were "no longer opposed to Mouton Rothschild being accepted as a premier cru." *Noblesse oblige* indeed. I handed the letter to Pauline.

"You've won. I always knew you would."

On June 21, 1973, the Ministry of Agriculture issued a decree promoting Mouton Premier Cru. The four wines must be presented in alphabetical order: Lafite, Latour, Margaux, Mouton and, finally, Haut Brion. Haut Brion always appears last on the official lists as it is the only premier cru outside the Médoc area. The rest of the 1855 classification remained untouched.

It was a great moment. Forget the long years of fighting, bitterness, and rancour, it was time to celebrate. We cracked a jeroboam of Mouton '24, and all the vineyard workers came to drink to the future, and their new motto:

Premier je suis, second je fus, Mouton ne change.
[First I am, second I was, Mouton does not change.]

Year of triumph, and a Picasso label.

While the newspapers of the world were still descending on us, trying to add a few juicy bits to our story, and the local papers were caricaturing Battling Philippe, I thought I might as well start another fight. It was a situation which had vexed me for a long time.

Under our windows, just outside the courtyard, was the village street. It had once been a cattle track, but was fast becoming a noisy thoroughfare. There seems no end to the stupidity of modern planners. The ancient villages around us grew up in pleasant situations, well chosen by the first-comers. As you approach Le Pouyalet, crossing the fields after an evening stroll, you see a cluster of homesteads. They look sheltered and serene, but, on arrival, you have to cross a dangerous road which cuts the village in two. It is not long since our villages were as tranquil as cloisters, and their streets were gardens. Instead of avoiding the villages, the road builders destroyed them. I would make a bid to save our part of Le Pouyalet at least, so I tackled the local authority—I told them they should take the heavy traffic away from Mouton and the adjoining street.

To my astonishment, my powers of persuasion worked straightaway, perhaps my ferocious reputation helped. The lorries and speeding cars now use the motorway beyond the park, and our street is a pleasant place again.

Pauline and I settled in and soon we were a wonderful target for gossip in the Médoc and everywhere else. "They don't even live together," they said. Of course we didn't. We were both free. She would go off to Norway or London or New York, but alone. She talked more and more of life being wasted without creative work, said she wanted to be by herself and write.

We spent our summers together on a tiny Swedish island, which belonged to our friend Lars Schmidt who adored Pauline, in Denmark at Isak Dinesen's home, or in the Highlands of Scotland, where we had many friends.

Pauline preferred the north. She loved rain and snow, avoided the summer sun and disliked sunsets. For her the day should never end. She left things lingering on, forgotten, unfinished.

In 1963 we went to Russia.

> One night in December a man decided to leave his house and his vineyards, his work of translating English poets into French, to spend two months in a country unfamiliar to him. He and his wife would leave for Russia, the day after Christmas. . . .

I was amazed and delighted when a book appeared, a short, beautifully written account of our visit. Up till then she had only produced fragments. She called her book *The Irrational Journey*. She had fallen in love with Russia, the landscape, the works of art, the memory of her Russian lover perhaps, but most of all the people, the kindly, warm, erudite people who seem to have so little to do with their governors, Tsarist or Soviet.

Pauline dreamed of going back, of finding a dacha, of becoming a real writer; she even began to learn Russian. The book had only been a series of vignettes, she said.

I didn't stand in her way. I encouraged her and gave her everything a man can give, except fidelity, though the others knew what she meant to me.

In 1970 so did I. She had to have heart surgery; the disease was a heritage from her pathetic childhood. We had flown to Boston to visit the world-famous cardiologist Bernard Lown. Pauline could not bear the idea of a plastic valve in her body, and Lown told her that the only surgeon who used animal replacements was in New Zealand.

She went, and though the operation appeared to be successful, it was not. Back in the United States they found that the valve had only been repaired; it would have to be replaced, and this time in Boston, where all the new techniques were then in use. Again she submitted to the drastic operation, the opening of the rib cage, the long period of convalescence. As she slowly recovered, the faint heartbeat had to be sustained with a new drug, Tolamol.

From that time on Pauline was an invalid. She could hardly climb the stairs. Some days she couldn't move. We treasured her sleep and tiptoed past her door. She gained a little strength from time to time, but she was never again the Pauline I had known.

She began to dress simply, in clinging trousers and loose shirts, a bright scarf at her neck in the evenings.

My adventures were curtailed by her condition, there is no doubt about that—my life was governed by Pauline's condition, her often dragging gait, her darkening looks.

Just when we'd settled for a quiet life at Mouton, stories of our extravagance and eccentricity began to appear. When *Time* had a dig at Pauline for never moving without twelve servants, she wrote them a charming letter and asked them: "Have you ever tried following a migrating tribe through Persia, as we did two years ago, with twelve servants?"

There was no reply to the British media's film of best steak on a silver dish for my dog, cut in after a gloomy shot of a disabled man raking the gravel in the courtyard. It was cleverly produced.

If one enjoys the Rothschild myth, as all in our family do, one has to take the rough with the smooth.

One day Pauline told me she had had enough of Mouton, of me, of everyone; she was determined to go away and write. Without any sadness she told me she would have to hurry if she meant to master a new skill, her time was getting short.

She had taken a flat in the eighteenth-century chambers in the heart of London—Albany, Piccadilly. She settled there to write, but it was not long before a new court gathered round her, young designers, town wits, writers, old friends from America—and my grandchildren, thirteen-year-old Camille and her younger brother, Philippe, arriving in London to prepare for their English school. Her last refuge was Mouton. We were there together when in 1976 Lown cabled, "Come to Boston. Stop the Tolomol." We went. He told us that the drug was now suspect. It had caused cancer in some cases, he advised a new drug. The routine examination revealed that it was too late. She already had it—and she knew. Boston, the hospital, the hotel, were now a part of a deadly daily routine. I decided to take her to Santa Barbara for a change of air. We stayed at the Biltmore and were at once surrounded by friendly people. My poor Pauline, so many wanted to know her, to lionize her.

March 8th was sunny, she sat on the beach all afternoon watching the rolling Pacific, I swam. When I came in, she was dead. She had collapsed in the foyer of the hotel.

I found that she had not touched the new drug Lown had prescribed for her.

I brought her back to rest at Mouton. She is buried in the cemetery at Pauillac. Six vignerons in their work-a-day blues were her pallbearers. No one wore black, she wouldn't have wanted that. They carried her past the vines to a tractor covered with spring flowers. All the tractors on the estate followed.

Each year on her birthday the staff from Mouton carry branches of white lilac to her grave.

She was a beloved woman, beloved of everyone, not just the many gifted men and women who came to pay court to her, talk over their problems with her, or relax in her sweet company. She had shared every aspect of my life, and devoted herself to Mouton and to me. How could I go on without her?

I renamed the wine of d'Armailhacq Château Mouton Baronne Philippe as a small tribute to her memory.

It took all the strength I had to carry on. Work was the only solution.

Each day I walk in the park with my dog, Rajah. I am never on my own there. On summer Sundays, wedding parties stroll up from the village, after the *vin d'honneur,* to take their family photos by the urns. At every season, it's a favorite trysting place for lovers of all ages.

On the drawing board there are new projects, a reception room for tourists, arriving each year in increasing numbers, a decanting room for Raoul, a new *atelier* for Eusèbe, a new loft for my doves, a new gateway worthy of Mouton. These will soon be accomplished, but ideas for the future are still budding in my brain . . . a Mouton village, with shops, covered walkways, a restaurant and a *salle des fêtes*, lakes, gardens, trees.

I hope I shall be spared to see some of it. Meanwhile, there are everyday details to be watched: the design of the labels, the embellishment of forgotten corners, the daily decisions and chores which an estate employing three hundred people entails.

Mouton prospers. Thanks to the sturdy individuals who work in my vineyards, the old wisdom is still there, helped now by modern know-how and good guidance at the helm: many of them are sons or grandsons of the original crew, no longer prematurely old, no longer insecure. These are proud people, from a proud land, the Médoc, and, I might add, the girls are very good-looking.

Now I've got all that off my chest I feel a lot better. You may not know much more about wine than you did at the beginning, but at least I may have satisfied a little of that curiosity we all feel about the affairs of our fellowmen.

About the Rothschilds

Mankind is stubbornly curious of genealogy.

EVELYN WAUGH

I had made up my mind to be original, cut the family background and just talk about me, but as it happens, I change my mind more often than I change my socks, so when a letter arrived from Germany the other day asking, "Who are these Rothschilds?", I felt quite piqued. "The richest and most powerful family in the world," I wanted to tell them. I decided, then and there, to jot down my favorite part of the story as it was told to me, so many times, when I was a child. My grandmother, with her comical German accent, always began with: "Once upon a time," and I thought it was a fairy tale.

"Once upon a time there were five brothers, born very poor and humble, who, in their day, attained such dizzy heights of power and wealth as never have been heard of before or since."

But my story begins more precisely in 1743, when Amschel Meyer the peddler was born. Meyer was our family name; Rote Schield which became Rothschild was tagged on later, a nickname. Amschel was the father of the five famous sons represented by five arrows on my wine labels and on the family coat of arms. Some say the family had lived in the Frankfurt ghetto since the sixteenth century, the Jews had certainly been there since the thirteenth. We know this because the introduction of the ghetto is recorded. Someone even claimed to have seen them crossing the Danube ten centuries before that.

However that may be, it was Amschel the peddler and his progeny who put the family on the map and finally entered the language with:

"Mom, it's Saturday. Can I have fifty cents for the pictures?"
"Who do you think I am? Rothschild?"

I am descended from four of the five brothers, though strangely enough I have never thought of myself as a Jew, nor even primarily a Rothschild. Is that true? Reading the page again, I wonder. We often deny the truths which deep down mean most to us. However:

1. My great-great-grandfather was Nathan of London, son of Amschel.
2. My great-grandfather Nathaniel, Nathan's son, married Charlotte, his cousin, daughter of Jacob of Paris, son of Amschel.
3. My grandfather, James, son of Nathaniel, married Thérèse of Frankfurt, granddaughter of Kalman of Naples, son of Amschel.
4. (This is stretching it a bit.) Betty, wife of Jacob of Paris, father of Charlotte, my great-grandmother, was the daughter of Salomon of Vienna, son of Amschel.

Their story opens at the wrong end of the Judengasse, the ghetto's one street, twelve feet wide—between the city wall and a trench, said Goethe.

You entered the ghetto by a huge iron door, bolted from outside at night, on Sundays and on Mother Church's holy days. Once inside you came upon a human rookery, impossible to tell where one family dwelling began and another ended. Signs identified each section: Red Shield, Green Shield or some such, but if you belonged you asked for Jacob son of Moses,

Isaac son of Esau and so on. For the tax gatherer, hunting his prey could be a daunting exercise. Should the Jew leave the ghetto he had to wear a yellow star. If he encountered a Christian he had to step aside, raise his hat and bow. He was forbidden to enter public parks. He was not allowed to own land, practice law, enter the civil service, the army or the teaching profession. He was forbidden to sell handicrafts, fine cloths, fresh fruit, or marry a Christian.

What could he do? You may well ask. Make the best of it, concentrate on the few activities open to him and excel at them. In any case, living on the alert kept him on his toes. The ghetto was frequently raided, so an alarm system had to be devised and shelters dug underground. If the inhabitants were caught napping, the raid could develop into a massacre despite the thirty-two thousand florins each family paid for protection.

The massacres helped to keep the population down, especially since many of the survivors were inclined to move on. The toughest and the richest often managed it.

When the first ghetto was built the Jews were already dispersed over all the world: everybody had relatives or friends somewhere or other, somebody to whom they could turn when times were bad. And times were often bad. The Christians went on blaming them for everything: J.C.'s crucifixion, a missing daughter, the latest war, the weather. They carved their hatred into the stones of their cathedrals and sang it in their ballads. Amschel the peddler sometimes caught the words of these merry songs as he rode his donkey round the countryside beyond Frankfurt, selling bits and bobs, trifles, scraps of second-hand junk—he liked to have his young son Amschel with him. In a day's trot they might have to cross several frontiers. Germany was divided into many principalities, each with its own coinage. The boy Amschel could soon translate money from one currency to another at lightning speed. He was a serious child, his only hobby collecting any small, rare coins which fell into his father's leather pouch. When he was ten his father packed him off to a Talmudic school 175 kilometers away at Fürth, near Nuremberg; it was thought he had the makings of a rabbi. Three years later, both parents died of smallpox. Poor Amschel wanted to return home to be with his two younger brothers, Moses and Kalman, but the relatives said, no, he must finish his studies, a scholar is respected in the community. His future will be assured.

Amschel did his best, but after another eighteen months of chanting the Talmud he'd had enough. He folded his phylacteries and hitchhiked home.

"What's to become of him? He's a man, nearly fifteen, but no gelt, no prospects; he can't even speak good German with all that Hebrew knocking around in his head."

"Ah, but have you heard him at his calculations? What a gift."

A cousin got him a job in the Oppenheimer bank in Hanover, a step up.

Amschel sorted out his frugal belongings, not forgetting his precious collection of coins, tied up his bundle, embraced his brothers and was off.

He was going north to a different climate altogether. Hanover was the homeland of the Protestant kings of England and said to be more liberal than Hesse. Amschel didn't have much chance to find out. It was 1756. Louis XV was fighting a few rounds with Frederick the Great, and Hanover was in his path. Amschel had sometimes to dodge a running saber fight on his way to work, or wait for a thick, black pall of smoke to drift away. These new shells turned day into night, so that nobody knew who was killing whom. Among the dead soldiers strewn across the street were twelve year olds, part of the army Prince William of Hesse hired out to the highest bidder; he charged more in the event of death or mutilation, so the corpses were carefully checked. Amschel added a new column to his calculus, the market value of a life.

One day when the fighting had lulled and business was slack, Amschel sat idly polishing his coin collection as an old general wandered by. He paused to look over the boy's shoulder; he was a collector himself. "Not much there, but what he has is good and rare."

He asked the boy to bring him any unusual pieces he might find when rummaging round the flea markets and gave his name, von Estorff. Amschel had made a useful contact. When the war was over, in 1763, the general and the boy found themselves back in Frankfurt, von Estorff working for Prince William of Hesse, Amschel back in his old home, the Iron Pot in the Judengasse.

Despite its repressive race laws, for a young man who had yet to make his way Frankfurt was the place to be—set on the junction of ancient trade routes where goods arrived from London, Manchester, Amsterdam, Bremen, Copenhagen and Prague; it was far livelier than Hanover, and for the cost of purchasing a pair of balance scales, Amschel could open up a little exchange business. He also had contacts in the ghetto for coin collecting and would be able to find rarities to please von Estorff.

Chance is a fine thing, and Amschel knew how to make the most of any occasion. In 1765, Prince William, heir to the principality of Hesse-Cassel, was bored; he wanted a new hobby, preferably profitable. As he sat brooding in his over-furnished salon, a diffident young man was ushered in, prodded by General von Estorff.

Prince William was peculiar even among German princes: in the first place he had grown very rich, mainly through his trade in human flesh. His soldiers were in good shape when hired out—he liked to measure their pigtails personally. Then they would be packed off to any current schemozzle. Some of his twelve year olds finished up fighting for George III against the Americans; the mad Hanoverian king was William's cousin and his best customer.

William also had a passion for needlework, servicing willing women and collecting—collecting any old thing. Von Estorff had persuaded him that rare coins were a good investment. So here was Amschel bowing graciously as he untied his kerchief and let bright coins roll across the table.

Fixed. Amschel was to employ himself building up a collection for Prince William.

Of course he took care, when he presented the prince with his finds, to ask only bargain prices, and, the prince being very rich, Amschel always threw in a little gift.

Four years later the young man's thoughts were turning toward matrimony—but the father of his chosen one didn't think much of his prospects until, on September 29, 1769, the crowd passing in the street stopped to watch Amschel nailing up a sign:

MEYER AMSCHEL

COURT FACTOR

BY

APPOINTMENT

TO

HIS SERENE HIGHNESS

PRINCE WILLIAM OF HESSE.

All Judengasse came by to take a look, even the prospective father-in-law was impressed. A flattering letter had done the trick, phrased in good German, written by the local letter writer. The arrangements for the marriage went ahead, and on August 29, 1770, Amschel Meyer took as his wife Gütel Schnapper, in the ghetto of Frankfurt am Main, in the principality of Hesse. She was a neighbor's daughter, a spruce little maiden of seventeen. Amschel was twenty-seven. They were married under the *huppah*, the ritual canopy, and the bridegroom broke the ritual glass severing all previous ties. The marriage contract, the *ketubah*, was printed on parchment, the whole affair having been properly arranged by the local matchmaker, the *shadchan*. Amschel took his bride home to the house where he was born, at the sign of the Iron Pot, and after the wedding night, Gütel cut off all her beautiful red hair and shaved her head. Then she put on her married woman's wig for the first time. A woman's hair, her crowning glory, was considered very sexy; there are always allusions to young women combing their long hair in Jewish love songs. Once married and in the arms of her husband, she wasn't supposed to attract other men.

Amschel and Gütel lived in the same poor dwelling for fifteen years. When Gütel was nursing her sixth child, Amschel's prospects improved and they moved to the House of the Green Shield. It was a very old house, tall and dark, and even here they had to share with another family, but at least they had their own pump plus a small balcony at the back which looked out beyond the ghetto. Of the four rooms, one became the office, shop and *bureau de change*, in fact, the first Rothschild bank.

Gütel gave birth to twenty children, ten of them died in infancy, five boys survived, and five girls, Schonche, Belche, Brienliche, Jentle and Jitle. Jentle died when she was twenty-six.

In his old age Amschel said that this was the happiest time of his life, "watching my sons grow up around me."

Each morning would begin with a prayer, Amschel wearing his prayer shawl and winding his phylacteries, the boys in their yarmulkes—the small skull caps that good Jewish boys wear at all times—Gütel with one eye on the stove.

Good, now eat. The Jewish mother's cure for all ills: nourishing borscht, blintzes, smetane and kez.

On Seder night the boys' Hebrew had to be perfect as they read each in their turn from the Haggada.

As the girls grew up they helped their father with his bookkeeping and clerical work. In such families the women worked as hard as the men to make a living, or a fortune; then when the time was ripe they were married off to suitable contacts with a suitable dowry. Among the Meyer girls, only the youngest, Jitle, tried to break the mold. She worried everybody by running after boyfriends of her own choice, but it wasn't long before she too settled down and made what they called a good marriage.

In 1789, when news of the revolution in France reached the Judengasse, Amschel was doing well, trading in wine, tea, coffee, tobacco and cotton goods from Manchester. He had contacts all over Germany and had been careful not to let fall his tenuous connection with William, the eccentric prince. "War to the palaces, peace to the cottages," meant very little to Amschel and the rest of the ghetto people. Such protection as they enjoyed tended to come from palaces.

One day when Amschel arrived at William's palace with his little gifts and his latest display he found his prince, a busy factotum at his side, wading through a heap of bills and bad debts, searching in vain for some banknotes, which William swore had disappeared or, more likely, had been stolen. Amschel looked on, amazed at the confusion. William's assistant, Carl Buderus, had been tutor to one of the prince's many broods of illegitimate children. Very delicately, Amschel offered to help. The two men were amazed at the speed with which he put things in order, and his wizardry with figures.

Buderus had an idea: the clever Jew, with his comical accent and his outlandish clothes, was obviously ambitious, yet still patently honest—just the man to collect William's bad debts. Could he be persuaded? He could. It would be an honor to collect in the name of the prince.

Amschel took his boys along with him, to let them see the ways of the world. The Rothschilds were on their way. They were financing their first prince, while the French were proclaiming their belief in Liberté, Égalité, Fraternité, and liberal spirits all over the world were cheering them on.

Not for long. Utopia didn't sound so good when aristocratic refugees began to arrive with their stories of the guillotine and the terror. Prince William's guest rooms filled with émigré French, travel stained and penniless, seeking allies, hoping to raise an army of intervention to bring their crazed countrymen to heel. William kept away from his guests—he was afraid they might have brought some disease with them.

In 1792, Austria and Prussia got together to suppress revolutionary France, and Prince William reluctantly pledged his support.

Down in the Judengasse, Gütel, now thirty-nine, gave her last child to the world; they named him Jacob.

The war of liberation started out as a perfect muddle, as wars will. The French got bogged down in Belgium, the Austrians and Prussians were kicking about in Champagne, waiting for someone to give them an intelligible command. The French occupied Frankfurt and called on the natives to rise against the tyrant William, who sold their blood to the English. William got cross and threw them out, but in 1795 he changed his mind and made peace with France. He had a lot of money stashed away in England, but those damned French, shouting their revolutionary slogans, were camped under his window.

Amschel looked on; he'd seen one war and noted all its foolish waste. At night after prayers he'd lament the ways of the world. Wars and revolutions were the business of the goyim. Let them come, let them go, trade goes on forever.

During the day, the boys would have been out foraging for the English goods which were still appearing in the byways of Frankfurt, on a farm cart hidden under an old coverlet, or falling off the back of a wagon.

In 1796, the French bombarded Frankfurt and destroyed the ghetto. Nearly all the old wooden houses went up in flames. The authorities were forced to house the homeless. At last the Jews were allowed to move out into the city, so the Meyers promptly set up an office in the center of town, and became M. A. Rothschild und Sönne. In fact, their ghetto home had survived, being better built than those at the poorer end of the street. Gütel lived in it for the rest of her life.

Amschel made good in his new depot and married his eldest girl, Schonche, to a neighbor in the same line of business. The countryside might be impoverished and stink of war, but there were people prepared to pay any price for good German wine and good English cloth. Amschel was doing fine until the price of cotton goods from Manchester suddenly rocketed sky high.

The black marketeers were laughing. Amschel's boys were frozen out. What was to be done? At the family council they had an idea: if Amschel paid William good gulden and William repaid Amschel in England, all that was needed was a clever operator on the spot to buy the goods cheap and get them to Frankfurt. Here is Nathan's version: "One big trader came who had the market to himself. He thought himself quite the great man, and that he was doing us a favor if he sold us goods. Somehow I offended him, and he refused to show me his patterns. This was on Tuesday. I said to my father, 'I will go to Manchester myself.' On the Thursday I started out."

At that time Manchester was the workshop of the world. It had all the coal it needed for its blast furnaces, rain from the surrounding hills to keep the spinning cotton humid, and canals had been dug to link mill, mine and sea routes. Raw cotton was bought cheaply in India and spun and woven into all manner of material, from fine muslin to gun cotton. The mills were working round the clock to meet the demand, and the town could not accommodate the multitude who came flocking there looking for work in the new mills and mines. The manufacturers spoke the same language as their workpeople, a new class —driving, ruthless and successful. Manchester was the classic soil of capitalism and a dirty, filthy place but, where there's muck, there's brass, as the man said. It was the right place for an ambitious young man of twenty-one, with plenty of fight in him and a zest for money making.

Tuesday to Thursday before Nathan's trip must have been very busy down in the Meyers' crowded home. First there was the problem of financing the undertaking. Amschel's resources were not unlimited, but his son was a good investment. The sum Nathan was given varies with each storyteller. Who knows? The family always kept two sets of accounts anyway—one for the taxman, the other unintelligible except to the family. Nathan carried a few letters of credit for his father's contacts and Prince William's, and cash for his personal use. The girls brought down Nathan's warmest coat and opened the lining.

A ten-year contract was drawn up between father and son, and a system of communication plotted. There were friends and relatives on the continental side; Nathan would have to set up an English network. Letters were to be in Hebrew and unsigned, no proper names to be used, a code had to be agreed upon. The family started to laugh again as Nathan fished out old family nicknames: Uncle for Prince William, rabbis for gulden, honey cake for good news. There was no need for Amschel to read a homily on the snares and temptations awaiting young men abroad. Nathan had but one thought in his head—success, money. The father must have felt a twinge of envy as Gütel stitched the coins into Nathan's coat.

At the last moment they decided that Sigmund Geisenheimer, a bookkeeper, should accompany him. Bookkeeping was Nathan's only weak point; he might need a little help there. Then came the farewells and the tears—it was the first break in the family circle. Nathan gave a specially fond embrace to his youngest brother, Jacob, only six years of age but bright as a button. Gütel prayed to God to preserve her boy and keep him safe and told him to keep his feet dry, get his socks darned and send back his old shirts when he bought new, so that she could make the old ones over. Nathan's only English came from the fruity lingua franca of the markets, but he had Yiddish, a despised language though useful everywhere, and he could spout exchange rates and market prices off the top of his head.

After a few months in London, Nathan took the coach to Manchester. He lodged with a good Yiddish family in the pleasant suburb of Ardwick and settled down with them. They fed him well, took him to the synagogue and showed him the ropes. He took an office in Mosley Street in the center of the city, and daily, barring Shabbat of course, a steaming kosher meal was carried to him at midday. Manchester was a grim but friendly place, and beyond the smoking factory chimneys, one could see the glorious hills of Derbyshire.

Within a year, Nathan was buying cotton goods in the markets of Nottingham, Leeds and Glasgow, as well as in Manchester and the surrounding towns. The pattern book he produced was a work of art, and he took infinite pains over the quality of the printing and the prompt delivery of his cottons. They were costing him far less than the German traders had been asking. When the family sold them, cut-rate, in Frankfurt they still made a good profit. Nathan knew how to buy and how to organize.

In the ghetto, the Rothschilds had many rivals fighting to climb the same ladder. Nathan in Manchester had the field to himself; the small Jewish colony there—the Cohens, Isaacs, Jacobs, Joels, Levis and Samuels—were teachers or dealers in ostrich feathers, flowers, pencils or brushes, no threat to Nathan. Not long after he had established himself, there was an invasion of German merchants, among them a German merchant's son, Friedrich Engels, who visited the stock exchange each day in his father's interest, at the same time working on an international link-up very different from my ancestor's.

Nathan soon had his empire staked out. His cottons traveled to Frankfurt via enemy France or Holland. His brothers were kept on the hop.

Music and speculation were the diversions of the new cotton lords; Nathan just speculated, to such effect that when he moved to London six years later his capital amounted to £50,000. Soon he acquired a handsome bride and some very good connections in Amsterdam. Hannah Cohen was the daughter of one of the richest men in England, Levi Cohen, linen merchant of Amsterdam and Throgmorton Street. When Nathan asked for Hannah's hand in marriage, Mr. Cohen asked him about his prospects. "If that's all that's worrying you," said Nathan, "you would do well to give me all your daughters."

Hannah brought him a dowry of £10,000 and bore him seven children. She was his only confidante, the family his only joy—and pain.

In London Nathan stopped trading in goods and concentrated on money. In 1809 he became a naturalized Englishman and in 1810 established the bank of Nathan Meyer Rothschild at New Court, St. Swithin's Lane, in the City of London. He and Hannah lived above the shop.

Twelve years since he'd left papa and mama, but what a move it had been. N. M. R., the financier, highly successful merchant banker, now had contacts all over Europe—in Lyon, Metz, Basel, Copenhagen—but communication was too slow. He needed reliable information for his business, and he needed it fast. So he set about organizing an army of trustworthy messengers who knew their geography and could evade excisemen, policemen, and any bands of soldiers on the loose who might be pillaging around. In Dover, he had small ships belonging to smugglers standing by, ready to set sail at a moment's notice with Rothschild messengers aboard.

At the continental ports, a corresponding army went into action. Nathan's system operated with unbelievable speed, efficiency and secrecy, especially between London and Frankfurt. It must have cost him a trifle, and it was a tightrope on which the Rothschilds were to risk their millions, often precariously.

Over in Europe the scene had changed radically since Nathan left. In 1799, on the brink of a new century, the little corporal from Corsica had seized power and the title of first consul. At first he wished to be known as citizen consul and had a statue of Washington erected in the Tuileries, then as an afterthought he added Caesar and Alexander. Like the Rothschilds, he was an alien in the country he adopted, and never completely mastered its language. He and Amschel were inspired organizers and both wished above all to found a dynasty, but there the resemblance ends.

"It is against the policy of our house to give money for war," the Rothschilds said. They became the world's top money spinners, Napoleon, number one at the war game. When he took over, the Republican army was no more than a rabble; the veterans of the Bastille and the American campaign were still wearing their tattered uniforms, faded liberty caps, and odd boots. He cleaned them up and restored the hierarchies, dishing out shining insignia, epaulets, gold lace and plumes.

Till then you hadn't been able to tell an officer from a rank-

and-file man. Now both were given their bits of tinsel. "It is with such baubles that mankind is governed," said Napoleon later, when Republicans objected to him restoring the Legion d'Honneur.

Anyway, the trimmings did the trick. The men might be hungry but they looked like somebody; the girls turned their heads as the soldiers passed on parade. And there were lots of parades, with silver bands playing the stirring old revolutionary songs, while Napoleon brooded on his dais, wondering where the army of liberation should go liberating next. Well, there was Italy "groaning under the Austrian yoke." A walkover? Could be. Soon the soldiers were being issued new boots to ready them for the long march. To Italy—or death.

William of Hesse didn't care for all this disturbance, especially since he couldn't make up his mind which side he was on. But he found a solution—he took to his needlework, leaving Amschel and Buderus to cope with his affairs.

In 1803 William was breathing fire and brimstone against Napoleon, when he was suddenly summoned to meet the great man himself in Paris. He went. Some of the German princes were to be softened up, temporarily. William came back with the title of elector and a large slice of someone else's land. He was delighted, but not for long. William could change sides at the drop of a cocked hat.

In 1804 Napoleon was crowned, not once, but twice: On May 10 by the archbishop of Paris, then, in case this wasn't good enough for the people, he dropped a line to the Pope who duly obliged and turned up at Notre-Dame on November 29. The Pope lifted the crown of Charlemagne from its cushion to place it on Boney's head, only to have it snatched from his grasp: Napoleon crowned himself. He straight away got down to solving the unemployment problem; along the Normandy coast he had men dredging harbors, readying them for the heavy barges which would carry him to England. William of Hesse trembled for his money in London; Amschel trembled for his son Nathan. Nathan wrote to his father, "Don't worry, he won't last," which seemed very optimistic. A French engraving, the Emperor's Triumphal Entry into London, was going round the coffee houses. England had the wind up, the farm laborers were set to work building warning beacons along the white cliffs. "Nonsense," said one old admiral, "they'll never get here by water."

One forgets that Napoleon was regarded as the Bolshevik menace of his day. Even so, it took a year's planning and prevaricating before the tsar of all the Russias finally threw in his lot with Austria, and they set out to cut Napoleon down to size.

The plans for invading England were dropped, Napoleon raced his men across Europe, savaged the Austrians and the Russians, capturing thirty thousand of them, chased them to Austerlitz and beat them to a frazzle. When Prussia objected to the Grande Armée being camped on its frontiers, Napoleon gave them a taste of the same medicine, and with Prussia finally crushed at Jena, he planted his jackboot on the map of Europe.

Now for a little much-needed plunder. William of Hesse was known to be the greediest princeling in the pack and a double dealer. Also, like most rich men at that time, he kept all his loot under his own roof. Napoleon cast his eagle eye on the castle near Frankfurt, which was said to be a gold mine. William panicked, out came the coffers, trunks and assorted bridal chests. The family coaches disappeared into the night, heading for Copenhagen or Prague; his border guards rushed round nailing up notices: Neutral Territory. It was a race against the clock.

In truth, William had too much of everything; objets d'art, molting furs, brocades, moth-eaten velvet gowns, jewels and junk had to be stuffed pell-mell into sacks. But where could he pack the heavy bars of gold and silver he'd been hoarding? He'd never get it all away. Buderus and Amschel calmed him down. The best thing would be to hide what he could on the spot. Amschel was willing to take the risk. Mysterious convoys arrived in the Judengasse and vanished.

Well, you can't stash away a king's ransom without somebody noticing. Napoleon's hounds were everywhere. And there were jealous friends. Rothschild und Sönne were sitting on dynamite. Sure enough, one night, someone came pounding on the door. "French police, open up." One of the girls slid back the bolts. Gütel was waiting for them. "We've come to arrest your husband."

"You can't do that. He's ill in bed."

"Well, his accomplice Buderus is in prison. Did you know that?"

"I know nothing."

The family had been tipped off by the Jewish chief of police, recently appointed by Charles Theodore, Baron von Dalberg, an unusual character—at once Napoleon's administrative man at Frankfurt, archbishop and friend of the Jews, especially of Amschel's who had lent him a great deal of money.

The French police turned the house over and Amschel turned his face to the wall.

Salomon graciously answered all their questions. William of Hesse? As far as anybody knew he was in Prague. Someone in the ghetto had been financing the Resistance? Certainly not his father—Amschel Meyer was a man of peace. Amschel groaned pitifully. In fact the Meyers had given money to the guerrillas. Amschel hated Napoleon. The questioning went on, Salomon waiting till he was given the proper cue. The bribe did the trick. All that appeared in the police report was that Amschel Meyer had helped the elector to invest his money. It was well invested, some of it was already safe and sound in Nathan's vaults at St. Swithin's Lane, London, and the rest was on its way. Quite a flitting. If you can trace the route you will have done better than the French police and secret agents, who never succeeded in intercepting the Rothschild traffic between Frankfurt and London.

Napoleon might be lord of Europe, but who can lord it over every hidden path or short cut, or watch every creek along the coast? "There always seems to be a Rothschild at the back of

the elector, as manager, ambassador, carrier or secret agent"—
French police report.

"Risk is the soul of commerce," said Nathan one day as he
went sailing on the windy side of the law, supremely confident
that he could tack back before anyone was the wiser. With
William's English money he had capital to play with. He risked
his father's reputation and his own and shuffled the money
around. When Napoleon's war was over and William returned
to his castle, every penny was restored to him, with interest.
Nathan was none the poorer either.

Nathan was the cornerstone of the family, a tough, irascible,
impatient man. "Don't tell me about your broken leg, I want
the market prices," he wrote to James. And they all bowed to
him. "You are the general, we are your lieutenants," said Salomon.

"Right," said Nathan, and involved the whole family in the
gamble of a lifetime.

In 1810 Napoleon was blockading England very successfully.
The duke of Wellington, stranded with his armies beyond the
Pyrenees, unable to pay his starving troops, wrote a furious
letter to London. "Send us money or disband us." The last
convoy carrying bullion to Wellington had been sunk and London couldn't find any more.

Nathan could. He heard that there was gold worth £800,000
on a frigate which had just docked in the port of London. It
belonged to the East India Company. "I knew England needed
that money," he said, "so I bought the lot. The government
sent for me. They said they knew I had the gold and they must
have it. I sold it to them, payment deferred."

The French were swarming the seas; how could they get the
gold safely to Spain? Nathan said he could fix it. How? "The
family. I'll send it through France." Salomon and Kalman were
already practiced fixers. They knew Austria and Germany inside out, and they were not lost in France either.

The territory from the Pas de Calais to Paris Nathan allotted
to Kalman, Salomon took over from Paris to the Pyrenees. But

Paris was the crux; Nathan needed a very sharp operator there. He asked his father to arrange for Jacob, the youngest, to enter France. Quite a tall order.

Back in Frankfurt, Amschel Meyer, father and son, pulled strings . . . ropes. They were in luck, the archbishop, Baron von Dalberg was a sucker for a grand occasion. He would have to be in Paris for the event of the year. Napoleon had divorced his naughty Josephine—his soul, the one thought of his life— to be free to marry into royalty. In this case, Marie Antoinette's niece, Marie-Louise of Austria. "Now I shall be Louis XVI's nephew," said General Nap from Ajaccio, as he jumped into bed with his new bird.

Nine months later she obliged him with a son and heir. One in the eye for all those gossips who'd been saying he was impotent. Napoleon was planning a glorious knees-up.

Von Dalberg was broke of course, so Amschel provided the coach, the flunkies, the gold braid and an amusing traveling companion. Once within sight of Paris, Jacob waved good-bye to the baron and made off to register with the Paris police. It was March 18, 1811. He found rooms at 5 rue Napoleon, and took a quick look round as the fireworks burst over the Seine and the dancing began under the floral arches. He had no time for dallying—the first shipment of gold was arriving in Dunkerque at any moment, but he must have walked on air, moving freely in a fine city where there were no race laws.

The Rothschilds were sufficiently well known by now to arouse the interest of the secret police. A report reached Monsieur Mollien, Napoleon's finance minister: "British bullion is being shipped through France by a . . . " But he scarcely had time to wipe his spectacles before a young man, the Frankfurter mentioned in the report, appeared on his doorstep.

Jacob may have had broken French but his talk was smooth and he had been well briefed. Nathan knew that Napoleon was a peasant when it came to money and trade. He had demanded gold from every state he conquered, and he was hoarding the lot. The economy was paralyzed, European trade was at a standstill. Nothing moved. The idle ports of France were turning royalist. "I have all the gold," announced Napoleon in 1811. "The bank is full. Austria is already bankrupt, Russia and England will soon follow suit."

And just at that moment Jacob appeared with his cock-and-bull story. "The bullion arriving in France will drain England dry," he told Minister Mollien. "My brother in London tells me that the English will have to devalue their currency." Mollien was impressed. Wishful thinking. "I think you will find that my family can best conduct the operation. We are well placed," said Jacob.

Mollien told Napoleon and Napoleon smiled. An amusing way to give England the coup de grâce. So Jacob was given letters of introduction to several French bankers and went off well pleased with himself.

The gold began to arrive in Paris. The chief of police became very suspicious and wanted to arrest Jacob, but the young man swore he had government sanction for the business and produced his credentials. Other police chiefs said nothing, but it was observed that they began to live in surprising luxury.

There was still a great deal of fixing and fiddling to be done, but by now the brothers were experienced hands. The money had to be disguised, laundered, exchanged and transferred without arousing suspicion. They managed it. The French police were hoodwinked. Wellington fed his army. Nathan was very proud of the whole affair. "The best business I ever did," he said long after.

The brothers were improvising, laying tracks, using their wits and their contacts, and they were beginning to operate on a multinational scale.

This much Papa Amschel knew as his life drew to a close. His end seemed to be as quietly organized as his life had been. He made a new will, then he went to the synagogue. It was the Day of Atonement. He fasted and prayed all day. Then he went home and died. It was September 18, 1812. He was sixty-nine.

My daughters, sons-in-law and their heirs having no part
whatever in the existing firm of M. A. Rothschild und
Sönne . . . nor the right to examine the said business, its
books, papers, inventory, etc. . . . I shall never forgive my
children if they should, against my parental will, take it
upon themselves to disturb my sons in the peaceful posses-
sion of their business. . . . You are a family, you are the
family. All the brothers should stand together, all shall be
responsible for the action of each. Nothing must be allowed to destroy this harmony. Respect it. Keep it whole.
Honor your faith. God bless you.

Amschel had made a success of his business and his life. He
had founded his dynasty. His sons' future promised fair. He
could not have imagined the power and glory which was to
come and indeed much of it he might not have approved.

His private life was simple and strictly religious. He died
where he was born. He was loyal to his friends and to his patron, William of Hesse.

Amschel was always opposed to any deviation from the customs of his race and religion. It was only after his death that
Kalman became known as Carl, and Jacob as James. Successful,
smart, tough as they had to be, none of his sons had the quiet
charm of Amschel Meyer of the Judengasse.

Amschel did not live to witness the downfall of Napoleon,
something which would have warmed the cockles of his heart.
A month after his death, in October 1812, the terrible retreat
from Moscow began. In London, Nathan's son Nathaniel was
born, my great-grandfather, and in Paris, Jacob gave up kosher
cuisine and pomaded his hair à la française.

Despite their father's strict injunctions, and Nathan's favorite
tag, "There are only two nations, the family and the others,"
once Amschel was gone the family ties began to strain, suppressed resentments rose to the surface, as they so often do at
such times. Salomon was always the peace maker. He seems to
have been a wise and gentle soul. "We are like the mechanics

of a watch," he told his brothers, "each part necessary to the others."

The world believed that they always worked in total harmony. The myth of an almost telepathic understanding was created, but of course it was untrue. Amschel, the eldest, clung to his father's ways, methodical and deeply conventional. Little brother Kalman was the runaround, James was up and coming, but Nathan was the boss and a very fierce and demanding one. "You are the general, we are your lieutenants," said Salomon, but sometimes brother Nathan was too much even for him. "Your letters make me ill," he wrote. Nathan had been hurling insults at Frankfurt for accepting too low a rate of exchange. "We are not drunk or stupid," Salomon replied and put in a dig of his own. "We have something here that you in London obviously do not have, good bookkeeping."

Their father had often scolded Nathan for his untidy ways. His only filing system seemed to be in his head. On this occasion he owed Frankfurt a matter of £100,000. Salomon's letters, like his father's, were exquisitely polite. Nathan's prose style wasn't improved by his constant mixture of German, Hebrew and Yiddish, plus a peppering of the family code.

Amschel, too, was upset by Nathan's angry criticisms and countered by accusing his brother of "dirty little speculations." Insults and abuse came winging back. Salomon tried to calm the storm. "Surely we are rich enough, thanks be to God, not to quarrel over two or three thousand pounds. If my tears were black I would write a lot easier than with this ink."

But they were not so foolish as to let the world know of their differences. The combo never broke up. In that respect they were true to their father and one another, and they never let anyone else into the firm, not even their in-laws. Of course when they were going at full tilt, the squabbles died down, and they had plenty to occupy them in 1814, with Napoleon fizzling out.

Young James had been treading on eggs in Napoleon's Paris but with the ex-emperor safely stowed on the island of Elba, and a gouty old Bourbon, the eighteenth Louis, restored to the throne, he registered his bank at 17 rue Pelletier, depositing funds from Russia, Prussia and England to be used for the maintenance of their occupying armies. The brothers' skill as international conveyors was now famous and they were reckoned honest and prompt. Their commissions grew with their reputation.

The Peace Conference in Vienna, brilliantly staged and well provendered, was deciding the fate of France and the repartition of Europe when, in its fifth month, the debates were suddenly interrupted. "Napoleon has escaped from Elba." The hundred days runaround he gave them all came to a bad end at Waterloo. James and Nathan financed a Bourbon comeback. Louis XVIII, who had been sitting it out in Belgium, asked five million francs to do his command performance in style, and got it.

Big brother Nathan had been watching the moves in Europe like a master chess player. He was the most respected businessman in London. In Paris, James had Louis in his pocket, but the other three brothers were sitting on a rickety branch in Frankfurt, now part of the Jew-hating Hapsburg Empire, with Prince Metternich at the helm.

"You need a safeguard. The Austrians must give you some sort of recognition," Nathan told them. "After all they would never have laid hands on English money for their war without us."

So Salomon wrote Count Stadion, Austrian minister of finance, a wonderful letter full of curlicues and honored sirs, reminding the gentleman of the Rothschilds' services to the empire during the late troubled times, and the minister passed it on to the emperor, with a note: "I would recommend a von."

And the Emperor passed it on to the privy counselor who doled out the titles, and the privy counselor said:

"What! Aren't the brothers Rothschild Israelites? A gold snuff box is good enough for them." Stadion wouldn't have it, he needed the boys. They got their von and a coat of arms, but it was severely edited, not at all the one they'd asked for.

Worse was to come. With all the grand illusions of a new Europe shattered, and rusting cannons and moldering bones all over the place, the old order came tottering out of the ruins looking for scraps: penniless princes, daft old dukes with greedy doxies and all their train of procurers and pimps, closely followed by the bankers of the old regime. "France will have to pay," they cried. There was a summit conference. Castlereagh from London, England. Shelley knew him: "I met Murder on the way, he had a mask like Castlereagh." The Duc de Richelieu from Paris: "Rothschilds? Coin changers." And Prince Metternich, chancellor of Austria, a supple character, formerly an admirer of Napoleon. Between them they would restore Europe's shattered economy, without the Israelites.

Of course this didn't mean that Metternich could do without his own household Jew, his secretary and financial adviser, Friedrich von Gentz—a brilliant fixer, whore master, student of Kant and very greedy man. "I wouldn't like to tell you how much he cost me," said Salomon when von Gentz composed a good publicity brochure for the family, "but it was worth it."

The old-style bankers had come to the conclusion that squeezing France dry might not be such a good idea; a loan would be more to the point. An enormous number of government bonds were issued. The bankers were delighted when these were quickly snapped up, puzzled when they disappeared altogether and horrified when they woke up one morning to find the bonds were being dumped, sold for a song. And who do you think thought that one up?

The next loan was floated by the Rothschilds.

All the same, back in Frankfurt the family was still vulnerable. Brother Amschel, watering his mother's window plants of an evening, would hear the roars of the Jew-baiters as they hurled bottles and stones at the closed iron gate, only a few yards away. One fine day a gang of young heroes gathered outside his banking house in the city, and began piling a mound of bricks and stones on the cobbles. He went out on to the balcony. "Good day to you."

There were the usual cries of: "Do your duty, Jew." "Blood-sucker." "Usurer." "Who murdered Christ?"

Amschel smiled and bowed. "So you take me for a rich man. Do you know then how much I possess?"

"Thousands. Millions. As many gulden as there are Germans in Germany."

"You are right, and I have a coin for each one of them. Here, you may have yours now." And he threw down a shower of silver.

There was a roar of applause. In the scramble they forgot about Amschel and set about fighting among themselves.

But by 1819 violence had grown uncontrollable. Was it to be a pogrom? Many of the poorer Jews took flight. The Rothschild bank in Frankfurt was invaded. James said, "Come to France," and the rumor went round that the family was packing up and leaving. It came to the ears of Chancellor Metternich and he was worried: the Rothschilds were useful people. One day Salomon received a letter marked with the Austrian eagle, actually inviting the brothers to desert Frankfurt and make their home in Vienna. It was from Metternich.

When they got over their surprise, Salomon said he would go himself and sound out the situation. Once closeted with Metternich he found that, as usual, protection would be rather expensive—fifty-five million gulden. Surely Salomon could raise a small sum like that?

Back home he talked it over with Amschel and Kalman. "That hospitality offer was a joke. The Jews are still not allowed to own property in Vienna."

"Rent the best hotel."

"And the fifty-five million?"

"Quite a problem."

"Another impossible job, and what thanks do we get?"

"Tell him we'll raise it, if . . ."

"If first they give us our due. Without a title you can't open a carriage door in Vienna, let alone a bank."

"And the gulden?"

That needed a little thought. They put their heads together, consulted Nathan and came up with a new idea, a public lottery. Salomon went back with the scheme in his pocket and quoted his price.

Metternich dropped a note to his emperor: "The great and rich house of Rothschild is threatening to leave Austria for France. It would be in our interest to keep them here. . . ." Without waiting for a reply, Metternich assured Salomon that his request was as good as granted, there would be no more shilly-shallying. Salomon took him at his word, rented the best hotel in Vienna, the Romischer Kaiser—the whole of it—and went to work.

The Viennese nobility tripped over each other gazing up at the windows of the big hotel. In company they turned their backs on that frightful Frankfurter, but Salomon was used to such manners—in any case he was much too busy to waste time among such idlers.

He was still putting the finishing touches to his lottery scheme, when in 1821 Metternich tried to hand him another little job. There was trouble in Naples. The locals were demanding a constitution, and their old king, Ferdinand of Naples, and the two Sicilies were giving in to the people, granting them everything they asked. This couldn't be allowed to go on.

Metternich called a conference of kings and their like. The best thing, they decided, would be to send in a neighborly army of Austrians to occupy the place. "Where will we find the money?"

"Rothschild," said Metternich.

But Salomon refused to help, said he had enough on his plate selling lottery tickets. Nevertheless the brothers considered the matter—it was a pity to let any opportunity slip. Couldn't they keep it in the family? After all, Naples could open the door to Italy. James and Nathan thought up a

scheme, but who could operate it? Well, there was still Kalman.
Send little brother. So they did. Kalman went to Italy, became
Carlo and on March 21, 1821, rode into Naples in Ferdinand's
coach, escorted by the entire Austrian army. No blood was
shed. The Neapolitans simply looked on—they wanted repre-
sentation not revolution, peace and a little prosperity. Carl was
pleased with his new self. He went to see the Pope—who,
thanks to the Rothschilds, could now sign his own checks and
buy a few badly needed vestments—and asked him to use his
influence to abolish the Roman ghetto; His Holiness agreed.
Little brother decided to settle in Italy with his handsome wife
Adelheid. He built a palace for her below Vesuvius.

By 1822, Salomon's fund raising was finished. Despite the
usual accusations of bribery and fiddling, the lottery had done
the trick: Salomon took twelve million gulden for his pains.

As a sideline he had been fixing a pension for Marie-Louise,
Napoleon's wife, and her bastards. She had been busy cuckold-
ing her imprisoned lord but didn't know how to feed the kids.

One day Salomon walked into Metternich's *salle de réception*
with a large scroll. "What's that?"

"Our reward. The Rothschild coat of arms. It has taken a lot
of work. I trust Your Highness will like it. The lion which you
see on the coronet is for Hesse. We have always been loyal to
Hesse. The leopard is for England, on a nice red, and of course
we had to have the Austrian eagle. The stork? He's for piety,
the greyhound for loyalty, the star for Jewry, plus Concordia,
Integritas, Industria—that's our family motto. What about
that?"

"Isn't this the one you were granted with your von?"

"No, no, no. They cut the best bits: the greyhound, the stork,
half the Austrian eagle and the coronet."

"I think the coronet is only awarded with baronial dignity."

"Well?"

"I'll see what I can do."

"With regard to the loan, Your Highness, I mean your personal loan, the nine hundred thousand guldens—I consulted

my brothers and they agree, you need only consider repayment at the end of seven years. And I'll tell you something else, Your Highness, I'm not crazy about that stork. If they are going to cut anything this time, I wouldn't be sorry if he went."

Six days after this meeting, by imperial decree, the five brothers became barons of the Austrian Empire. The title to be theirs and their heirs forever.

The only brother who had no use for a barony was Nathan. He thanked Prince Metternich and the emperor kindly, but he preferred to remain himself, plain N. M. R. of St. Swithin's Lane. Nathan was Nathan; he had no need of any other title. He wasn't particularly impressed by rank and station anyway. One day a character burst into his office when he was very busy. "Take a chair," he said.

"You do know who I am?" said the gent, indicating the royal crest on the lining of his top hat.

"Take two chairs," said Nathan, and carried on. In another age and place he could have joined the Marx brothers.

"How did you make your fortune?" somebody asked him.

"Minding my own business," Nathan replied.

James had thoroughly enjoyed the ennobling game, writing to his brothers as dear barons, accusing them of all sorts of frivolity, asking whether Amschel had changed his tailor—Amschel, who dressed like a rabbi all the days of his life and only thought of the credit titles might bring to the Jewish community. James had been the first to throw off the old orthodox ways. He worked as hard as anybody but he liked to dress in the height of fashion and of an evening he'd be off to enjoy the best of French cooking and French *amour*. Everyone knew he was flying his kite among the pretty girls.

The brothers were worried. James was thirty-two and showed no sign of settling down. Salomon wrote him a few stern letters telling him it was time he did his duty, married and reared a family. He dwelt on his own happy state, how soon he would be celebrating twenty-five years of connubial bliss. He had married Gelche Stern, a careful girl.

James retaliated by marrying Salomon's daughter, Betty. She was nineteen, spoke French with only a slight German accent, could write a decent letter and had acquired a touch of poise with mama in Vienna.

James could now receive Paris with a good-looking young wife at his side, and he decided to teach the Parisians a thing or two about Rothschild hospitality. It must have taken all the Rothschild stamina to survive their social life. Thirty to lunch each day, sixty to dinner, three-to-five soirées a week. No respite when they went to the country—all the pots and pans went with them, so did their chef, Monsieur Carême, who had found the English royals too bourgeois and the tsar too stuffy. All very well, but it took two strong waiters to carry in one of his cake confections. No wonder James developed a pot belly. Betty kept slim rushing around locating the gilded brocades, figured velvets, laces and embroideries with which she rather over-draped their palatial homes. James introduced what came to be known as the Rothschild style. Salomon warned him, "Too much show, Jacob. You will create anti-Semitism with all this display of wealth."

It was true: Paris society was shocked. "Monstrously vulgar," they said, and schemed to get an invitation to the next meal. "Gorgeous but how greedy," they cried, stuffing themselves with ortolans. "And the accent! My dear!"

Monsieur Henri Boucher left us a description of their house warming, at the Palais Fouché, rue Lafitte, formerly the home of the chief of police who had wanted to arrest James over the bullion smuggling:

All Paris had been invited. Would they come? The lady of the house was nervous, restlessly touching the flowers, flicking the cards at the gaming tables, inspecting the salon, where all manner of clockwork toys were laid out, imported from Germany for the amusement of the guests. The whole house had been transformed, staircases enlarged, walls knocked down, a ballroom big enough for three thousand dancers erected in the garden. In one corner a low platform, festooned and brightly garlanded, seated an orchestra of forty. The candelabra were lit. It was getting late. The lighted façade of the house shone through the evening mist. The police had been on duty since eight o'clock. Carpets had been laid across the pavement, uniformed lackeys lined the steps awaiting the guests' arrival. The clocks, synchronized that morning, struck nine. At that very moment the jingle of harness was heard, three or four carriages were arriving, preceded by grooms clearing the way. Soon a stream of carriages blocked the surrounding streets; the horses forced to a halt, voided their hot breath on the shining boots of the footmen on the carriage in front. Paris was arriving.

The guests advanced through a wide hall ablaze with light, the walls were hung with gold-fringed drapes, the windows transformed into Gothic arches, the only furniture, occasional blue and gold stools and sofas. Relieved of their cloaks and scarves, the guests advanced to meet Monsieur de Rothschild, a young, slim person with short sidewhiskers, bold features and clear eyes. Yesterday ignored, today the whole world wants to know him and his attractive, young wife.

James liked to mix business with pleasure. He admitted that he learned everything he wanted to know at his dinner table and he always knew how to put a finger on the person he needed. It amused him to mix ministers, generals, crowned heads of Europe with writers and artists. At his house you enjoyed good claret, good food and a little wit with the dessert. His literary friends made hay with him behind his back, the Goncourts never stopped criticizing his taste, Heine couldn't visit the Palais Fouché without bitching his host. "I went to see Monsieur de Rothschild this morning. A gold-laced lackey was bringing the Rothschild chamberpot along the corridor. Some speculator from the Bourse who was passing raised his hat to the impressive vessel."

"Only a Jew could have thought that one up," said Salomon.

He was right; Heine too was a child of the ghetto—only he had made his escape through German literature, rather than economics.

Balzac wrote James into his Comédie humaine, caricaturing his accent and his amorous exploits. But James admired Balzac, amazed by the writer's insight into the workings of French law and banking. Not that Balzac knew a thing about making money for himself. He was always broke. James helped him from time to time, gave him shares in his Chemin de Fer du Nord and interested himself in his affairs, all his affairs. "Is she pretty?" James would ask Honoré, à-propos his latest.

"If she were, you should have her," said Honoré, as they sat together comparing notes and discussing the jealousy of spouses. James was the only Don Juan among the brothers and liked to boast about it to his cronies. "I have yet to meet the lady who refuses me her favors," he said.

He went bald in early middle age, developed a pot belly and took cures, but still: "Uncle James is running after all the girls; the waters seem to have done him a power of good; in fact we are speculating on Aunt Betty producing another little one"— Nathan's son, Anthony, writing to his brother in London.

Nathan's new home at Stamford Hill was quietly conventional, with Jewish feast days and holy days strictly observed. The sons were always comparing it unfavorably with Uncle James's scintillating social life in Paris.

During his cures James developed another obsession—collecting. He would travel fifty miles to view a few ancient stones dug up by a farmer who knew he was in the neighborhood. He had already bought a houseful of paintings, old masters rather than new. Nathan bought only one picture in his entire life, and that under pressure. An art dealer turned up at New Court; if he hadn't been armed with a letter of recommendation from the chief rabbi Nathan would have thrown him out. "Give me a thirty pound one," said Nathan.

"Which one?"

"It doesn't matter which. Good morning."

Meanwhile Betty, Baroness James, was having her portrait painted by Ingres and filling her house with sweet music. She could lionize Chopin and Rossini without a word of complaint from James, but poor Hannah couldn't do a thing with Nathan. Ludwig Spohr, the greatest violinist of the day, asked Nathan to name his favorite music. "This," said his host, jingling the coins in his pocket. All the same, he bought his little daughter Hannah a solid gold harp for her birthday. It is not known whether the yellow metal improved the tone or not.

In 1830 Nathan was giving brother James the rough edge of his tongue over more serious matters. Another French king on the run—was James asleep? "England has no confidence in your ministers; do they dream of nothing but revolution?" The refugee king this time was the old Bourbon, Charles X, who had succeeded his brother, Louis XVIII, six years earlier. James was banker to both brothers, but despite the fact that he was negotiating a large loan for him, Charles disliked James and, faced with economic crisis, decided that he would find his own way out. His solution? A right-wing junta foisted onto his volatile subjects. Revolt threatened, a general election had to be called. The king and his party were voted out. The Rothschilds' rivals were plotting a coup, and Paris was on the boil, so Charles X dissolved Parliament. Up went the barricades, the military was called out and the streets were littered with bodies. Then the troops revolted. The terrified, old king fled. James could hardly have been very welcoming when Charles came to beg a loan. The rash old man had already cost him a fortune.

While the country was in chaos, the rival bankers produced their trump card, a citizen king, Louis Philippe, born Duc d'Orléans. He had fought with the Republican Army and earned his living in exile as a tutor in Switzerland. He turned up with a green umbrella, a red, white and blue cockade in his hat, sang the "Marseillaise" with the people and addressed the national guard as comrades.

"Rothschild is out," crowed the anti-Royalist press, and Louis Philippe's performance made banner headlines all over Europe. The news was blown up beyond recognition. There were uprisings in Poland, Germany, Italy and Belgium, "To arms, brothers, France inspires us!" Even Switzerland and England felt the shock waves. Thrones were shaking, banks were rocking; Napoleon was nine years dead, but should such another arise at this time he could easily spark off another conflagration. Had Louis Philippe a length of fuse in his pocket? Austria appeared to think so: Metternich had been dragging out the cannons. The French were glaring at each other, suppressing the Republican press, arresting foreign dissidents. Angry letters from Nathan kept arriving. James wrote to Salomon in Vienna: "We are holding eighteen million francs worth of government bonds. If peace is preserved they will be worth seventy-five, in the event of war, forty-five. What is your prince doing? If the powers are arming, we shall have to do likewise." Salomon went to work on Metternich with a lot of soft soap.

The Rothschild bush telegraph was continually humming, their private eyes were everywhere. The brothers worked overtime. Gradually revolts were scotched, ministers calmed, golden oil was spread on troubled waters. Nathan organized the pacifying flow. Then he wanted to know why James hadn't been to see his new king. James dutifully attended Louis Philippe's first *levée*, as a representative of the Societé des Antiquaires. The courtiers bowed low, the bankers even lower, felicitating their new lord on his accession. He didn't seem too good at court protocol. Who was he waving at? It couldn't be James de . . . It was.

When they were alone, the citizen king asked the baron to be his banker-in-chief. Monsieur Lafitte, who'd held the job, had just gone broke.

Once in the saddle, Louis Philippe's Republican fervor faded clean away. His government was run as a joint stock company, and James fixed all the big loans. The fires of revolt burned low, or were trodden out, though some smoldered for a long time. Baron James received the Legion d'Honneur for his services to peace. He also managed to recoup his losses and make another fortune. At the end of Louis Philippe's reign he had more resources than the Bank of France.

"It might be a blessing if all the kings were dismissed and the Rothschild family put on their thrones," said Ludwig Borne, another jealous neighbor from the Judengasse. But by now the Rothschilds had kings for pawns and chancellors for joint stools. The world was dazzled, shocked and envious. "Rothschild has it, I want it." Few knew how Rothschild got it in the first place and, what's more, kept it, which as Nathan said was the harder part.

Till now the rich had been the titled few, the owners of great estates. The poor could only dream of wealth—Aladdin's cave glimmering with jewels, an ever-ready banquet nearby, laid on plates of gold.

Wasn't wealth entrenched in land and titles anymore? How had this upstart family made it? What were those messengers about, careering between Madrid and Moscow, Amsterdam, London and Brazil? Well, the boys had simply tuned up Papa Amschel's system, learned when they had ambled with him across divided Germany in his little donkey cart. The courier had replaced the donkey, and the check, the family code. In the new age of industry and technology, good management and business acumen could outweigh social standing: "The Rothschilds are vulgar, ignorant Jews, but they are endowed with a remarkable instinct, which causes them always to choose the right, and of two rights, the better. Their enormous wealth is entirely the result of this instinct"—Friedrich von Gentz to Prince Metternich.

Of course as their power and wealth increased, attacks on the family grew vicious. Anti-Rothschild, anti-Jewish cartoons appeared all over Europe. Nathan collected them and stuck them on the wall of his office. He had been a target for the racists and diehards since 1815 when he was accused of suppressing the news of Waterloo and making a fortune. The story was too far-fetched, but it stuck. Any dog or bird story goes down well in England. So Nathan was supposed to have been seen amidst the smoke of battle releasing his carrier pigeons from a large basket. He had abandoned his pigeon experiment years before in favor of more reliable messengers, but people never forgot those pigeons.

It was all the same to Nathan. He made millions before, during and after Waterloo. He was the great gambler who understood the rules of the game, and that headpiece of his was kept constantly in use, fed with data from his universal information service.

The story of Napoleon's escape from Elba reached him long before the politicians were awake, and when Waterloo was won they were still asleep. "Lord Castlereagh is not to be disturbed, he is at his repose," said the flunkey when Nathan took the trouble to call round with the news of Napoleon's final defeat.

"Too bad," said Nathan. He left a note for his lordship and went on to the stock exchange to buy up a few British bonds. "I close my bargains on the spot. I'm an offhand man," he said. "Prepared for anything."

In any case, when Lord Castlereagh finally got the message he didn't believe it. He didn't like Nathan. He didn't like Jews. So much the worse for him. Nathan didn't put himself out to court anyone's good opinion. You'd as soon get a crack as a compliment in his company.

"Victory? Yes, but how terrible the loss of life."

"As well as for you, major, or you'd still have been a drummer boy." Nathan's table talk.

Like most highly successful people Nathan was obsessed with what he called his work; in fact it was his pride and joy. "I don't read, I don't play cards, I don't go to the theater. . . . "—etc. etc. But he had a gorgeous time and the secret fun of seeing the goyim jumping around like cats on hot bricks whenever he made a move. "If they're pleased with the way I manage their affairs they let a few crumbs fall." His commission amounted to a king's ransom but the queue grew ever longer; princes, chancellors, the powerful men who usually stand in the shadows. There they were hoping for an audience, edging past the wagons unloading bullion in the yard at St. Swithin's Lane.

Nathan addressed them in an amazing mixture of languages, peppered with wisecracks.

He couldn't write a decent letter, let alone a diplomatic one, and he had as much tact as a bull in a china shop, but he was the only man who understood how capitalism worked, and profited by his knowledge. Karl Marx, who lived down the road, had a fair idea as well, but he was a poverty stricken genius with no seat to his pants. Nathan had no time for that. "If they cannot do good for themselves, how can they do good to me?" He was not inclined to move outside his own realm, so he didn't grasp the significance of George Stephenson's little locomotive puffing along the Stockton–Darlington track in 1802. When the railways began to spread over England in the early thirties, Nathan was kicking himself. Luckily for the family, Europe was way behind England at the time, so in 1835, he wrote the brothers telling them to get in on the act over there, and be quick about it. The brothers jumped to it.

The railroads of Europe were Rothschild built, and Salomon erected a life-size statue of himself in the waiting room at Vienna.

In 1836 all business activities were cancelled for a few days. The Rothschild clan was to be reunited for the first time. Nathan's son Lionel was marrying Charlotte, Carl's daughter, and to please grandmama Gütel, now eighty-three, the wedding was to be celebrated in Frankfurt.

The carriages could not pass for the throng that turned out to watch the return of Amschel's boys, the now world-famous Rothschilds. They and their distinguished guests were arriving from the four corners of Europe. The flags of all nations were hung from the balconies, and the crowds cheered as princes and potentates passed by, then roared with delight as they identified the middle-aged men who had once lived amongst them. Now they were richly dressed, with beautiful women at their sides. Broods of children and grandchildren gazed wide-eyed at the strange town where their parents or grandparents were born.

Nathan's carriage came last. He could hardly raise his head, he had a vicious swelling on his neck and had been forbidden to travel, but he would not disappoint the old lady. By nightfall he had a high fever, but insisted on standing by his son's side at the wedding. After the ceremony, he collapsed. Hannah, his wife, sent to England for the family doctor. The local physician did his best, but it was too late. When the rabbi came to read the prayers for the dying, Nathan interrupted him. "I have no need to pray so much. I have not sinned," he said, and died. He was fifty-nine.

Gütel stood silent as they took his body away, the twelfth of her children to die before her. "Why does God not take me now?" she asked. Nathan was to be buried with great honor in the country of his adoption, England.

Gütel lived on till she was ninety-six, never moving from the house where she had passed the best part of her married life. Her eldest son, Amschel, bought a fine place with a deer park and gardens full of flowers, but she would not leave the ghetto —for fear it might bring her boys bad luck.

Poor Gütel, superstitious, believing in signs, omens and the evil eye, like so many Jewish mothers who passed their lives never knowing from which quarter the next attack would come. The mezuzah nailed to your door would save your house from harm perhaps, a prayer to Adonai might bring you to the homeland: "Adonai, our father, our king, bring our scattered ones among the nations near to thee, gather our dispersed from the ends of the earth and lead us with exaltation into Zion."

Crowns and coronets could have meant little to you, dear lady. In your small world you reigned supreme and confident. "My boys won't let them go to war. They won't give them the money." And they honored you. In times of hardship there were always tasty morsels for your plate. No desperate search for love or sex ever troubled you. Amschel was your all; I'm sure you had lovely times with him. It was in the nature of things. Lovemaking was always highly prized among our people and a woman's privacy respected. At your time of the moon you slept apart. As you listened to the stories of the Exodus,

Amschel would pass the wine cup first to you. Even in that dark street you celebrated the harvest. Did you manage an arbor of fruit and flowers? Hardly.

I see you lighting the candles on Shabbat eve, placing them everywhere for Hanukkah, the Festival of Light, praying over the memorial candle, lit for your lost ones on the anniversaries of their deaths and busy about the house with your girls, repeating Nathan's jokes till the house would be full of laughter.

I hope you enjoyed your old age, at least sometimes, as I do. You became one of the honored dowagers of Europe, a port of call for the young aristocrats making their grand tour.

We had the good luck to see the old mother of the Rothschilds, and a curious contrast she presented. The house she inhabits appears not a bit better than any of the others. It is the same dark and decayed mansion in the narrow, gloomy street, and before this wretched tenement, a smart calèche was standing, fitted up with blue silk; a footman in blue livery was at the door. Another carriage waited at the end of the street. Presently the door opened, and the old woman was seen descending a dark, narrow staircase, supported by her daughter-in-law, the Baroness Carl.

Two footmen and some maids were in attendance to help the old lady into the carriage, and a number of the inhabitants collected to see her get in. A more curious and striking contrast I never saw than the dress of the ladies, their equipages and liveries, with the dilapidated locality in which the old woman persists in remaining. They say she never in her life has been out of Frankfurt, nor will she leave this house, in which she is resolved to die.

—Charles Greville's diary.

So, your sons' admirers came to pay court to you. Princes and poets came to call, and you received them in your small sitting room.

There I must leave you, as the honey cakes and sweet wine are passed round and you sit there, still and dignified, receiving the homage due to you. I do not see you smiling; compliments would mean nothing to you, flattery less. Life had been a serious business. "God can have me when he will."

Sometimes, I'm sure you would be moved to tell stories of your boys, especially their childhood tricks in the golden days of your young womanhood. Then you might smile and shake your head, because the courteous stranger listening could not understand a word of Yiddish.

Mazeltov, Gütel. Shalom.

I've strayed from my story, but there you are—Gütel's Rembrandt face, with the resigned expression and the voluptuous lips, could always set me dreaming.

The only other one pushing his way into this book is great-grandfather Nathaniel. He moves center stage in 1836, hand-in-hand with his pretty sister, cocking a snook at the family. Hannah wished to marry out, outside the faith, that is. Nathaniel encouraged her. She was twenty-two, and had already had at least one dazzling lover. An Austrian prince had asked her hand in marriage when she was seventeen. He had danced with her at her uncle's house in Paris. Nathan was furious. "I will never allow my daughter to marry a Christian." He went further, added a codicil to his will! "My daughters shall be disinherited if they marry without the consent of their mother or their brothers."

Hannah had to get over her prince, but this time, with her father dead and gone, she thought the younger generation would have no objection to her marrying the man of her choice, another Christian, Henry Fitzroy. She couldn't have been more mistaken. "No," said three of her four brothers. "Oh no!" said her mother, and wept. Hannah pleaded and reasoned. Her mother forbade her to see her suitor for six months. "It's like scarlet fever, you'll get over it."

Hannah sent Henry away and kept to her room. Of all the family only Nathaniel was sympathetic. "She is pining away," he told his mother, and tried to persuade the old lady to change her mind.

She couldn't, she didn't dare. The brothers were adamant, and the sisters and all the rest of the family, but the lovers were adamant too. Two years later they were married in a Christian church, St. George's, Hanover Square. Mama cried again, but she didn't attend the ceremony. Nathaniel was the only member of the bride's family in the church. Luckily the marriage was a success and probably compensated Hannah for her family's behavior.

"Neither my wife nor my children will ever see Hannah again. She will be erased from our memory," said Uncle James. The whole family cold-shouldered her from that time on. Worse, when she lost her three-year-old son, they declared that it was a judgment on her.

Nathan's sons had set about enjoying the money their father had made, as is the custom. They feathered their nests, went gadding about, gave money to charities and took to huntin', shootin' and fishin'. Nathan must have been spinning in his grave, especially when Lionel planted a tombstone, on it marked Baron Nathan de Rothschild, and started touting for an English title for himself.

Nathaniel hung about London for a while, the bank didn't attract him, nor did his family's dull social life. He tried hunting but fell off his horse and crippled himself for life. What was he to do? He had always preferred Paris to London, and his youngest uncle, James, to his stuffy brother Lionel, so he decided to leave England, and with his uncle's help became a Parisian *bon viveur*, diehard dilettante and soon, an attentive son-in-law. In 1842 he married his cousin Charlotte, my great-grandmother. She had a sweet face, sad but pretty. Chopin even wrote a song to cheer her up; she preferred to escape into her painting. Nathaniel, meanwhile, cared more for books than business. Together they made the fabulous collection of Chardin's works, which my father inherited. Neither of them seemed to have anything in common with the rest of the family.

"My worthy Uncle James works from seven in the morning till five at night. When he isn't seeing all those railway gentlemen, he's rushing from Dieppe to Lyon and thence to Strasbourg. I couldn't do it."

Despite his poor half-paralyzed body, Nathaniel still enjoyed many of the good things in life, among them: wine, especially the *vin clair* wine of Bordeaux which he had tasted at his father's table. Nathan had been an abstemious man, but hospitable, his guests enjoyed the wine most favored by the English, claret. They could not pronounce its French name, *clairet.*

In 1851, Nathaniel and his gentle Charlotte visited the Great Exhibition at the Crystal Palace, London, where the Bordeaux wines stole the show. To have such an elegant wine at their table? How delightful.

So when an obscure property, Brane-Mouton, was put up for auction—sixty-five acres of vineyard plus stables and out houses—the people of the little town of Lesparre in the Gironde were amazed when an unknown agent at the back of the hall kept pushing up the bidding.

"Any advance on 1,125,000 francs?"

Every head turned.

"Who's he acting for?"

"Sold to Baron Nathaniel de. . . ."

The auctioneer couldn't pronounce the name.

"Who is he?"

"Whoever he is, he's well-heeled."

"Where is he from?"

"How many hectares?"

"How much did he say?"

"Sold to Baron de Rothschild in the auction rooms at Lesparre, this 11th day of May, 1853."

They couldn't spell the name either. They still can't.

Great-grandfather was obviously the maverick of the family. Perhaps that's why he doesn't loom so large in all those Rothschild histories. He was a terribly crippled man, but, in 1840, stirred to anger by the persecution of his race, he wrote and agitated against the tsar when poor Jews, expelled from Russia, were left stranded at the frontier. And in the same year he demanded justice when the Jews of Damascus were tortured and massacred. In 1848 when Paris was having yet another revolution, he stayed at his uncle's side.

"Everybody is frightened, and with good cause," he wrote. "Paris is not so cozy, the town has gone wild. The weather is fine so all Paris is out on the streets forming processions, planting trees of liberty. God knows where it will end. Our worthy uncle has gone to his beloved Ferrières. It almost breaks one's heart to think that a place which has afforded us so much pleasure will be taken from us, one day or another."

Nathaniel had good reason to fear the worst. The 1848 revolution was not confined to France, it blazed all over Europe. Salomon's house in Vienna was vandalized. He was lucky, down the road the minister of war was hanging naked from a lamppost. Prince Metternich scrambled into his housemaid's old clothes, dashed round to borrow five thousand gulden from his dear Salomon and fled to England. Salomon returned to Frankfurt and never set foot in Austria again.

In Naples, too, the people were on the streets. Carl acted smartly. He persuaded a reasonably liberal government to grant concessions, fast. Revolution was postponed.

In Paris, the people set fire to the throne and, draped in the royal finery they'd found in the cupboards of the Tuileries, paraded in the streets. Louis Philippe grabbed his umbrella and fled to England—"like a bankrupt fleeing his creditors," said Prosper Merimée. On February 25, the day after Louis Philippe's flight, the Chemin de Fer du Nord was attacked. A band of angry men invaded the railway station at Valenciennes, not sure whether they were out to intercept the fugitive Louis, fraternize with the railwaymen or, as one of them suggested, "burn everything belonging to Rothschild." In the end they contented themselves with digging up a few railway sleepers and smashing some windows.

Nathan, who generally knew what was in the wind, was dead.

The others were taken off guard. "We made fifteen million in 1847," wrote James. "All being well we shall make twenty this year." A few days later the Rothschild château at Suresnes was methodically sacked and burned, and the insurgents were marking the Paris properties with a cross. Behind their palace walls the Rothschilds had been more effectively sheltered from the gathering storm than ever they had been in their ghetto.

But 1848 was no pogrom. The gaunt men and women on the streets were disease ridden, near starvation—and with no more say in their fate than the alley cats. The franchise extended to a mere ninety thousand voters, governments came and went like April showers. In Paris a workman earned one franc for a thirteen-hour day.

This time when the hungry poor took to the streets, there were armed men among them, and the national guard refused to fire or disperse them.

When James heard of the sacking of Suresnes, he called his household together. "My friends, if they come, open the doors, do not try to resist them. My nephew Nathaniel and I will stay with you. I know you have deposited all your savings with me. If you lose them, I shall share my last crust with you." That same day a young man wearing an armband of the People's Militia noticed two well-dressed men strolling arm-in-arm along the Rue de la Paix while bullets whistled by, coming from every art and part. "Monsieur le baron," said the young man, "I'm afraid you haven't chosen a very good time or place for your promenade. They're shooting in the Place Vendôme and all along the rue de Rivoli. I would advise you to return home."

"Thank you, my young friend, but tell me, what are you doing here? Your duty, no? Well, I am here for the same reason. You are trying to protect peaceable citizens, I am trying to find your minister of finance. I think he may be needing some help." And so saying he and his nephew went their way.

In England the demand for reform had grown up much earlier, concessions had been made and the most persistent reformers imprisoned. London was a safer place than Paris, so James sent his wife and children to nephew Lionel's house, and Lionel joined his brother Nathaniel in Paris to give Uncle James a little moral support.

The citizens of Paris grew tired of parading and shouting and settled down long enough to elect a provisional government. It was made up of journalists, lawyers, one poet, one astronomer, one mechanic, one banker's son and Adolphe Cremieux, the man who had been to Istanbul to intercede for the Jews of Damascus.

The Rothschilds had helped finance Cremieux's trip to Istanbul; perhaps it was Cremieux who persuaded James to finance the new Republic to the tune of twenty-five million francs—or maybe there was no choice. Whatever the reason, James paid up.

Despite his resilience and his brusque manner, the baron was a moody character, easily depressed. For once, at this moment in his life, we catch a glimpse of the private man. He wrote to his dear angel, Betty, in London, telling her how much he missed her. "We could take a little house somewhere," he wrote, "live quietly." Was he tired of the big show? Did he really want to disappear into the wings, or was it just a black cloud, which would pass? More than anything, he dreaded the thought of his eldest son being forced to bear arms for the Republic. He need not have worried. The revolution was short-lived. The people planted their trees of liberty, sang their songs of hope and waited for the government to bring them better days. There were no better days for them, so when after a few months Napoleon's nephew arrived from England to serve under the flag of freedom, they welcomed him and elected him president They still loved the name.

Between the Rothschilds and this uneasy parvenu there was no love lost. Louis knew that his uncle's imperial crown had been merely another tinsel bauble, and that he'd better subscribe to a few Republican principles if he meant to stay the course. "A third-class Napoleon," James called him.

Louis returned the compliment. The Rothschilds were old hat, there was to be a new style in banking, available to a wider public. "Are they all going to be rich then?" asked James.

The enemy, the Pereires, were invited to run the new show. James looked on. "An insignificant lot," he called them, and occupied himself with his own affairs, extending his railway, making new business contacts in far-away Havana and New York. James never became a naturalized Frenchman—the world was his oyster; his true métier was being a merchant of capital, directing the flow of money across the world.

In 1852 he took the trouble to warn Louis, now known as Napoleon III, that his financiers were on a disaster course—an astute letter, but it was ignored.

By 1860, Napoleon III's adventures in Italy and Mexico had come to a bad end. Two years before he had narrowly escaped his own, when a bomb had been thrown at him outside the Paris Opera. Finally his new economic policy collapsed like a house of cards, as James had predicted, and not without a little help from the family.

James decided that the time had come to move in again, not to rescue his liege lord, but rather the country he loved. "I am first a Rothschild, then a Jew, but my heart is French."

At this stage in the journey, Napoleon III was only too pleased to grab at any lifeline, so James threw a little party at Ferrières to celebrate the reconciliation. It was quite an affair. A green carpet embroidered with Bonaparte bees was rolled out for the arrival, and Betty stood on it to welcome her guests, wearing a violet velvet frock. Behind her stood the entire Rothschild family, assembled from all over Europe. After luncheon, served on Sèvres china, Louis planted a cedar and went shooting. It was a Rothschild custom for visiting royalty to plant trees.

Nine hundred pheasant bit the dust that afternoon, and as the chasseurs strolled back to the house, the chorus of the Paris Opera burst into a paean specially composed for the occasion and conducted by Rossini himself.

Everybody agreed that nobody would ever forget it, and best of all, it was one in the eye for the "insignificant lot."

James, now in his seventies, showed no sign of taking it easy. He had taken over Nathan's role, rousting the family when they missed a good deal, ruling his sons with a rod of iron, rushing about all over Europe to be sure he wasn't missing anything, and complaining of old age.

When he was seventy-six he bought Lafite, which borders on Mouton.

It was 1868, and Nathaniel was boasting that he'd sold his "extraordinarily good wine at the fantastic price of 5,000 francs a barrel."

Uncle James had been trying to buy the neighboring Lafite property for years, but the owners wouldn't sell. In August of that year he tried again and he was successful, but they must have seen him coming.

"How much?"

"Four thousand, one hundred and forty thousand gold francs."

"My uncle hasn't sold his wine yet, he thinks the price will rise still higher."

Whether it did or not, James did not live to see it. He died in November, 1868 a few weeks after he bought Lafite. He was seventy-six, the last of the pioneers. Amschel, Salomon and Carl had died all in the same year, 1855. Like the mechanics of a watch, each part seemed necessary for the survival of the others.

James had survived two Napoleons, two revolutions, two Bourbons, and a citizen king. He lived on to hear Offenbach's music and see the steamships crossing the Atlantic. He outlived four brothers and four sisters, the loneliness of old age mitigated by the grandchildren he adored. And, even in his decline, he still enjoyed flirting with the pretty girls.

Nathaniel on the other hand was very much the married man. He lived with his talented wife, Charlotte, and their three children beside him. In 1870 his elder son, James, had to go to war; the old men were brandishing their muskets again. À Berlin. Nach Paris. James bade good-bye to his young wife,

Thérèse, my grandmother, and rode off to join his regiment. When he returned to a defeated France, he found that his father had died during the siege of Paris. Napoleon III had fled to England, and Paris was controlled by the Commune. He had to abandon all hope of continuing his career—he was a barrister—and try to safeguard his father's estate. When the French and the Germans combined to slaughter the Communards, James retired to his father's library; books seemed friendlier than people. He added to his father's collection, and his library became world famous. So did his *moutons*.

The children of the innovators seldom equal their fathers, though often they carry on their work well enough. Many of the new generation were astute financiers, cleverly using the know-how instilled in them by their wise fathers. Whatever advantages inherited wealth may bring, there is no doubt that many of the great achievements of this world have come from a strong impulse to free oneself from poverty or the chains of race prejudice.

The brothers never forgot that they were Jews. "We made our fortune as Jews, Jews we remain," said Salomon, and they never lost an opportunity to further the Jewish cause. Even staid elder brother Amschel was instrumental in abolishing the laws forbidding intermarriage in Prussia; Nathaniel's brother Lionel was the first Jew to take his seat in the British parliament without renouncing his faith. It took him eleven years. Three times he was elected by the City of London, and three times he was refused admittance because he would not take the Christian oath. "I will swear as a Jew or not at all," he said, and in 1863, thanks to the tireless efforts of the Whig, Lord John Russell, and the Tory, Benjamin Disraeli, a baptized Jew, Lionel was at last allowed to take his oath according to his faith, head covered, a triumph for British Jewry, they said, and he took his seat with due ceremony. He never opened his mouth thereafter. So, in the 1874 elections, when his friend Disraeli became Prime Minister, the voters, tired of their dumb representative, gave him the push.

His other claim to fame was the Suez Canal affair. The canal had been designed, constructed and financed by Frenchmen, but it was the Khedive Ismail who held the controlling shares and England wanted them. Suez was her short-cut to India.

Disraeli, "the only brain in England," according to Bismarck, heard that the Khedive, who had wasted all his money on women, wine and useless projects, was now touting his shares. Dizzy would have to act fast to beat the French to it. A quick flip around London—the Rothschild mansion in Piccadilly? Four million for the shares. Buckingham Palace? A medal to pin on the Khedive's chest. Bob's your uncle. England had control of the canal and Baron Rothschild, member of Parliament, collected his 100,000-pound interest on the loan.

Lionel was the perfect specimen of second-generation wealth: better educated, better spoken, better behaved than his father, he became the smooth operator par excellence. When his beloved mother passed away (as they say) he had her tombstone inscribed with these words: Baroness Hannah, relict of the late Baron Nathan.

In the 1890s Lionel's French cousin Edmond was buying tracts of land in Palestine to harbor refugees from Poland. He had no Zionist ideals at the time; like all the Rothschilds he believed that you had to pay for what you got and that was that. "Zionism," he said, "is an American Jew giving money to an English Jew to bring a Polish Jew over to Palestine." His friends suggested Abyssinia, Argentina or even lakeside Chicago as a Jewish national home, but Edmond went on buying bits of Palestine, and ran them like a dictator. In his declining years he moved closer to Zionism. In 1914 on his last visit he was deeply moved by the progress of his settlements. "I am old and weak now," he told the colonists, "but I will send my son James to you and he will address you in Hebrew."

Nathan's bank, New Court, St. Swithin's Lane, London, still flourishes. It is the only bank that determines the price of gold each day, a heritage from Nathan, and everything is still "so noiseless and efficient that the only sound one hears is the occasional creak of the floorboards." And I think they'd got rid of that the last time I was there.

Carl's branch in Naples was transferred to Frankfurt in 1861 and lasted until 1901. Vienna was taken over by Hitler, and the head of the bank, Louis von Rothschild, was arrested. Louis arranged his own ransom terms with Himmler and left for France. The Paris bank is still there, though, in this year of grace 1981, nationalized.

The family's great days may be over, or perhaps a new era is now beginning, but whatever happens, the Rothschilds will not be forgotten. They have given too many extraordinary characters to the world: champion wastrels among them, money grubbers and spendthrifts, collectors and donors, scientists and dilettantes, gardeners and entomologists, organizers and gamblers, Don Juans and respectable fathers of families, lovers of good eating and drinking . . . and me.

> Philippe, que fais tu?
> Je me fuis et me prête
> Déshabillé vêtu
> Des oripeaux du vent sous un chapeau sans tête.

Monsieur de Rothschild's Works

Diagrammes (published privately).
Paris-Paris, a story (Éditions René Laporte).
Aile d'argent la magique, a fairy-tale (Éditions Gallimard).
À l'Aube d'une guerre, poems (Éditions Henri Javal).
Eclos à l'aube, poems (Éditions Henri Javal).
Le Pressoir perdu, poems (Éditions Mercure de France).
Vivre la vigne (Éditions Presse de la Cité).

TRANSLATION:
Théâtre pour trois saisons, three plays by Christopher Fry: *The Lady's not for Burning, The Dark Is Light Enough, Venus Observed* (Éditions Calmann-Levy).
Théâtre hors saison, three plays by Christopher Fry: *Curtmantle, A Phoenix Too Frequent, The Young Man in the Cart* (Éditions Calmann-Levy).
Elizabethan Poets, bilingual anthology, French Academy Prize (Éditions Seghers).
Dr. Faustus, by Christopher Marlowe (Éditions Seghers).
Tamburlaine, by Christopher Marlowe (Éditions Albin Michel).

For permission to reproduce black-and-white plates the author and publishers wish to thank the following: Atelier 53/SPADEM, no. 26; Mme. Brassaï, no.28, which is copyright © Brassaï 1953; Anne-Marie Gonsalves, no. 37; Dmitri Kasterine, no. 31; Photo France-Illustration (photo: Henri Parnotte),no. 30; S & G Press Agency Ltd, no. 35; Sotheby & Co. (photos: Cecil Beaton), nos 29,39,40. The remaining plates are reproduced from photographs in Philippe de Rothschild's family collection.

For extracts which appear in the text we are grateful to: Chappell Music Ltd, for allowing us to reproduce the lines on page 101 from "Shall We Dance?" by George and Ira Gershwin, and the lines on page 245 from "It's All Right With Me" by Cole Porter; Columbia Pictures Publication, for kind permission to reproduce the line on page 195 from Duke Ellington's "Don't Get Around Much Any More," Redwood Music Ltd, for permission to reproduce the lines from Buddy de Sylva's "If I Had a Talking Picture of You" on page 167; Ludlow Music Inc., New York and TRO Essex Music Ltd, London, for the lines on page 172 from Woody Guthrie's "Talking Columbia," © 1961 and 1963 (international copyright secured; all rights reserved); and Williamson Music Ltd, for the line on p. 51 from "Oh What a Beautiful Morning" by Richard Rodgers and Oscar Hammerstein II.

About the Author

BARON PHILIPPE is the project of a unique collaboration between raconteur Baron Philippe de Rothschild and writer Joan Littlewood, one of the founders of Britain's Theatre Workshop. A pivotal force in the development of twentieth-century theatre, she now lives in Vienne, France.